GW00401532

OXFORD RESEARCH STUDIES IN GEOGRAPHY

General Editors

J. Gottmann   J. A. Steers
F. V. Emery   C. D. Harris

The Western Pyrenees

DIFFERENTIAL EVOLUTION OF THE
FRENCH AND SPANISH BORDERLAND

Daniel Alexander Gómez-Ibáñez

CLARENDON PRESS · OXFORD
1975

Oxford University Press, Ely House, London W. 1

GLASGOW NEW YORK TORONTO MELBOURNE WELLINGTON
CAPE TOWN IBADAN NAIROBI DAR ES SALAAM LUSAKA ADDIS ABABA
DELHI BOMBAY CALCUTTA MADRAS KARACHI LAHORE DACCA
KUALA LUMPUR SINGAPORE HONG KONG TOKYO

ISBN 0 19 823216 0

© *Oxford University Press 1975*

All rights reserved. No part of this publication may be reproduced, stored in a retrieval system, or transmitted, in any form or by any means, electronic, mechanical, photocopying, recording or otherwise, without the prior permission of Oxford University Press

Printed in Great Britain by
Fletcher & Son Ltd., Norwich

For

JOSÉ D. GÓMEZ-IBÁÑEZ

EDITORIAL PREFACE

The Pyrenees are a high, massive, forbidding range, generally regarded as an effective barrier between France and Spain. The ancient proverb *'Hautes sont les Pyrenees'* illustrated the political function of these mountains in French folklore. However, two ethnic groups have long straddled the fence: the Catalans at the eastern edge of the Pyrenees and, even more so, the Basques on both sides of the Western Pyrenees. There may be more in common between the opposing slopes of the range than its reputation would suggest.

Professor Gómez-Ibáñez has studied the Western Pyrenees with loving care. His book fills a gap in the scholarly literature in English on the area. It draws heavily on the abundant literature published in both French and Spanish, but focuses on the question, little examined in recent times, of the differences and linkages existing on both sides of the boundary. The approach in historical as well as socio-economic.

The author has paid special attention to the communities living in the valleys inside the range and to their evolution due to the political situation or to technological change. The book contributes to clarifying the historical geography and the economic history of a region where the communities sheltered in the deep folds of the land have managed their destiny with more autonomy than was suspected from the much larger political systems that met and contended in the region. Chapters V and VII add new material and ideas not only to the Pyrenean literature but also to the study of the human geography of mountain regions and of the political geography of boundary areas.

Social organization at first appears largely conditioned by the difficult environment of the mountains; but the valley communities have evolved according to the opportunities offered by the networks of relations they had developed outside the region. The interplay between two environmental systems, the local and the external, is well illustrated here by Professor Gómez-Ibáñez. The present mosaic of the region is shown to be determined by societal and political factors at least as much as by physical circumstances. While the author's emphasis is on regional facts and trends, his conclusions suggest ideas of general portent concerning man's organization of space.

Oxford, Spring 1975   J.G.   J.A.S.
                                                         F.V.E.   C.D.H.

PREFACE

I first saw the Pyrenees during the summer I was seventeen. For two months, my father and I walked half the length of the range together, going from village to village, pausing frequently to talk with people we met or to look at the landscapes they lived in. I remember the walk, of course, as much for what my father and I learned about each other as for what we learned about the villages and people of the mountains. But it left me with a love for the region which drew me back again and again, and which eventually encouraged me to write this book.

In 1967 and 1968 I returned to the Pyrenees with my wife and daughter. We lived in the mountains for a year and a half while I gathered material for this study. We spent the first summer and autumn in Mont, a tiny village perched high above the Vall d'Arán, the Spanish valley which is the source of the Garonne river. There we rented a large house, with windows which opened to views of the great Maladeta massif to the south. Its fieldstone walls were 8 feet thick at their base; made without mortar. Grey slate roofed it.

Our house belonged to a family who had moved to the town of Viella, the capital of the valley, three kilometres away. Their son had become a carpenter there, and with his income the family had left farming for town life. Indeed, in moving to Mont we joined only six families in a village which once had been four or five times as populous. Like most other Pyrenean villages, since about 1860 Mont had had fewer inhabitants at each successive census. A thirst for the opportunities of the modern world drew the youth from a place which for centuries had subsisted on the fruits of its fields, pastures, and forests. Unlike that of some other villages, Mont's agriculture was too remote, too marginal, to fit into the metropolitan economy into which it had been thrust. Most of our neighbours were old, and long since resigned to the death of the traditional ways of the village. Yet with pride they still kept their cattle and sheep, and threshed their grain, as they might have done three hundred years ago. From them we learned a great deal.

The next year we took a house in St. Étienne de Baïgorry, a French village in the Atlantic Pyrenees; primarily because by then I had decided that a study focusing on the borderland would be easier to do in the Western than in the Central Pyrenees. Baïgorry, as the village as well as its valley is called, was centrally located in the new study area, which stretched from the Somport Pass to the Atlantic: approximately a third of the whole range. Our new house in France was very close to Spain. From the bridge by Baïgorry's church it is 8 kilometres to the border along the narrow road that twists upward to the Ispéguy Pass, between the valleys of Baïgorry and Baztán. The road led past our house, which was on the outskirts of the village, just beyond the small French custom-house near the bridge.

Baïgorry was larger than Mont: 700 inhabitants in the village itself and twice as many more living in farmsteads dispersed throughout the commune. Mont had been a tightly clustered settlement, where every house touched its neighbours. Baïgorry looked more like a gathering of farms, strung out for two kilometres along the road which ran up the valley of the Nive river. The dispersed settlement was characteristic of the Basque country.

Baïgorry differed from Mont in other ways. Its houses were whitewashed sandstone, roofed with red tile, instead of the Central Pyrenees' grey fieldstone and slate. The pines and alpine meadows above Mont were replaced by beeches and heaths here. The region was well-watered and green. Its mountains were gentler than the peaks which had surrounded us in Mont. Life looked more prosperous. So it was. Although this region, too, had suffered a century of depopulation, its rural economy was adapting to the enlarged markets of the twentieth century. The farmers who remained were shifting away from their fathers' subsistence polyculture to more specialized forms of livestock husbandry. Tourism and small industries had grown important.

The pace of change in the Western Pyrenees was quicker, but there were still people who preferred the old ways. Thus Manech, the farmer who lived above us on the road to Ispéguy, spent several afternoons teaching me how to mow smoothly with a scythe. His neighbours used machines. Nicolás, whose son-in-law was the commune's *garde champêtre*, still gathered chestnuts in the autumn. He remembered hard winters. From Nicolás I learned how close were the ties between the traditional husbandman and the land. Nicolás had been born in Esteríbar, the Spanish valley south of Baïgorry, and had moved to France before World War II. Once after I had returned from a trip to Esteríbar I showed him a series of wheats I had picked from fields in the valley. Each stalk differed slightly from the others, because these were local varieties, each peculiar to a single village. Nicolás looked at the wheat and his eyes widened. Holding the stalks he exclaimed, 'These are from my valley! —Look! Here is one from Zuriáin! And this is from Larrasoaña . . . and this from Urdániz! . . .'

These insights into traditional ways were valuable because I was interested in studying the borderland's changing cultural landscapes. About a third of my working days, however, I spent not in the field but in libraries and archives in Toulouse, Pau, Bayonne, Bordeaux, Pamplona, Saragossa, or Madrid. I also discussed the region and the methodology of my study at length with scholars in both France and Spain, and interviewed numerous government officials on both sides of the boundary. Thus much of the study was based on excursions to cities, or days spent copying cadastral ledgers or manuscript censuses. But I knew my archival work must be grounded on an intimacy with the area which only residence and much travel within the region could give. So I visited widely, and paused often to talk with people.

We were living in the Basque country, and although I could not speak

Basque, I found my French or Spanish (or sometimes a combination!) served in all but a few cases. In fact, being an American sometimes turned out to be an advantage. I often met Basques who had relatives in the United States, or Basques who had been there and later returned. The practice of primogeniture left a 'surplus' of younger children, and many Basques emigrated to the sheep ranches of the western United States or the Argentine pampas. In fact the association of Basques with sheep raising in the Far West is almost legendary. In 1965 and 1966, I had met many Basque ranchers and sheepherders while making a study of transhumance in the West. In the Pyrenees, two years later, I sometimes found that someone in Elko, Nevada, or Buffalo, Wyoming, was a mutual acquaintance. Many conversations started on just such a note, once my American origin became apparent.

We stayed nearly a year. Acquaintances became friendships and the landscapes grew familiar. Of the many persons we met in the villages of the Pyrenees, so many of whom helped me grow in my understanding of the area and its people, particular thanks must go to the Monge family, to Justin Mourguiart and his wife, and to M. & Mme Sauveur Bidart, whose hospitality and friendliness we will never forget. And for much scholarly insight and criticism, I am especially indebted to Professor Jean Sermet of the University of Toulouse, whose kind guidance and support has been without measure, and to his colleagues, both in France—Georges Viers (Toulouse) and Pierre Barrère (Bordeaux)—and in Spain—Manuel Terán Alvarez (Madrid) José Manuel Casas Torres (Madrid), and Alfredo Floristán Samanes (Pamplona). At the University of Wisconsin, Professors Richard Hartshorne, Andrew Clark, Stanley Payne, and Edward Gargan, also read the manuscript and offered much valuable criticism.

1. IBARRONDO IN OSSÈS (FRANCE)

Pierres Etcheverri and Jeane Indart were the first masters of this house. The lintel's inscription tells the date they built it: 1839, when population densities in the Western Pyrenees were at their highest levels.

2. VENTA AT THE ISPÉGUY PASS

Located between Baïgorry (France) and Baztán (Spain). This is not the Spanish customs-house but a Spanish store selling wine, sausages, fruits, and dry goods to Frenchmen. The line of stone posts and trees marks the international boundary. The French customs-house is 8 km. away in St. Etienne de Baïgorry, and the nearest settlement in Spain is Errazu, also 8 km. distant.

3. DISPERSED FARMSTEADS IN THE BAZTÁN VALLEY (SPAIN)

The circular clearing of the farm in the foreground, called a *labakis*, gives a clue to its origin during the eighteenth-century expansion of population and settlement, when new farms were created by usurping patches of what had been common land.

4. ANHAUX IN THE VALLEY OF CIZE (FRANCE)

A typical Basque small hamlet: more a loose gathering of farmsteads than a compact settlement. It is late March, and sheep graze on meadows around the farms. In a few weeks they will leave the village for upland grazings.

CONTENTS

LIST OF FIGURES

LIST OF PLATES

ABBREVIATIONS

RGPSO	*Revue géographique des Pyrénées et du Sud-Ouest*
Actas, I CIEP	Refer to the partially-published proceedings of the congresses of the
Actes, II CIEP	Union internationale d'études pyrénéennes: I: San Sebastian, 1950
Actas, III CIEP	(pub. Saragossa: Instituto de Estudios Pirenaicos, 1952); II: Luchon–
Actes, IV CIEP	Pau, 1954 (Toulouse: Union internationale d'études pyrénéennes,
Actas, V CIEP	1956–64); III: Gerona, 1958 (Saragossa: Instituto de Estudios
Actes, VI CIEP	Pirenaicos, 1958——); IV: Pau–Lourdes, 1962 (Toulouse: Union inter-
	nationale d'études pyrénéennes, 1964——); V: Jaca–Pamplona, 1966
	(Jaca: Instituto de Estudios Pirenaicos, 1966–8); VI: Bagnères-de-
	Bigorre, 1971 (Jaca: Unión Internacional de Estudios Pirenaicos,
	1972——).

CHAPTER I

Introduction

In the south of Europe the great mountain arcs enclosing the Mediterranean basin sweep westward to meet the Atlantic. Westernmost rise the Pyrenees, where the Iberian peninsula joins the rest of Europe. They span the 435 kilometres from the Mediterranean Sea to the Atlantic Ocean. In the centre their breadth attains 140 kilometres, separating Spain's Ebro valley from the Aquitanian lowland of France. Like other mountains, the Pyrenees make a world of high peaks and pastures, remote valleys and villages, and an economy based on grazing, tillage, forestry, and tourism. They form a region remarkable for its diversity. Their situation between France and Spain, Atlantic and Mediterranean, has made them a meeting place of contrasting climates, cultures, and landscapes.

From the Atlantic to the Mediterranean, the Pyrenees' most readily identifiable contrast is political. Here Spain marches with France, except for a few kilometres where Andorra, remnant of feudal times, lies tucked between. Stones, crosses, and custom-houses mark the boundary in the mountains, which follows the watershed for almost two-thirds of the way.[1] The line is more than markers. It separates two administrations, two sets of political institutions, two official languages, two economic areas, and therefore two ways of life.

This political pattern was superimposed on an earlier arrangement of many economic, cultural and linguistic areas, usually corresponding to valleys. These were most important before Paris and Madrid extended their influence to the farthest corners of their realms. Local dialects, many confined to a single valley, were widespread before the advent of modern communications. In the absence of effective central governments Pyrenean valleys organized themselves into what were almost oligarchic republics.[2] It was also common for adjacent valleys on the northern and southern slopes to conclude treaties with one another, treaties which regulated the usufruct of adjoining alpine pastures and the intercourse between valleys, and which bound the valleys to mutual peace, whatever the quarrels of their titular sovereigns.

This independence, of course, gave way to modern international agreements covering grazing and communications in the boundary zone. Except for Andorra, the valley republics became large municipalities, or syndicates which manage the common lands of several communes in a valley. Scraps of the old local cultures survive, or are consciously preserved, in the ceremonies, traditions, folklore and dialects which can still be studied, especially in the more secluded valleys on the Spanish side.[3]

Of the language areas which remain, the Basque country in the west is most striking, because the language spoken there is a rare instance of a surviving non-Indo-European tongue. Its extent, and the zones occupied by the language's various dialects and sub-dialects, show little concordance with modern administrative units. *Euskalleri*, the land where Basque is spoken, straddles the international boundary for 100 kilometres eastward from the Atlantic.

In the Mediterranean Pyrenees there is another linguistic region lying astride the border. There Frenchmen and Spaniards alike speak Catalan, a Romance language like French and Spanish and the various local dialects still sprinkled through the mountains.

Although Basque and Catalan remain more or less vigorous, the dialects are moribund. And very few people, most of them elderly or extremely isolated, speak a local tongue exclusively. Compulsory education or, where that has been absent, the need to communicate with outsiders, has taught French or Spanish to almost all the inhabitants of the Pyrenees.[4] The distribution of the languages people learn in school corresponds almost exactly to the administrative division of the mountains between France and Spain. 'Almost', because children from a few isolated farmsteads walk across the international boundary to go to school.

The Pyrenees also include contrasting climates. In general the northern slope is well-watered and green with moisture from the Atlantic. To the south the influence of the Mediterranean dominates: the mountains are drier and relatively barren. It is easy to appreciate the difference in the Central Pyrenees. Talking with a herder on a high mountain pasture in summer, one learns that here the Pyrenees have two skies. There is the French one, to the north; it is probably grey with drizzle, or there may be a low bank of clouds at one's feet which hides all but the crests of the mountains. The herder turns to the south and points to Spain's sky: it is blue and luminous.

It is not difficult to find exceptions to this rule. For example, in the east, both Ampurdán and Rousillon have Mediterranean climates. Then westward, past the Pic d'Orhy, the mountains gradually subside, and the contrast between the rainfall of the northern and the southern slopes is less pronounced. And in the Central Pyrenees, where most peaks rise above 3,000 metres, the highland zone constitutes a distinctive region characterized by its alpine vegetation, by the relatively lower temperatures and abundant precipitation, and by the importance of summer grazing.[5]

A complex layering of regions gives the Pyrenees their fascinating diversity. The Spanish Vall d'Arán illustrates this quality in microcosm. Located in the very centre of the Pyrenees, it is a place where different cultures have met and mingled. One finds relics of the ancient presence of Basques in some of the valley's place names, like Montgarri, Artiga de Lin, or Arán itself. Many inhabitants speak Spanish, French, and Catalan, as well as their local dialect, Aranese, a derivative of Gascon. The valley also demonstrates the significance of political division in the mountains. Elsewhere in the Central Pyrenees, the climatic contrast between the northern and southern slopes seems to explain the different quality of life one finds in France and Spain. The administrative differences appear less important. But the Vall d'Arán is lush and green, the source of the Garonne: a valley on the 'French' side which belongs to Spain. The Aranese enjoy the generous climate of the northern slope. However, most of them have a lower standard of living than their French neighbours. A common sight in Arán are the old women who spend their days watching three or four cows graze unfenced meadows near the village, whereas a few kilometres away in France, electrified fences keep the cows from straying.

Administrative division emerges as a fundamental component of the modern Pyrenean landscape. It has two aspects. First, there are differences between the Spanish and the French Pyrenees which reflect disparities in their national circumstances and governmental policies. Second, the very presence of an international boundary influences life and landscape in the borderland. The nature of the adjacent nation and its economy may make trade or smuggling profitable, or garrisons necessary, or the boundary may mark a hindrance to communications. Furthermore, the boundary's influence upon the borderland has changed with time.[6] One variable is the degree to which all parts of the nation have been affected by the fortunes of the whole. Another is the changing national circumstances and governmental policies.

These ideas underlie this examination of the Western Pyrenees. Its aim is to analyse and explain the relation the international boundary bears to various economic and social distributions or associations. It assesses the significance of political division for life and economy in the borderland.

This is also a regional account. It belongs to the south-western fringe of France and the northern edge of Navarre. It describes the western third of the Pyrenees and the people living there, and it grew from a long-standing affection for this mountainous land. A study in political geography was combined with this regional account, because the area's outstanding trait, political division, provided the framework for the analysis of its characteristics.

As far as possible, the analysis is historical. A static view, one which only described the area as it is now, is inappropriate when the objective is to clarify the effects of political division in the area. Historical series of observations are more useful. This is not only because present patterns are best explained as the result of historical processes. It is also because the rates of change of phenomena on either side of the boundary provide measures which can more easily be correlated with corresponding developments in France or Spain. For example, present population densities in the borderland do not show much difference between France and Spain, but an historical analysis does bring out marked differences in their rates of change during the

last century. These can be related to the history of each country, showing
that the boundary does indeed mark an important discontinuity in the area's
demography.

This is not the method adopted by most geographical studies of
borderlands.[7] Some consider boundaries in general.[8] Of those concerned
with a particular borderland, a few virtually ignore history altogether.[9]
Others include an historical review even though they do not employ
historical analysis.[10] An exception is Andrew Burghardt's study of
Burgenland, Austria.[11] He saw Burgenland as a border between east and
west and examined the history of the forces which passed through or
commingled there. Less interested in trans-boundary differences than in the
opposing currents which moulded the area, he considered only one side of
the boundary. His work is relevant here because it shows how the tensions of
the march and the melding of cultures imparted character to the area. This is
also an important theme in Pyrenean history.

One work illustrates the use of historical methods to uncover trans-
boundary contrasts: Suzanne Daveau's doctoral dissertation at Lyon.[12]
There are more sophisticated ways to manipulate data than those she
employed ('rates of change' hardly appear); nevertheless, the work is
admirable historical geography. Daveau recognized the same two problems in
the Jura that were raised for the Pyrenees. First, how has nearness to the
boundary affected the area's inhabitants? Second, how has political
partition in a physically homogeneous area influenced the character of the
landscapes of either side?[13] Her answers depend upon a description of the
Jura's demography, agriculture, land use, and economy over several
centuries. Time after time patterns emerged which she explained by invoking
economic, social, or political conditions in one country or the other.[14] The
boundary's character changed, too. Relatively permeable at first, it gradually
became a greater and greater social and economic discontinuity as the people
on both sides were more and more securely bound to the affairs of their
states. This widening of the border gap, as it were, has also occurred in the
Pyrenees.[15]

Only a few authors have explicitly recognized the importance of the
international boundary in the Pyrenees. Instead it has been more common to
link the peculiarities of local economy and culture to climate and land
forms, or to the traditions of formerly isolated valleys. Excessive concern
with the influences of physiography has obscured the differentiating effects
of the French and Spanish governments, even though since Napoleon's rule
their characters have diverged widely.[16]

In a review of Daveau's dissertation, Michel Chevalier discussed its
relevance to the Pyrenees.[17] It was difficult, he said, to imagine applying
these historical and political methods in the central Pyrenees where an
extensive highland zone of rocks and pastures obliterated the idea of a
'border population'. Here too the climatic contrast overwhelmed the

political. He thought the French and Spanish Pyrenees lent themselves to international comparison only at the eastern or western extremities of the range.

Maximilien Sorre's doctoral dissertation at the University of Paris studied both slopes of the Eastern Pyrenees.[18] It was not specifically a comparison between Ampurdán and Rousillon, but Sorre noted the ancient contrast between the two, a contrast which is still apparent. Today Rousillon grows fruit and vegetables on irrigated fields for the markets of northern France. The hallmark of the Spanish side is its textile industry, spread northward from Barcelona, which mingles with a traditional polyculture based on the Mediterranean triad: olives, vines, and cereals.[19] But these contrasts did not interest Sorre so much as the altitudinal zonation of nature and human activity in the mountains. Elevation structured his 'ecological' approach (this is what he meant by *biologique* in the title).[20]

The only regional monograph straddling the boundary in the Central Pyrenees is Pierre Birot's comparison of Pallars and Couserans.[21] Birot recognized the importance of government efforts to develop communications—roads in particular. The early extension of all-weather roads in Couserans freed French farmers from the need to produce wholly for their own subsistence and allowed them to specialize; to sell and buy in larger markets. In Spain an archaic and insufficient infra-structure denied these possibilities to most of the peasants of Pallars. The difference Birot attributed not only to the rugged topography of the Spanish slope but also to the French government's prodigious road-building programmes.[22] But everywhere else in his comparison he came up against the problems posed by climatic, geological, and pedological inequalities without finding any satisfactory way to cope with them. Chevalier cited Birot's difficulties to show that international comparison was not feasible in the Central Pyrenees.[23]

This view is probably wrong. An historical study which used rates of change as a comparative measure might successfully explore the effects of Spanish or French administration in the Central Pyrenees. Using rates of change tends to attenuate the influence of different base levels. Although the present study deals only with the relatively homogeneous Western Pyrenees, it should be possible to extend it eastward to the rest of the range.

In the Western Pyrenees one major study includes both Spain and France; it is Théodore Lefebvre's dissertation at the University of Paris in 1932.[24] In his huge area (it extended westward to include part of the Cantabrian Mountains), it was the contrast between the northern and the southern slopes which stood out. It might still. The southern slope falls away to the Ebro valley. There are only two towns, Pamplona and Vitoria. Between them the road runs for sixty miles, past villages dusty from the hooves of sheep, past men bent over the harvest. It is a land of vast grazings, wheat, olives, fruits, and dark wine; a rural landscape. But north of the mountains, along the coast, Basques built the industries of Bilbao, San Sebastian, and the valleys in between: shipbuilding, hardware, coal, iron and steel. The ports are busy. To fish or trade, the Basques have sailed as far as Newfoundland for perhaps 800 years.

Within this compass, France was represented by only a small and undeveloped portion of the northern slope, agricultural like the northern edge of Navarre. To Lefebvre, thinking of his whole area and writing when the influence of the environment was given greater weight than it is now, the international boundary seemed insignificant.[25]

Much has changed in the fifty years since Lefebvre began his study. The very land looks different. There are new crops, new tools, more pastures, fewer fields, and fewer people. It is appropriate to write again about the Western Pyrenees. It is also appropriate that the account should focus upon a neglected but essential aspect of the Pyrenean landscape, its division between two nations, especially at a time when their governments are so different: authoritarian in Spain, republican in France. The purpose is twofold: to describe the land and its people, and to show how administrative division has become a major component of the landscape.

[1] In the area studied here, the Western Pyrenees, boundary and watershed coincide only rarely. Most of the area lies on the mountains' northern slope.

[2] Henri Cavaillès, *La Vie pastorale et agricole dans les Pyrénées des Gaves, de l'Adour et des Nestes; étude de géographie humaine* (Paris: A. Colin, 1931), pp. 74–96. This is Cavaillès' doctoral dissertation at the University of Paris.

[3] See: Ramón Violant y Simorra, *El Pirineo español; vida, usos, costumbres, creencias y tradiciones de una cultura milenaria que desaparece* (Madrid: Plus-Ultra, 1949).

[4] Andorra's official language is Catalan. Bi- or trilingualism is widespread there.

[5] For a good introduction to the physical geography of the range, see: Luis Solé Sabarís, *Los Pirineos; el medio y el hombre* (Barcelona: A. Martín, 1951), pp. 7–194.

[6] Of course it is not the boundary itself which is influential, but rather the two administrations which it delimits.

[7] For introductions to the study of boundaries, see Jacques Ancel, *Géographie des frontières* (Paris: Gallimard, 1938); Julian V. Minghi, 'Boundary studies in Political Geography; review article', *Annals of the Association of American Geographers*, LIII (1963), 407–28; J. R. V. Prescott, *The geography of frontiers and boundaries* (Chicago: Aldine, 1965); and id., *The geography of state policies* (Chicago: Aldine, 1969), chaps. 2 and 4. The last three items have bibliographies.

[8] e.g. Stephen B. Jones, 'Boundary concepts in the setting of place and time', *Annals of the Association of American Geographers*, XLIX (1959), 241–55; Ladis K. D. Kristof, 'The nature of frontiers and boundaries', *Annals of the Association of American Geographers*, XLIX (1959), 269–82.

[9] e.g. Robert S. Platt, *A Geographical study of the Dutch–German border* ('Landeskundliche Karten und Hefte der G. K. W.'; Reihe, Siedlung und Landschaft in Westfalen', No. 3; Münster: Geographischen Kommission für Westfalen, 1958); id., 'The Saarland, an international borderland. Social geography from field study of nine border villages', *Erdkunde*, XV (1961), 54–68.

[10] Richard Hartshorne, 'Geographic and political boundaries in upper Silesia', *Annals of the Association of American Geographers*, XXIII (1933), 195–228; Arthur E. Moodie, *The Italo-Yugoslav boundary; a study in political geography* (London: G. Philip, 1945); J. W. House, 'The Franco–Italian boundary in the Alpes Maritimes', *Transactions and papers of the Institute of British Geographers*, XXVI (1959), 107–31.

[11] Andrew F. Burghardt, *Borderland: a historical and geographical study of Burgenland, Austria* (Madison: University of Wisconsin Press, 1962).

12 Suzanne Daveau, *Les Régions frontalières de la montagne jurassienne; étude de géographie humaine* ('Mémoires et Documents', no. 14; Lyon: Institut des études rhodaniennes de l'Université de Lyon, 1959).

13 Daveau, p. 12.

14 There is a brief summary of the study in Prescott, *The geography of frontiers and boundaries*, pp. 96–9.

15 For an example see: Michel Chevalier, *La Vie humaine dans les Pyrénées ariégeoises* (Paris: Génin, 1956, pp. 975–6. This is his doctoral dissertation at the University of Toulouse.

16 An exception is Georges Viers, who stressed political division in the introduction to his book, *Les Pyrénées* (Paris: Presses Universitaires de France, 1973), pp. 5–6.

17 Michel Chevalier, 'Le Jura, montagne frontière', *RGPSO* XXXI (1960), 425–35.

18 Maximilien Sorre, *Les Pyrénées méditerranéennes; étude de géographie biologique* (Paris: A. Colin, 1913).

19 On Ampurdán see the doctoral dissertation (University of Madrid) of Alberto Compte Freixanet, 'El alto Ampurdán', *Pirineos*, XIX–XX (1963–4), 5–283. Pierre Deffontaines discusses the cross-boundary contrasts in 'Parallèle entre les économies de l'Ampourdán et du Roussillon: le rôle d'une frontière,' *RGPSO* XXXVIII (1967), 243–58.

20 The theme also permeates his book on the whole range: *Les Pyrénées* (Paris: A. Colin, 1922).

21 Pierre Birot, *Étude comparée de la vie rurale pyrénéenne dans le pays de Pallars (Espagne) et de Couserans (France)* (Paris: J.-B. Baillière, 1937). This is Birot's *thèse complémentaire* for his doctorate at the University of Paris.

22 Birot, p. 8.

23 Chevalier, 'Le Jura, montagne frontière'.

24 Théodore Lefebvre, *Les Modes de vie dans les Pyrénées atlantiques orientales* (Paris: A. Colin, 1933). Lefebvre's unusual epithet for the Western Pyrenees (and the Eastern Cantabrians) resulted from his belief that the range extended through the Cantabrian Mountains to Galicia. Despite his environmentalist's bias, Lefebvre was a good observer. His dissertation is an excellent historical source. He did his field work in the 1920s; much of the material is fifty years old.

25 He was taken to task for his environmentalism and for his failure to acknowledge the boundary's importance in the review of his thesis by Daniel Faucher and Henri Cavaillès, *RGPSO* V (1934), 337–48– see p. 347.

CHAPTER II

The Setting

West of the Pic d'Anie the high and continuous crest of the Pyrenees breaks
down into a series of lesser ridges, peaks, valleys, and basins. The differences
between the rugged Central Pyrenees and the Western Pyrenees are
immediately apparent to even the casual traveller. From the Lazar pass, for
instance, between the Spanish valleys of Roncal and Salazar, one can see
both types of landscape. The view to the east is towards jutting, naked
peaks, with the first traces of Pleistocene glaciation in the U-shaped valleys,[1]
and uplands higher than the timber line. But to the west stretch gentle
summits capped with forests or meadows, and rolling hills and ridges, sloping
steeply to incised valleys or broad basins.

In the middle of this region of lower mountains, the international
boundary leaves the divide between Atlantic and Mediterranean drainage and
turns from its westward course to run north-westward toward the ocean.
Thus the area is bisected twice: once by the watershed, which runs nearly
due westward across the whole region, and once by the political boundary,
which after crossing and recrossing the watershed between the Pic d'Arlas
and the Ibañeta pass, there turns away to leave a large part of the north slope
to Spain. (See Figure 1.) The two lines, one physical, the other political,
divide the borderland into three broad regions. The first is the French sector,
almost entirely on the north slope. The second and third regions are Spanish.
One is the western half of the Spanish sector, on the north slope like the
French sector, and largely consisting of the drainage basin of the Bidasoa
river. The third region is the eastern half of the Spanish sector, on the south
slope. These divisions should be borne in mind when reading the descriptions
of the physical geography, in order to appreciate the distinctions between
the eastern and the western Spanish valleys, or between the northern and the
southern slopes. The eastern Spanish valleys comprise the southern slope,
whereas the northern slope includes all of the French sector plus the western
half of the Spanish sector.

As the divide between Atlantic and Mediterranean drainage decreases in
altitude, especially west of the Pic d'Orhy,[2] it ceases to dominate the
interfluves. A collection of uplifted massifs replaces the axial spine. Some of
the massifs are as large as 20 x 15 kilometres, like the Massif des Aldudes.[3]
They have been dissected by a complex network of streams whose valleys in
many places are deeply notched into the uplands. The striking characteristic
of the upwarped blocks is the uniformity of their higher elevations. From
vantage points they present a smooth-topped panorama of even summits and
ridges separated by only very shallow cols. The crest-line diminishes

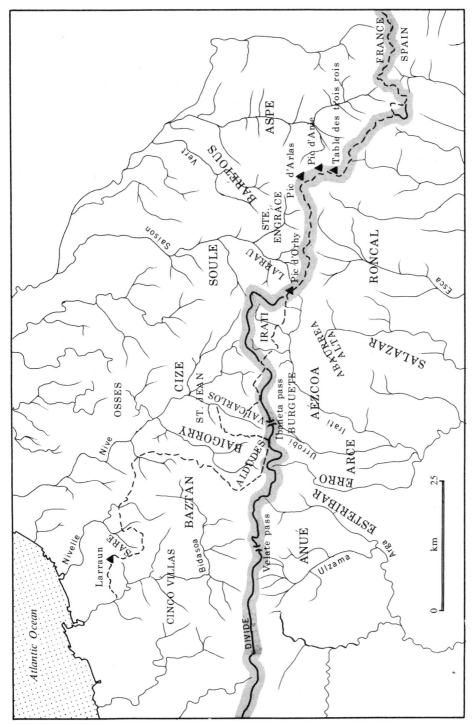

Fig. 1 The watershed and the boundary.

gradually from about 1,600 metres above sea-level near the Pic d'Orhy (which at 2,017 metres is the westernmost peak to exceed 2,000 m) to about 1,200 metres in the Massif des Aldudes, half-way to the Atlantic. The regularity of the surface one sees suggests a peneplain, uplifted and then dissected, but although the concept is useful to understand the look of the land, Georges Viers's studies show that as an explanation of geomorphic process it is over-simple.

The upland surfaces, if not forested, provide summer grazings for the flocks of the region, especially east of the Velate pass, where the summits are high enough to support alpine meadows.[4] The lower crests and surfaces between the Velate pass and the ocean may be heath (used as rough grazing in spring and autumn) or may even be settled with dispersed farmsteads.

In addition to their usefulness as pastures, the gentle crests make the most practicable routes in a region where the valleys are often narrow, twisting gorges. Many of the oldest tracks in the area, but almost none of the modern roads, follow crests. Distances between settled basins along crest lines are generally shorter than by valley, and no bridges or fords are necessary. The defeat of Charlemagne's rear-guard near Roncesvalles perhaps depended upon the Basques' familiarity with the crest-line trails. Roland and his foreign soldiers, thinking the deeply-incised Nive river marked the logical route to the lowlands, strung themselves out along its narrow length and were overwhelmed by Basques moving above them on the heights.[5] Today the old paths serve primarily as drove-roads and local footpaths. Many are passable by four-wheel-drive vehicles, and this is how jeeps reach the highest summer grazings to collect ewe's milk for the cheese factories in the valleys.

Tectonic depressions punctuate the uplands, nestled between or within the massifs, separated from them by steep slopes or cuestaform escarpments. Most people live in these basins, the sites of the earliest and best agricultural settlements. Into these lowlands mountain streams emerge from gorges to meander slowly for a few kilometres before re-entering the narrow valleys separating one basin from the next. The basins have various shapes. For example Sare's or Maya's are like bowls, about five kilometres across. St. Jean Pied-de-Port's trough is 18 kilometres long; its ends are often lost in haze. The little plain of Aldudes is much smaller, surprising the traveller with the tranquil contrast it offers to the twisting narrow valley leading to it, and to the peaks which rise around it.

Most of these lowlands are largely devoted to cultivation. Farmsteads scattered on the terraces or at the basin's periphery overlook their meadows and fields of maize. Somewhere along the stream the houses cluster sufficiently to be called a village. The basins make natural nodes of activity for the life of the mountains. They are the locations of the market towns, the focuses of routes, the centres of local government. Because their relatively flat terrain has been more amenable to mechanized farming methods, they are also the centres of modernization and prosperity. In the

summer tourists enjoy their peaceful, well-tended look, their gently
undulating landscapes framed by mountains.

In addition to the populous lowlands there are two areas of upland
plateau, the plains of Burguete (about 900 metres above sea-level) and of
Abaurrea Alta (about 1,100 metres). Each of these plateaux covers about 6
to 8 square kilometres, and each is the site of a village. Meadows and
pastures dominate the plain of Burguete, but Abaurrea Alta's plateau
includes much arable. Unlike their lowland counterparts they also have some
forested land.

None of the valleys in the Western Pyrenees has been extensively
glaciated. Most of them exhibit a V-shaped profile. They are generally deep,
narrow, and steep-walled, except of course where they open into basins. The
northern slope, narrower and therefore steeper than the southern slope, is
drained by a series of relatively short streams whose circuitous paths to the
Atlantic delineate a complex of valleys and basins without any dominant
orientation, or 'grain' to the topography. For example, Spain's Bidasoa river
flows first southward, then westward, where it receives a major eastward-
flowing tributary before turning northward to empty into the Atlantic at
Hendaye. Interfluves on the northern slope may be as prominent as the
divide between the Atlantic drainage and the tributaries of the Ebro to the
south.

On the southern slope, in the eastern part of the study area, the streams
resemble the pattern found in the Central Pyrenees: direct, descending to the
lowlands at right angles to the axis of the chain. They are the Esca, Salazar,
Irati, Urrobi, Erro, and Arga rivers.[6] This region is also distinctive because it
lacks the basins characteristic of the northern slope (except around Erro; and
at Zubiri, in Esteríbar). It includes the upland plateau areas of Burguete and
Abaurrea Alta. The climate is somewhat drier, a bit more Mediterranean in
character, than that of the rest of the study area, although enough
precipitation from the Atlantic reaches the upper portions of the valleys to
keep them green all year. Descending these Spanish valleys on the south
slope, one notes contrasts with their French counterparts to the north. The
villages are fewer but larger, and there are almost no dispersed farms. The
valleys look narrower and more thickly forested; their settlements are spaced
at intervals of two or three kilometres, situated usually where the valley
widens, with houses perched on a spur overlooking the fields on terraces
below. In the easternmost Spanish valleys, Salazar and Roncal, and also in
the French valleys of Soule, Barétous, and Aspe (the three easternmost), the
whitewashed walls and red tile roofs of the Basque houses yield to grey
fieldstone walls and slate roofs. The scenery in the east seems more rugged,
more 'mountain-like'.

West of these valleys, both in Spain and in France, the farmsteads
characteristic of the humid Basque regions reappear. If in the basins the
farms find room to coalesce and form villages or hamlets, in the narrow

valleys there is generally not enough contiguous space to allow anything but dispersed settlement. Set above a winding road which clings to the valley wall, the farm may be located on a terrace, spur, or lobe, its fields crowded on the slope around it. Nowadays these are the least favoured farms. Their sloping fields often cannot be worked with machines. Here one still finds the scythe, the sledge, the hoe, and the pack-frame in daily use. The terrain may be so steep that only a footpath links the farmyard with the road. Indeed, communications along many streams are so difficult that the less important valleys lack even a road. In some places the valleys become true gorges, as where the stream cuts through a sill of resistant rock.

Except near farms, most of the steep slopes in the valleys and around the edges of the basins are heaths, used for rough pasture. In places this zone extends to the crests. Other slopes and summits remain forested, especially those that are remote from farms.

CLIMATE

In common with other coastal regions of Atlantic Europe, the Western Pyrenees enjoy a climate characterized by an abundance of precipitation and a relatively narrow annual range of temperatures. The mountains, however, modify this temperate maritime regime according to the influence of various local factors such as elevation, aspect, and orographic barrier effect. The influences of the Ebro valley's Mediterranean climate and the 'continental' regime of the Iberian *meseta* can also be discerned in the region, especially in the south-east. In general the northern slope is maritime: well-watered and temperate. The leaden skies of autumn, winter, and spring, the steady gentle rains and the deep-green meadows are characteristic. West of the Arga river the divide between Atlantic and Mediterranean drainage is low enough to permit this oceanic weather to spill over and affect the southern slopes. Eastward from the Arga, however, the divide between north and south rises, and the southern slopes gradually acquire some of the Mediterranean characteristics of the central area of the Spanish Pyrenees, especially in the valleys' lower reaches, where summer aridity is more pronounced. Throughout this region the highlands remain well-watered and cool, as in the west, although winters in the more 'continental' eastern highlands are more severe.

Figure 2 presents data on temperature and rainfall for three stations: a coastal town (Biarritz, the resort just west of Bayonne); an inland city on the lowlands at the north-eastern margin of the area (Pau, capital of the Pyrénées-Atlantiques);[7] and another inland city, on the southern edge of the region (Pamplona, in the valley of the Arga, the capital of Navarre). All three lie just outside the region studied here, but it is roughly the climate they encompass which is modified by the mountains of the Western Pyrenees.

The yearly rainfall is everywhere greater than 1,000 millimetres, except that Pamplona receives somewhat less (914 mm) and experiences more summer drought than the northern stations. Were there a station at the

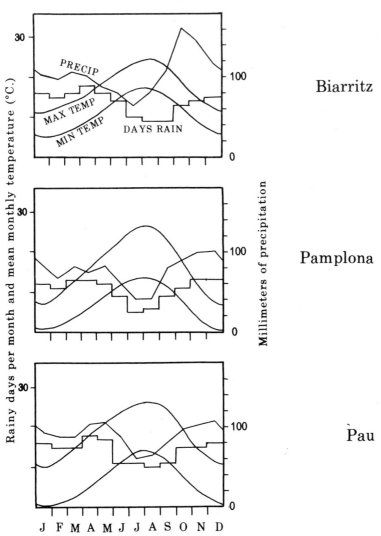

Fig. 2 Precipitation and temperature.

south-eastern corner of the region, it would probably show even more aridity. Maxima occur in winter and spring, generally as the result of cyclonic disturbances passing eastward across Europe.[8] Summers are driest, when the Iberian peninsula is influenced by the Azores subtropical high pressure, often in combination with a continental low pressure cell over the *meseta*. Enough rain does fall in summer to keep the mountains green, however; it may be associated with the rapid passage of fronts across France and the British Isles, or with orographic precipitation from north-westerly winds blowing off the Bay of Biscay towards the Iberian low pressure.[9]

The maritime influence upon temperatures is evident from the curves for Biarritz: both daily and annual variations are low. Inland, annual temperature ranges are wider (Pau has a range of 14·6°C.).[10] The annual range in Pamplona is even greater, 16·1°C.[11] Jaca, at the southern gateway to the Somport pass, is quite 'continental', with a range of 18·7°C.[12]

Except in the south-eastern corner, the temperatures are generally mild. Only during five months in Pamplona, four in Bayonne, is there likely to be a single day with a minimum below freezing. It snows only occasionally at lower elevations in winter, rain being more usual. What snow there is lasts only a few days on the ground. In March, 1970, the schoolmaster of St. Étienne de Baïgorry wrote to the author in Madison, Wisconsin, 'We have had a very severe winter. It hasn't been excessively cold, but since the end of November even Baïgorry has had several snowfalls. Of course they remained on the ground only a day or so, but even so, it must have snowed at least three or four times this winter. When you return to visit us again you must be sure to come in summer.'

Various factors modify this temperate maritime climate within the mountains. The altitudinal variation of temperature is the most apparent. Generally temperatures diminish with increasing elevation above sea-level. Since the stations depicted in Figure 2 are all at relatively low elevations, their average temperatures tend to be higher than those recorded in the mountains. For example, the temperature of Urdos, in the Aspe valley, south of Pau and 600 metres higher, averages about 2°C. lower than that of Pau.[13] The frost-free season at higher elevations is correspondingly shorter, but not so much as to constitute an impediment to agriculture except in a few eastern villages. The earliest frosts in the area occur in late September in the upper reaches of the Spanish valleys east of the Arga. Larrau and Sainte Engrâce (France) may experience freezing temperatures in early November, but elsewhere in the region the frost-free season extends from March until December. There may be frost as late as April in Larrau and Sainte Engrâce, as late as June in the higher parts of the eastern Spanish valleys.[14]

The snow-fall at various elevations reflects the local differences in temperatures. Although snow in Baïgorry occasions comment, Baïgorriards are used to seeing it on the summits surrounding their valley during much of the winter. The limit above which more than half the precipitation takes the form of snow lies at about 1,500 metres.[15] Snow is thus more important in the higher eastern part of the region, which also experiences somewhat greater annual variations in temperature due to its location further inland. As was evident from the dates of the first frosts, winters in the eastern Spanish valleys, less subject to the moderating influence of the ocean, tend to be harsher. From time to time, snow-storms there cut off communications to the higher villages. In France, snow-falls occasionally isolate Larrau and Sainte Engrâce.[16]

Besides being cooler, higher elevations receive more precipitation than lowlands. The humid air masses from the Atlantic cool as they flow upward over the mountains, and this tends to produce unstable atmospheric conditions and rain or snow. Such orographic effects raise the rainfall totals of stations in the mountains to at least 1,500 mm per year. Arette, in the Barétous basin, surrounded by mountains, receives that much.[17] Banca, in the valley of Baïgorry, receives 1,800 mm and may experience 200 days of rain in a year, even more than the coastal stations.[18] Other mountain stations produce similar figures. If the mountains are high enough, they may create climatic divides, as they do in the Central Pyrenees. Most precipitation occurs as the moist air ascends the windward slope (the north slope in the case of the Pyrenees) and little is left to fall leeward of the crests. The greater aridity of the south-eastern part of the region is due both to orographic barrier effects and to the penetration of the Ebro's Mediterranean regime northward through the valley of the Aragon.

The effects of topography are also felt in the *Föhn* winds[19] which affect primarily the valleys on the northern slope. The Basques call this wind the *haize-hegoa* (south wind), and the Béarnese call it the Spanish wind, for it comes to them from the Iberian peninsula. It is characteristic especially of autumn, winter, and spring, when air from the Castilian *meseta* may flow northwards towards cyclonic disturbances passing to the north of the mountains. The *hegoa* lasts anything from a day to two weeks: warm, dry air funnelled down the valleys, causing temperatures to rise rapidly. Its prevalence on the northern slope raises average temperatures there. It melts the winter snow (it is the *hegoa* which prevents snow from remaining on the ground for more than a few days at Baïgorry). It dries the standing maize for harvest, ripens the grapes, rattles shutters, and turns the grey sky pure blue. On October and November days its warmth brings flights of wood pigeons on their southward migrations over the Pyrenees. Basque hunters wait for them near the cols, forewarned by the hot breeze. But the *hegoa*, a Basque proverb says, has its wing in the water, *hegoak hegala urean du*.[19] As the cyclones to the north pass eastward, it is often followed by westerlies and then by the very rainy north-westerlies (*haize-beltza*, the black wind) which bring winter conditions back to the mountains.[21]

Other micro-climatic factors common to mountainous areas modify the local climates of the Pyrenees. Thus some valleys experience diurnal alterations of wind direction—katabatic and anabatic breezes. In the eastern Spanish valleys the heat of summer days can be accentuated by the anabatic mountain breezes: hot air blowing up the valleys from the sere plains to the south. The reversal of wind direction in the late afternoon gives relief as the valley winds bring cooler air downhill.

On the highest slopes, the greater amounts of precipitation, the increased ultra-violet radiation, wider daily and annual ranges of temperature, and exposure to strong winds, are conditions which encourage the alpine vegetation which is used as summer pasture. The lowlands also are subject to special climatic conditions. For example they may receive cold air slipping downhill on clear, still nights, producing shallow fogs. Driving down into the basin of Cize on early spring mornings one often sees the shallow pool of frost and fog on the valley bottom. By mid-morning it is gone. Because of their vulnerability to such frosts in April, vineyards are located for the most part on somewhat higher ground.

Besides elevation, aspect is the most important factor influencing the micro-climates of mountains, especially in the higher valleys. Where the valleys run exactly north-south, the insolation of either slope may be similar, unless of course mountains rise higher on one side than on the other. But the nuances of local topography generally cause the distribution and amount of sunshine received to vary considerably from place to place, and this naturally influences patterns of vegetation and land use. In a country where it is unequally distributed, sunshine acquires great importance. The most favoured farmsteads have sunny aspects. Those unfavourably sited have usually been settled later, and are more likely to be abandoned first.[22]

The sunny side of the valley of Larrau receives between 9 and 16 hours of insolation per December day, but the shady side only two or three. So important is aspect, especially in east-west valleys, that it is common to find the south-facing slopes cleared and settled, while the slopes opposite, in shadow much longer, colder and snowier in winter, remain forested. At Sainte Engrâce most farms are sited on the south-facing slopes; they are spared frosts until January and the snow cover lasts only a few days after each storm. The other side of the narrow valley is like another world, covered by a heavy mantle of snow for as many as six weeks, and subject to frosts from November to April.[23]

The Basques, like most mountain people, have words to describe the difference. They term the sunny (northern) slope *eki-begia* or *eguzki-begi*, the eye of the sun. The opposite slope is simply the shady place, *itzalbe* or *itzal-herria*. These terms correspond to the *adret* and *ubac* of the French Alps. The importance of aspect diminishes in the lower mountains nearer the Atlantic; it is much easier to observe its influence upon land use in the higher eastern valleys, as at Larrau or Sainte Engräce.·

VEGETATION

The vegetation of the Western Pyrenees is in most places the tangible expression of climate. In the mountains, substantial contrasts in climate occur over only short distances. To such closely spaced differences corresponds a diversity of vegetation, both in its natural state and as it has been modified by men. (Edaphic controls, while important on a local scale, are much less visible than climatic or cultural factors on a regional scale.) From the Atlantic, in the north-west, across the summits to the drier valleys of the south-east, or to the barren peaks in the east, one passes through a succession of vegetation zones which broadly correspond to variations in climate. Similarly, in a single valley, from stream to summit, one ascends through stages of vegetation (more or less clearly defined, depending on the valley's configuration and the degree of human interference) which reflect altitudinal changes in climate.

In the Pyrenees as throughout most of Europe, the so-called 'natural' vegetation is actually the result of a succession of climates and changes in local edaphic conditions (such as the draining of marshy areas) since the last glacial period. The millenia following the Würm glaciation were not characterized by uniform climatic conditions or even by gradual evolution towards the climate of the present day. Instead the climatic oscillations of the past 12,000 years or so favoured a variety of vegetation types, and the 'climatic climax' vegetation, besides being modified by local edaphic factors, presumably changed with time. It was only in about 800 B.C. that the present climatic conditions began to predominate, and with them the beech forests which are now characteristic of the Western Pyrenees.[24]

Although beech trees' pollen first appears in the palynological record around 8,200 ± 100 B.C.[25]   the lack of any ancient Basque word meaning beech may mean that the now widespread forests of beech grew up only recently. By the time they needed a word for the tree, the Basques seem to have known the Romans, and from them got *fago* (from *fagus*) to describe the beech. On the other hand, the prevalence of birch trees during the Boreal and Preboreal periods, and the long-lasting importance of oaks (confirmed by palynological studies[26]) is hinted at by the existence of ancient Basque words for them.[27] This is particularly striking in the case of the birch, because the tree is fairly unusual at present.[28] In Spain, the location of a few small groves of birch is kept secret by the makers of wooden utensils who depend on them for their raw materials. The *kaiku* is a vessel holding a gallon or two which is used for milking sheep. Although it is now made of stainless steel, it was traditionally made in one piece from a short length of the birch's trunk.

The Basque vocabulary for vegetation points to the presence of man. Man as an agent of vegetation and landscape change has influenced the environment of the Western Pyrenees since the beginnings of forest clearance, burning, and cultivation near the end of the Atlantic period.[29] This climatic period corresponds with the Neolithic, during which time the domestication of plants and animals spread to the Pyrenees.[30] From that time on, man was increasingly effective in altering the vegetation of the region, both by clearing for cultivating and grazing, and by planting and encouraging various forest species such as chestnut.[31]

Climatic change as well as man's presence therefore clouds the meaning of the term 'natural vegetation' in all but a few tiny spots in the Western Pyrenees. Nevertheless it is possible to outline zones in which certain types of vegetation predominate; and it is a useful exercise, since man's exploitation of these zones has given them economic significance.[32]

At the lower elevations, and nearest the Atlantic, the important trees are pines: maritime pines (*Pinus pinaster*) and even some umbrella pines (*P. pinea*). The maritime pines, far more prevalent in the Landes to the north, produce both turpentine and timber.[33]

Moving inland, and ascending, although there is here no clear-cut altitudinal zonation but rather an intermixture, one encounters oaks: pedunculate oaks (*Quercus robur*, L.[34]) and sessile oaks, (*Q. sessiliflora*, Salisb.). The pedunculate oak is often associated with the locally pre-dominant Pyrenean oak (*Q. pyrenaica*, Willd.)[35], although the Pyrenean oak has been decimated by human action and the ravages of Oidium disease. Pyrenean oaks (and other oaks) occur typically as pollards, massive but short trunks with young branches springing from the top. The slender boughs are harvested regularly from the old trunks for firewood or animal bedding, leaving a squat tree which is useless as timber and which cannot easily propagate itself. Pollards make a striking element in the landscape of the foothills. Some of them planted, some of them remnants of former forests destroyed by man,[36] they now punctuate the *touyà*, the heaths used as rough grazing in the foothills and on the uplands.[37]

The heaths[38] include furze or gorse, a spiny evergreen shrub with yellow flowers (*Ulex europaeus*, and a smaller plant, *U. minor*) and the heaths (*Erica vagans, E. ciliaris, E. cinerea*) and bracken (*Pteris aquilina* here), ling (*Calluna vulgaris*), and broom (*Sarothamnus scoparius*). With increasing elevation, and wherever the heathland rises above approximately 500 metres, the furze diminishes, leaving only bracken and heather and some grasses. The association at higher elevations is not known as *touyà*.

Virtually all the land in the Western Pyrenees which is not either forested or cultivated, or (in the east) alpine meadow, is heath. It is the heaths which are burned in the spring to provide better pasture. The farmers say this is what encourages the fine grasses of early spring on which the sheep graze before moving into the higher mountain pastures. In fact the heath, dominated by bracken, is a fire-climax community, maintained by human intervention.[39] The *brûlis*, as the burning is called in French, is forbidden by laws in both France and Spain—better enforced in Spain—but this does not seem to prevent the almost ubiquitous fires on the hillsides which on March nights look like thin strands of light flickering across the sky. The grass which turns the blackened hillsides green in April is soon overwhelmed by the bracken. In the autumn the ferns dry to a russet colour. Then farmers come with wide-bladed scythes to cut the ferns to make winter bedding for their flocks. In October they mow whole slopes, giving the very mountains a manicured look, and they gather the bracken there in tall stacks until winter when it will be brought down to the stables by ox-sledge. Burning, grazing, and the destruction of the Pyrenean oak and the beech on higher slopes, have tended to perpetuate and even extend the heath. The category 'lande' in the most recent French cadasters (this includes some alpine meadow) accounts for 53 per cent of the total area. 'Pastos' (also including some alpine meadow) in the 1962 Spanish agricultural census comprise 39 per cent of the area of the Spanish Western Pyrenees. The difference is due largely to the greater importance of forests in Spain.[40]

Throughout the region, edaphic conditions produce local differences in the vegetation. For example, poplars grow along the streams, joined there and in other wet lowlands by willows, maples, ash, hawthorns, and brambles. These ribbons of moisture-loving plants may extend deep into the mountains along streams, up to elevations of 700 or 1,000 metres on the northern slopes, joined in places by birch and elm. On the southern slope, willow and poplar are the trees most often seen at the streams' edges.

In the forested areas from about 300 metres elevation to about 800 metres, on the northern slope, the pedunculate oak gradually gives way to the beech (*Fagus silvatica*) which is probably the single most important tree in the Western Pyrenees. In many places there are quite extensive pure stands of beech, as in the forests of Hayra and Irati. The beech also grows in association with the chestnut (*Castanea vulgaris*, L.), a tree important enough nearly to have attained the status of a cultivated plant.[41] The chestnut provides nutritious mast for pigs, but more important (even in the recent past) has been the use of the nuts for human food, perhaps since prehistoric times.[42] The chestnuts are dried, then ground into flour to make bread or flat cakes. Many Basques remember years when chestnuts got the family through the winter. Chestnuts were eaten during the First and Second World Wars.[43] The chestnut tree is also a source of tannin, and the wood is made into various articles.[44] When the chestnut blight reached the Western Pyrenees (from Portugal) in the 1860s its ravages seriously affected the diet of the poorer peasants. The disease was serious enough throughout Europe to provoke extensive research into substitutes, and the most successful replacements for the native chestnut tree were Japanese varieties. Most of the existing chestnut trees are therefore not native to the area.[45]

At higher elevations, thus primarily in the east, the oaks disappear, and above 800 metres the beech forest is often pure, its trees tall and impressive. In places, it intermingles with firs (*Abies pectinata*), and at elevations of 1,200–1,300 metres there are a few vigorous stands of fir in the forests of Sainte Engrâce, Irati, Isseaux, and Arette. It was the huge fir trees, some towering straight for 40 metres, which were sought by naval engineers in the seventeenth and eighteenth centuries for use as masts. Extensive logging operations, the first to be organized in the Pyrenees, met the navy's requirements until the exploitable forests were exhausted around 1800. The effects are still evident.[46]

Above about 1,100–1,300 metres the beech and fir diminish in stature.[47] The tree which thrives best at these elevations is the hardy hook-needle pine, (*Pinus uncinata*). But economically more important is the alpine vegetation which begins here. Grasses, such as bentgrass (*Agrostis*, spp.), fescue

(*Festuca*, spp.), nard (*Nardus stricta*), and bluegrass (*Poa*, spp.), and various sedges (Family *Cyperaceae*) and legumes (such as *Trifolium alpinum*) form a turf which transhumant livestock graze in summer. A few shrubs, such as rhododendron (*Rhododendron ferrugineum*), whortleberry (*Vaccinium myrtillus*), and mountain ash (*Sorbus aucuparia*), and numerous wild flowers add colour to these high pastures. Like the heaths below, which are maintained by burning, the association of species which constitutes the alpine flora depends upon transhumance. It is in fact a 'grazing-climax' community. Alpine vegetation is most common around the eastern summits. It diminishes in extent towards the ocean, and the last alpine species grow just west of the Velate pass, which also marks the westernmost limit of summer transhumance.[48]

The vegetation of the southern slope reflects its somewhat greater aridity. The range of the beech overlaps onto southern slopes, as does that of the pedunculate oak. But the beech and oak association of the northern slope's middle elevations is replaced on the south by Scots pine (*Pinus silvestris*)[49] and, lower down, by xerophyllic oaks such as evergreen oak (*Quercus Ilex*), the Ilex of the Romans, providing a hard and resistant wood, bark rich in tannin, and an abundance of mast for pigs. Also present is *Q. lusitanica*, which occurs in small patches on the northern slope, but not nearly so extensively as in the eastern Spanish valleys.

The heaths of the southern slope differ, too. The characteristic plant is the boxwood shrub (*Buxus sempervirens*). Its name in Spanish, *boj*, yields the name of the whole association, *bojeral*. In the driest areas *bojeral*, compared with its northern counterpart, *touyà*, is sparser, dustier, and woodier—all consequences of the greater dryness of the sub-mediterranean zone. *Bojeral* and evergreen oak are characteristic in the lower Spanish valleys east of the Arga, on the south-eastern edge of the study area. Other components of the *bojeral* here also evoke the Mediterranean: Spanish broom (*Genista hispanica*), Lavender (*Lavandula latifolia*), and thyme (*Thymus vulgaris*).

Higher up the valleys (thus within the study area) Scots pine replaces the oak, and the *bojeral* includes more hygrophyllic plants such as bracken, furze, heath (*Erica* spp.), and juniper (*Juniperus communis*). The vegetation of this zone is complex, blending Mediterranean with Atlantic elements according to the aspect of the slope, its elevation, and how far west or east it is. Thus west of the Arga, where the humid maritime climate crosses the divide, the vegetation zones resemble those of the northern slope. It is in the east that the dry heath is most common, but even here a south-facing slope covered with *bojeral* may face a north-facing slope of beech forest. And throughout the region, beech trees and bracken grow above the *bojeral* and the Scots pine.

1 There was some minor glaciation farther west, as in Soule. See Georges Viers, 'Le relief de la Haute Soule et du Haut Barétous et les influences glaciaires', *RGPSO* XXIV (1953), 73—95.

2 Basque has long been a language more widely spoken than written, and Basque toponyms have eluded attempts to systematize their spelling. Georges Viers, whose familiarity with the region convinces him of the worthlessness of many traditional spellings, writes, for example, Orri, or Yarra, or Baygorri, instead of the usual Orhy, Jara, and Baïgorry. But it seems prudent to adopt here the so-called 'traditional' spellings which appear on the official French and Spanish topographic maps at 1:50,000, even though in many cases they sacrifice the nuances of local pronunciation to a desire to make the names look 'French' or 'Spanish'. On the problem, see: Viers, 'Les études toponymiques dans les Pyrénées occidentales', *RGPSO* XXVI (1955), 151—4; and Pierre Lamare, 'Sur la toponymie dans les cartes géographiques', *Eusko-Jakintza*, III (1949), 450—5.

3 Georges Viers, *Le Relief des Pyrénées occidentales et de leur piémont; Pays basque et Barétous* (Toulouse: Edouard Privat, 1960), pp. 229—60. Viers's doctoral dissertation at Bordeaux; this is the most authoritative work on the geomorphology of the northern slope.

4 'Pseudo-alpine' in some cases, because not all of these meadows lie above the timber line. They are a 'grazing-climax' vegetational form.

5 The theme is developed further in a stimulating though somewhat deterministic article by Pierre Lamare, 'Milieu physique et condition humaine en Pays basque', *Munibe*, VI (1954), 70—81. Other discussions of the links between topography and human activity are: Lamare, 'La Structure physique du Pays basque (quatrième article)', *Eusko-Jakintza* V (1951), 165—75. Cavaillès, *La Vie pastorale*, p. 54.

6 Pyrenean valleys often bear names different from those of the rivers which run through them. Thus, although the Salazar valley is indeed drained by the Salazar river, one usually speaks of the valley of Roncal (drained by the Esca river) and the valley of Baïgorry (drained by the Nive des Aldudes). Most of the valley names also designate the corresponding traditional communities.

Name of the valley	River
France:	
Ossès	Laka
Baïgorry	Nive des Aldudes
Aldudes (part of Baïgorry)	Nive des Aldudes
Cize	Nive
Soule	Saison
Barétous	Vert
Spain:	
Cinco Villas	Bidasoa and tributaries
Baztán	Bidasoa
Anué	Ulzama
Esteríbar	Arga
Valcarlos	Nive d'Arnéguy
Arce	Urrobi
Aezcoa	Irati
Roncal	Esca

7 In 1970 the name of the department was changed from Basses-Pyrénées to Pyrénées-Atlantiques.

8 See Hermann Lautensach, *Geografía de España y Portugal* (Barcelona: Vicens-Vives, 1967), pp. 61—2 and Figure 10; and André Le Gall, 'Les types de temps du Sud-Ouest de la France', *Annales de Géographie*, XLII (1933), 19—43.

9 See Lautensach, pp. 60—61, and Figure 10; and M. Billaut, *et al.*, 'Problèmes climatiques sur la bordure nord du monde méditérranéen', *Annales de Géographie*, LXV (1956), 15—39.

10 J. Sanson, *Recueil de données statistiques relatives à la climatologie de la France* (Paris: Ministère des Travaux Publics, Office National Météorologique, 1945), p. 8.

11 Great Britain, Air Ministry, Meteorological Office, *Tables of temperature, relative humidity and precipitation for the world, Part III, Europe and the Atlantic Ocean north of 35°N.* M.O. 617c (London: Her Majesty's Stationery Office, 1958), p. 88.

12 Lefebvre, p. 103.

13 Sanson, p. 8. Urdos's average would be even lower were it not for the effects of local *Föhn* winds.

14 Chambre départementale d'agriculture des Basses-Pyrénées, *Enquête montagne* (2 vols.; Pau: Chambre départementale d'agriculture des Basses-Pyrénées, 1965), I. 14.

15 Lefebvre, pp. 107—8.

16For information on the relative snow-fall at various cols, see Emile Fornier, 'Le déneigement des cols pyrénéens', *RGPSO* XXXVIII (1967), 309—24.

17*Enquête montagne*, II. 3.

18France. Ministère de l'Agriculture, Direction Générale des Eaux et Forêts, Inspection de Bayonne, 'Rapport de M. Georges Duplan, Ingénieur des Travaux des Eaux et Forêts à Bayonne, sur la Forêt Syndicale de la Vallée de Baïgorry, dite d'Hayra—Rapport de son histoire et du projet d'aménagement (1961—1975)', typescript in archives of Centre de Gestion de Bayonne; n.d. but *c.* 1966.

19This name originated in the Alpine valleys of Switzerland. Also known as Chinook (in North America), the wind is common to many mountainous areas and is produced by the dynamic heating of air masses as they flow downhill. It is a hot, dry wind.

20From Lefebvre, p. 134.

21On the *Föhn*, see: Georges Viers, 'Le Climat et les types de temps dans la vallée de Baïgorry' (unpublished typescript; Université de Bordeaux. Faculté des Lettres. Mémoire secondaire pour le diplôme d'études supérieurs de géographie; Bordeaux: 1950), pp. 32—7.

22Aspect may be the quality Basques think of first when considering a farm. In the narrow valley of the little stream which runs eastward from the Ispéguy pass down to Baïgorry there are five farms, two abandoned, three still occupied. During almost three months each winter, one of them (on the south slope) lies in shadow. Neighbours like to remember a story of the first year the present owner's father and his bride lived in the farm. Winter had been hard. On the morning of 2 February, as he put on his coat to leave the house, the farmer told his wife to prepare a fine lunch. It was worth killing the rabbit, he said, for he was expecting an honoured visitor, someone they hadn't seen in a long time. The bride, wondering, cooked the rabbit stew, spread a clean tablecloth, and set three places. But at midday her husband returned alone. He sat down to eat. She asked, 'But where is your friend? '

He smiled, 'He is at the door.' Stepping to the threshold, she saw him: spring's first ray of sun shining on the lintel.

23Lefebvre, p. 133.

24For a discussion of Holocene climatic periods and vegetation changes, see: Karl W. Butzer, *Environment and Archaeology; an introduction to Pleistocene geography* (Chicago: Aldine, 1964), pp. 402—9; and S. R. Eyre, *Vegetation and Soils; a world picture* (Chicago: Aldine, 1963), pp. 136—46; and Emmanuel Le Roy Ladurie, *Times of feast, times of famine; a history of climate since the year 1000* (Garden City, N.Y.; Doubleday, 1971).

25Marie-Madeleine Paquereau and Pierre Barrère, 'Palynologie et morphologie quaternaires dans les environs d'Arudy', *Actes*, IV CIEP, IV. 19.

26Besides Paquereau and Barrère, pp. 18—25; see: Paquereau, 'Étude palynologique de la tourbière d'Ogeu (Basses-Pyrénées), '*Actes*, IV CIEP, I. 99—103; H. Alimen, F. Florschutz, and J. Menéndez Amor, 'Étude palynologique sur le Quaternaire des environs de Lourdes', *Actes*, IV CIEP, I. 7—26.

27Birch, *urkië*; Oak, *haritz* (also the generic word for tree).

28Birch is an early invader of heaths which are protected from fire.

29Paquereau, *Actes*, IV CIEP, I. 102—3.

30José Miguel de Barandiarán, *El hombre prehistórico en el País Vasco* ('Biblioteca de cultura vasca', No. 42; Buenos Aires; Editorial Vasca Ekin, 1953), pp. 125—59.

31On the importance of Neolithic clearing, see: J. Grahame D. Clark, 'Farmers and forests in Neolithic Europe', *Antiquity*, XIX (1945), 57—71.

32The paragraphs which follow are based on personal observations in the field, and on various published sources, especially: Aimé G. Parrot, 'Le paysage forestier au pays basque français', *Eusko-Jakintza*, VI (1952), 85—100; Henri Gaussen, 'Les forêts du Pays basque', *Travaux du Laboratoire forestier de Toulouse*, t. III, vol. I, art. XVI (1941); Lefebvre, pp. 141—70, Plate XXXIX; Cavaillès, pp. 36—51; and Salvador Mensua Fernández and Manuela Soláns Castro, 'El mapa de utilización del suelo de Navarra', *Geographica*, XII (Enero-Diciembre. 1965), 9—15 and Plate.

33A few Mediterranean oaks grow near the Atlantic, also: cork oaks, *Quercus suber*, and a subspecies, *Q. occidentalis*, Gay.; and evergreen oaks, *Q. Ilex*.

34Also known as *Q. pedunculata*.

35The English name is my invention. *Q. pyrenaica* is known to French authors as the *Chêne tauzin*, *Q. tozza*, Bos., but *Flora Europaea* gives *Q. pyrenaica* as the preferred form.

36Pierre Balié, 'Les forêts de Chênes têtards du pays basque', *Revue des Eaux et Forêts*, LXXI (1933), 741—53, 825—33, 905—15.

37From *toúye* and *touge* (Béarnese), the local name for furze (*Ulex europaeus*), characteristic of this plant association at lower elevations.

38 Except where restricted specifically to plants of the genus *Erica*, 'heath' is used in this book to designate an association of plant species. The French word is *landes*.

39 Aimé G. Parrot, 'L'incinération des landes au pays basque français', *Bulletin de la Société des sciences, lettres et arts de Bayonne*, no. 66 (jan., 1954), pp. 1–11, gives a description of the burning. Its effects are studied by P. Jovet, 'Influence de l'écobuage sur la flore des pâturages basques', *Annales de la Fédération pyrénéenne d'économie montagnarde*, XVIII (1952), 23–94.

40 France, Ministère des Finances, Administration des contributions directes et du cadastre, 'Matrice cadastrale des propriétés bâties et des propriétés non bâties. Commune de . . .' (MS. ledgers for 81 communes on file at regional offices in Bayonne and Pau); Spain, Instituto nacional de estadística and Ministerio de agricultura, 'Primer censo agrario de España, 1962' (Typescript tables of results by municipios (for 59 municipios in Navarre) on file in the Ministerio de Agricultura, Madrid.)

41 Both French and Spanish cadasters accord it a separate category of land use.

42 J. G. D. Clark, *Prehistoric Europe: the economic basis* (London: Methuen, 1952), pp. 59–61.

43 Earlier, Basques may also have made bread from the relatively sweet acorns of the evergreen oak, *Q. Ilex*

44 For example, because it splits so easily, it is quickly fashioned into the tines of hay rakes.

45 Henri Gaussen, 'Les Châtaigniers japonais au Sud-Ouest pyrénéen', *Travaux du Laboratoire forestier de Toulouse*, t. I, art, XVI (1932).

46 The history of the Pyrenean forests will be treated in more detail later.

47 Not everywhere. The Isseaux forest rises to 1,700 metres.

48 For a discussion of the alpine flora and a bibliography, see: P. Dupont, 'Herborisation aux confins basco-béarnais', *Actes, II CIEP, III. 23–43. Also: Claude Dendaletche, 'Le peuplement végétal des montagnes entre les pics d'Anie et d'Orhy (Pyrénées occidentales): notes écologiques, floristiques et phytocénotiques', *Pirineos*, CV (1972), 11–26.

49 *P. silvestris* grows in the French Pyrenees, but the Aspe valley marks its westernmost limit.

CHAPTER III
The Valley Communities

The importance of the valley as a fundamental unit of economy and society is a theme which permeates Pyrenean history and geography. Agricultural activity, social life, economic transactions, and exchanges of all sorts; all once took place primarily within the compass of the valley. Tradition made valley and community nearly synonymous in the mountains.

The typical valley community included about a dozen villages, located at intervals along its length on terraces, lobes, or where the flood-plain widened. But for the Pyrenean countryman it was the valley more than the village which bounded the world in which he lived and worked. His flocks, together with those from the other villages, grazed on commons belonging to the valley, not the village. He traded in the valley's market—usually its largest village—and there discussed news of the valley with friends from other villages. It was the valley he named when telling a stranger where he came from.

The valleys were politically distinct as well. Theirs were the most important administrations in the area until Spain and France effectively asserted their dominions. In some cases this happened only relatively recently, perhaps a century and a half ago. During the Middle Ages the Western Pyrenees were largely exempt from feudal obligations. Many valleys then functioned almost as autonomous republics, building long-lasting traditions of self government.[1]

Although the emergence of the modern nation-states and metropolitan economies after the seventeenth century diminished their importance, the valleys were able to preserve vestiges of their former independence, especially in their ownership and administration of vast common lands. Today these commons, lingering traditions, and the valleys' continuing importance as a locus for many daily economic and social transactions, maintain the sense of community.

While the valleys were proud of their peculiar identities, and jealous of their autonomy, they were not wholly self-sufficient. They maintained somewhat distant but nevertheless dependent trading relationships with the larger towns and markets which were located where the Pyrenean foothills met the plains to the north and south. And every winter transhumance took flocks from high mountain villages to distant lowlands. However, the complementary nature of mountain and plain was more important to the inhabitants of the Pyrenees than to their lowland neighbours, for whom the mountains long remained a marginal and relatively little-visited region.

The valleys also trafficked among themselves. Indeed, the relations between adjacent valleys constitute another important theme in Pyrenean history. The transhumance of summer brought herds and flocks from the valleys to graze together on the high pastures along the crests. Because they were located on the divides, the pastures were shared by more than one valley. Conflicts, sometimes bloody, frequently erupted over pastoral rights. From about the twelfth century it became common for neighbouring valleys to sign treaties with one another to ensure the peaceful use of their alpine grazings. These agreements between valleys, called *facerías* in Spanish or *passeries* in French, were long-lived as well as widespread, and many continue in force even today. Because they promoted harmonious relations they also served to protect the local ties of transaction and custom which bound the valleys together into a larger Pyrenean community. In their partition of summer grazings on the crests, the local treaties came to embody centuries of pastoral adjustment and compromise. Later, in the nineteenth century, they guided the demarcation of the Franco-Spanish boundary.

This way of organizing the territory into valleys and associations of valleys points to a relationship between livelihood and topography. In many places the range is narrow and thus the valleys are short. The generally simple hydrographic network, in which most streams descend at right angles to the axis of the range, and the high interfluves, tend to make the valleys discrete compartments. This concordance between physiography and community varies from region to region. In the central area of the Spanish Pyrenees the greater width and complexity of the southern slopes alter this simple pattern. There the valleys may be broken into several parts, often separated where the streams run through gorges. As one approaches the Atlantic Ocean, on the other hand, the mountains become hills, the valleys appear less distinct, and the notion of the valley as a community diminishes in importance. But in the higher mountains, and through most of the area studied here, the organization of the terrain into discrete valleys is very clear.

In the Western Pyrenees with which we are concerned, there are about eighteen valley communities, embracing in all about ten or fifteen times as many villages. That villages should consider themselves members of a larger valley community rather than independent entities doubtless grew from the close interdependence of the various agricultural areas within each valley. The necessity for give and take between the different parts fused the valley into an indivisible whole.

The physical basis for the traditional agricultural economy and the cohesive social organization of these valleys was the diversity of landscapes which each included. The arrangement of agricultural activities within the valley was roughly threefold, and corresponded approximately to three broad physiographic divisions. The first zone included the most fertile lands, in the basins or along the streams on alluvial terraces, talus cones, or (in the east) on moraines. There grew up the villages, surrounded by their fields and meadows. This was the area in which the most intensive cultivation of the land took place. The other two zones were arranged, schematically at least, around the gatherings of farmsteads and fields.[2] First came the intermediate zone of slopes: the spring and autumn pastures, heaths, and forests. Beyond these, farthest from the villages, lay the summer pastures: originally Alpine but extended by the felling and burning of the forests to include most of the upland crests and summits. Pyrenean agriculture depended on the integration of this variety of environments. From the tree-lined streams meandering through the basins, up through the woods and bracken on the slopes, to the high meadows above, each part of the valley was used according to the season.

As in modern times, sheep and cattle were the mainstay of the traditional agricultural economy. In spring the herds and flocks left their winter pastures and began moving upward, following the growth of the mountains' meadows. In the Basque country the burning of the heaths preceded the shepherds' departure from the home villages. Burning produced fine grazing on the intermediate slopes in spring, followed by the growth of bracken which was harvested in autumn.

In the Middle Ages, and until the introduction of maize in the seventeenth century, the principal crops were wheat and millet or barley. Kitchen gardens in medieval times were much more extensive than they are today, and vines and apple orchards more widespread.[3] From the produce of the last two the Basques made famous cider and a light wine called *chacolí*. Flax grew in fields accorded special care and manured most lavishly, in the days when it was necessary to produce one's own cloth. In the valleys the natural meadows yielded two or three crops of hay each summer, depending on their situation and the weather.

As the grass and the crops matured during summertime the livestock reached the high grazings at the valley heads. There the herders lived in small stone huts. Although remote, these were in fact outbuildings of the farms to which they belonged, the site they occupied on the common being rented from the valley. They comprised a sheepfold, a sleeping room, and another room in which the cheeses were made (from ewe's or cow's milk). Such a cabin is called a *txabola*, *borda*, or *korta* in Basque, *cayolar* in Souletin and Béarnese. Still used in summer, these cabins dot the mountainsides. Farms might own more than one, generally at different altitudes. Regulations in many communities prohibited locking their doors, so that anyone seeking shelter from a mountain storm might enter them.[4]

The herders remained on the mountains until the cold forced them down. Tradition in many places fixed their descent for St. Michael's Day, 29 September, but it might occur later where the climate were mild enough, on All Saints' Day (1 November) near the Atlantic.[5] The return to the villages followed the harvest, so in fields near to home the animals grazed on the rowen or aftermath as they manured the soil. Autumn was also the time to mow the bracken, now dry and russet on the slopes. It made winter bedding for the sheep and cattle.

If the climate were mild enough, the animals could be kept in the village, in stables at night and during the coldest weeks. But in the higher valleys, where winters were harsher or meadows less extensive (and thus the grass in the hay-mow less plentiful), the flocks made a winter journey as well. This time downhill away from their home farms, to grazings in the lowlands. Near the ocean short movements sufficed, as from a village high in the valley to one downstream. Inland, where mountains rose higher, the sheep moved farther. Those from the valleys of Salazar and Roncal in Spain found winter pasture in the Bardenas Reales, 80 kilometres to the south, a practice which continues to this day. Today such long journeys are exceptional, but formerly they were commonplace. The herdsmen of Ste. Engrâce once travelled as far as Bordeaux with their flocks, and villages sent their sheep to graze in the Landes, north of the Adour. A few flocks from the Ossau valley still travel far to the north, even to other départements. The moves are now made in trucks or trains.[6]

Thus the most important links between the different parts of the valley were pastoral. To a large extent the valleys' cohesion depended upon the complementarity of the summer pastures in the highlands with the meadows and fields in the lowlands. Transhumance, the seasonal movement of livestock, linked the two regions. The system permitted each village to enlarge its resources. A few cattle or sheep might live all the year round on the forage in the valley bottoms alone, but it was possible to increase greatly the number of animals a valley could support by sending flocks to graze the alpine meadows when they were free of snow in summer, the intermediate slopes in spring and autumn, and the lowland meadows and arable after the harvest. The to and fro of herds and flocks involved the whole valley in a common enterprise. In summer, the lower villages depended upon the alps near the higher villages, while in winter the high villages had to send their herds down to join their neighbours' in the more clement basins.

There is evidence that livestock husbandry and transhumance in the Western Pyrenees are very old practices. They may have been associated with the permanent settlement of the area during the Neolithic. Some support for this idea comes from the monuments left by the prehistoric inhabitants of the Western Pyrenees. The large number of late Neolithic dolmens located in the highlands, at cols and on alpine pastures, points convincingly to ancient transhumance. Many archaeologists assume only ritualistic motives for the dolmens' construction, and there is doubtless some truth in this view; dolmens were generally burial sites. But domestication itself, the growing symbiosis between animals and man, was probably charged with religious implications,[7] and the coincidence of transhumant livestock and dolmens in the summer pastures seems natural. At the very least the dolmens' locations imply knowledge of the high pastures, and this may mean that seasonal movements of sheep and cattle are very ancient.[8] To some archaeologists, and to this writer, the dolmens' appearance also strongly suggests their use as shelters for herders. In fact many modern *txabolak* are built on dolmens.[9] Herders still seek temporary shelter in dolmens or use them as folds.[10] And in many places prehistoric menhirs and cromlechs serve to delimit the high pastures of adjacent valleys; a few of them also demarcate the modern international boundary.

The Basque language also illustrates the long importance of animal husbandry in the valleys' economies. Livestock was the traditional measure of wealth. As in Latin, in which *pecunius* (wealth) was derived from *pecuus* (livestock), the Basque word meaning livestock, *abere*, is cognate to *aberatz*, wealthy. The Basque words for sheep, swine, and goats, and for the various qualities and kinds of their offspring, show little relation to other Indo-European languages, and are thus very old. Place-names in the mountains frequently evoke the pastoral qualities of the site. For example, La Rhune, the mountain overlooking the fishing town of St. Jean de Luz, is Larraún to the Basques, meaning 'good grazing'—an epithet, however, which its overgrazed and denuded slopes no longer deserve.

[1] The valleys were less independent in Navarre. See Chapter VI.

[2] Although today the Basque country is noted for its dispersed farms, the earliest settlements were probably villages, or at least small agglomerations of farmsteads (G. Viers, *Les Pyrénées* (3rd ed.; Paris: Presses Universitaires de France, 1973), p. 65). As will be shown later, most of the dissemination of settlement coincides with the introduction of maize and the increase in population during the sixteenth and seventeenth centuries.

[3] See Théodore Lefebvre, *Les Pyrénées atlantiques*, pp. 199—210; and Marie-Pierrette Foursans-Bourdette, *Économie et finances en Béarn au XVIIIᵉ siècle* ('Collection de l'Institut d'Économie régionale du Sud-Ouest, VII: "Études d'économie basco-béarnaise" ', t. V; Bordeaux: Ed. Bière, 1963), pp. 34—41.

[4] José Miguel de Barandiarán has written an interesting article on these cabins: 'Vida pastoril vasca. Albergues veraniegos, trashumancia intrapirenaica', *Anales del Museo del Pueblo Español*, I (1935), 88—97.

[5] In former times—but as recently as 1948 in some valleys (Ribagorza and Pallars) in the central area of the Spanish Pyrenees—it was the custom to begin the new year on this date. This resembles Celtic traditions cited by Sir James George Frazer, *The new golden bough* (abridged, ed. by Theodore H. Gaster; Garden City, New York: Doubleday, 1961), pp. 360—1. A saint's day (St. Mark's, 25 April) was also the traditional time to start the ascent to summer pastures.

[6] Théodore Lefebvre, *Les Pyrénées atlantiques*, pp. 187—97; id., 'La transhumance dans les Basses-Pyrénées', *Annales de géographie*, XXXVII (1928), 35—60 (includes maps); Ramón Violant y Simorra, 'Notas de etnografía pastoríl pirenaica—la trashumancia', *Pirineos*, IV (1948), 271—89; Henri Cavaillès, 'La transhumance dans les Basses-Pyrénées', *RGPSO* IV (1933), 490—8; id., *La Transhumance pyrénéenne et la circulation des troupeaux dans les plaines de Gascogne* (Paris: A. Colin, 1931); Bernard Hourcade, 'La transhumance hivernale du bétail du Haut-Ossau', *RGPSO* XL (1969), 253—65; Navarre. Diputación foral, *Las cañadas en Navarra* (Pamplona: Diputación foral, 1936).

[7] Erich Isaac, 'On the domestication of cattle', *Science*, CXXXVII (1962), 195—204.

[8] José Miguel de Barandiarán subscribes to this view. See pp. 130—53 in *El hombre prehistórico en el país vasco*. On the other hand, one of the most learned scholars of the prehistoric Pyrenees, Prof. L. Pericot García of the University of Barcelona, interprets Pyrenean dolmens as having been intended only as sepulchres. (Personal communication, 20 September 1971.)

[9] J. M. de Barandiarán, *Anales del Museo del Pueblo Español*, I (1935), 96—7.

[10] Jean Sermet, 'Nouveaux dolmens des Pyrénées basques', *RGPSO* XXV (1954), 84.

CHAPTER IV

Landscape, Society, and Economy
before the Industrial Revolution

The communal organization of the valleys is first evident in documents dating from the late Middle Ages. At that time there seems to have emerged a more rigorous organization of the valleys' landscapes and governments, and a gradual codification of rights of usage and customary agricultural practices.[1] It seems likely that these tendencies were one of the consequences of increased population pressure on Pyrenean resources. The regulations for the use of arable and common which were formulated then were not only manifestations of the valleys' powers of self-government; they doubtless also were the response of established interests—especially pastoral interests—to the threat of incursions on the grazings by the increasing population and settlement.

Like the rest of Europe, the Western Pyrenees seem to have experienced a substantial rise in population during the twelfth and thirteenth centuries. The corollaries of this increase were many. In Europe, the growth of population provoked a rise in the prices of foodstuffs, which in turn increased the value of arable land, and meant that it became feasible to cultivate previously marginal lands. In the Pyrenees during this period, farming in the valleys was extended farther up the slopes, pushing into what had formerly been the waste or common, turning heath and forest to arable. Indeed most of the area at present inhabited or under cultivation was settled by the end of this period.[2] Romanesque churches abound in the Pyrenees, handsome testimony to the antiquity of the settlements they serve. One of the most noteworthy examples, the former chapel of an abbey founded in the eleventh century, may be seen in the high and remote village of Ste. Engrâce, a village which grew up around a colony of monks. In Béarn, where demographic growth may have lagged somewhat behind European trends, about ten new villages (the *bastides*) were founded between 1282 and 1358.[3]

Besides the settling of upland villages there were other consequences of the growth of population. In the twelfth and thirteenth centuries the valley communities of the Western Pyrenees accumulated a complex of legal and social institutions in which the land held in common became one of the essential attributes of the valleys. Most of the forests and the high grazings—that is, all that was not arable—was included in the commons. In the Atlantic Pyrenees, where land held in common was more widespread than in the east, between 75 and 90 per cent of the land still is held in communal tenure.[4] The 'commons' also came to include rights enjoyed by the valleys' inhabitants. These made a long list: the common of pasture, by which every household's livestock might graze on the village's open fields after the harvest; the common of estover, the right to gather wood in the forest for fuel, building, tools, and repairs; rights to hunt and fish; to make hay in common pastures; to gather furze or bracken on the slopes; to plant fruit and nut trees on the common; to gather acorns and chestnuts in the woods; to harvest branches growing on pollards; to assart, that is, to clear or grub patches for arable on the common pasture, often restricted to temporary clearance;[5] and of course the right to pasture livestock on the common land. With the passage of centuries, many of the common rights gradually fell into disuse, but the common grazings remained vital to the region's agriculture.

The establishment of common rights over private arable around the twelfth century also points to dense settlement and the need to subordinate individual rights to the common good. In the late Middle Ages, much privately owned arable land in the Western Pyrenees was held in an open field system, especially around villages occupying broad, fairly flat sites on valley alluvium.[6] A few villages preserved their open fields until quite recently. The open fields supported a system of communal crop rotations closely linked to the requirements of transhumant pastoralism.

To each farm belonged one or several parcels in each of the large fields surrounding the village. These large fields were called 'open fields' because they contained no hedgerows or fences dividing one man's holdings from his neighbours'. They were worked as units, and looked like huge single fields, though in fact they were made up of many individually owned strips.[7] They provided the framework for the medieval crop rotation. In the Pyrenees the scheme mentioned in late medieval documents may have been a three-field or three-course rotation,[8] alternating winter wheat and spring wheat, millet, or barley, with a fallow every third year.[9] Excepting vetch and peas, grown with the wheat, fodder crops or cultivated meadows[10] were unknown then, but all the households of the village or valley had the right to pasture their livestock on the three fields in autumn and winter. The sheep and cattle grazed on the rowen (the stubble left after the harvest) or the aftermath (the grass which grows after the harvest or after the last mowing of a meadow).[11] In return, the animals manured the fields as they grazed. This meant that all plots in an open field had to be sown and cultivated in the same way, and the field harvested by a certain date, to be available as common pasture. Peasants, though their land was freehold, could not do as they wished with it. If they wanted to farm it differently than their neighbours they could not. The system is known as 'regulated' rotation, from the restrictions the community imposed on individuals' use of the arable. These and other regulations, which favoured livestock husbandry, probably were imposed only after the twelfth century, when population increases threatened the stability of the traditional farming community by usurping (or 'reclaiming', depending on one's point of view) former grazing lands.

Similarly, the use of the common pastures in the highlands came to be regulated. Along with their charters of autonomy the valleys acquired the power to control access to their grazing lands. The *devête* (*devèze*, *devès*) and the *vête* were the dates on which the summer pastures must be entered or abandoned. The valleys also claimed the right to exclude livestock from other valleys, and to seize (*carnaler*) trespassing animals or even to confiscate the offending herders' food, clothing, and carts (*pignoradge*). Infractions or usurpation, threatening as they did the basis of the valleys' livelihood, often brought violent reactions.

Most disputes arose where pastures of adjacent valleys met along the crests. The twelfth- and thirteenth-century *traités de lies et passeries* between adjacent valleys sought to replace these violent encounters with compromise. The treaties generally specified the limits of each valley's grazing privileges, often establishing zones of compascuity in which the two valleys' herds might graze together. They will be discussed more fully in a later chapter.

Thus in many ways it was the defence of the commons which gave the valley community its first *raison d'être*. In fact, Pyrenean communities may have originated with the need to administer the common, or perhaps they were born in the struggle to preserve control over it.

The legal origins of the communities and of their title to the common land are obscure. There are several theories: that the land was held in common since society began in the area; that the common was a legacy of Roman law; or that the communities held their land thanks to charters from medieval lords.

But it seems more reasonable to suppose that in the absence of outside restraints the communities assumed title to the land as soon as it became necessary to do so. When population was sparse, grazing and settlement in the highlands might be unbridled. Only as their numbers grew did the inhabitants of the mountains find both the means and the need to assert their 'title' to the territories, and to invest themselves with the trappings and regulatory machinery of government. In their twelfth-century litigations they claimed to have governed their territories freely since time without memory. Who could deny it?

Communities were relatively free to acquire autonomous control of their grazings in part because the Western Pyrenees had been little touched by the civilization of the Roman Empire or, later, by the feudalism of the Middle Ages.[12] In these respects their history differs from that of the Mediterranean Pyrenees. The Romans occupied the Eastern Pyrenees earlier and more completely than the rest of the range. Near the Atlantic, the Roman presence was evident in the lowlands but not in the mountains, and the colonization came later and was much less influential than it was in the east.

Roman agricultural estates, fortified against the incursions of barbarians after the decline of the Empire, became the manorial establishments of the Middle Ages. The system of peonage and tribute developed by the Roman landowners and their henchmen contained the germs of medieval feudalism: the *colonii* of the Romans became the serfs of the seigneurs. But as Roman influence in the Western Pyrenees was less, so was feudalism less completely developed there. In this way the Atlantic Pyrenees became a region of freeholders. In contrast to the east, for example, the remains of medieval castles and forts are almost completely absent from the western valleys.[13]

It is true that lords in the nearby lowlands attempted to assert their dominion over the mountainous districts, but they were never effective masters of what were for them relatively remote and unprofitable regions. Eventually they let their claims rest, or settled for tokens of fealty for which they granted charters (*fors*, *fueros*) to individual valleys. These charters were much like those given to medieval towns in that they recognized the *de facto* independence of the valleys and allowed them a large measure of self-government. Thus did the valley communities emerge as the most important units of administration in the mountains. This process, which lasted about two hundred years, was completed around 1300.[14]

There were a handful of Basque nobles. But the noble houses of the Basque mountains were few in number, and short-lived in many cases. They owned only a small fraction of the land.[15] These nobles were not endowed with all the perquisites their peers elsewhere in Europe enjoyed; rather they lived among their neighbours as *primus inter pares*. They were exempt from certain taxes, but otherwise held few special prerogatives or powers.[16] Their neighbours were not vassals, but free men, and sat beside them as equals on the valley councils. The largest estates had tenants, to be sure, but this was not the basis for class distinctions, for many tenants were also freeholders (by virtue of another property they owned). In fact many Basque 'nobles' were no wealthier than ordinary commoners. Most Basques were free, owning their farms outright. Indeed, noble status was frequently attributed to this yeomanry, and Spanish custom held, for example, that *all* the inhabitants of certain valleys (Roncal, Salazar, Baztán) were noblemen.[17]

Thus the valleys came to be governed by legislators chosen from the heads of households. In the valley of Baïgorry, for example, the earliest form of government may have been a general assembly of all the householders, but as the population increased, representatives from each hamlet, called *jurats*, met to debate and vote (at a place in Baïgorry called Berrogain—sunny hill—from which the assembly took its name). The form of representation gradually became more complex so that it comprised three distinct councils by the eve of the French Revolution. These were a general assembly of the hamlet, called the Biltzar, which usually took place after mass on Sunday; an advisory meeting of the *jurats*, called the Berrogain; and a legislative council at which each hamlet cast one vote. Other valleys in the region were similarly governed. Only heads of households—freeholders—were enfranchised.

The tangible evidence of this freedom was the family farm. It continues to be a crucial element in Basque culture. The Basque farmhouse was built of stone to stand for centuries. Broad and two-storeyed, it sheltered all: family, animals, tools and hay. Around the house and farmyard lay the meadows and fields; often walled with stone.

Nowadays the house is whitewashed, except for the wooden beams of the long porch on the second storey, the stone lintel with its inscription telling the name of the first owner and his bride and the date they built the house, and the blocks of sandstone at the angles of the walls. Red tiles roof the house.[18]

So important is the house in Basque culture that each has a name, and it is this name which identifies the family within. A man's legal surname, used in the records of the cadaster and other government documents, may be unfamiliar to acquaintances, but his farm's name, centuries old, is always recognized. This is just the opposite of Irish custom, where it is the farmer who gives his name to the land he works.[19] In the Basque country, even tombstones bear the names of their houses.[20]

Attached by sentiment and name to his family's farm and fields, the *etxekojaun*, or master of the house, saw as his first duty the careful husbanding of the property. Opprobrium met whomever failed to maintain the prosperity and integrity of the farm. To this end Basque tradition required that the farm should pass unfragmented from one generation to the next. The inheritance was thus almost never divided, but given intact to a child (usually, but not necessarily, the oldest son) selected by the parents as the most suitable heir. Despite eighteenth- and nineteenth-century French and Spanish laws prohibiting primogeniture and requiring the equal division of the inheritance amongst all children, this Basque tradition still survives, having kept farms and families together for centuries.[21]

Primogeniture created problems. The younger children inherited nothing but the prospect of working as a labourer on the family farm; emigrating; marrying into another property; or establishing a new farm by enclosing a piece of the common. During periods of population growth many dis-inherited sons chose the last option, often turning the family's *borda* into a permanent farmstead, and it was in this way that settlement was pushed uphill in the late Middle Ages and again in the period 1700 to 1830. As might be expected, such usurpations of the common were resisted by the older established families of the valley. Communities sometimes tried to restrict the franchise (participation in valley government) to the heads of the 'original' households, and so the republics became less democratic, more 'oligarchic'.[22] In some valleys a householder might even acquire more than one vote, as by marriage to the heiress of another enfranchised farm. Disenfranchisement might also mean exclusion from the rights of commonage, a situation which invariably provoked disputes.

Eventually, of course, the valley communities incorporated the new settlements, a process doubtless eased by the demographic reversal which apparently occurred after about 1300, and which characterized Europe as a whole. Most of the evidence for this population decline in the Western Pyrenees is indirect. For both the French and the Spanish slopes, 'census' material first becomes available only in the fourteenth century; thus unfortunately no comparison with previous centuries is possible. In the Catalan Pyrenees to the east, where earlier data are available, there does appear to have been a decline in the population, beginning in the fourteenth century.[23] In the west there seems to have been some retreat of settlements and arable. Disputes over the use and control of pasturage, which were probably an expression of increasing population densities, diminish in frequency after the fourteenth century, a sign perhaps that the pressure of population on resources was becoming less acute. An inquiry made in Navarre in 1534 (for fiscal purposes) revealed a significant number of formerly inhabited places which by then had lost all their population. In the valley of Erro, for example, fourteen villages were still inhabited, and four had been abandoned. There is no way of knowing the size of their former population, however.[24] In Béarn, the fourteenth century saw a reassertion of seigniorial control over lowland forests and pastures, to the detriment of the mountain valleys (Ossau, Aspe, and Barétous) which had greatly extended their rights and dominions in the preceding century.[25] In particular, the Ossalois had been able to acquire (and legitimize) the exclusive use of lowland heaths just north of Pau (the Pont-Long region) for winter pasturage in the thirteenth century. By the beginning of the fifteenth century, however, their interests in the lowlands had been curtailed by the viscounts of Béarn,[26] and their pastoral activities must have diminished accordingly. It is uncertain whether it was the forceful character of Gaston Fébus of Foix and Béarn (1343–91) or the recession of the mountain economy which was primarily responsible for these developments. Records also tell of the visitation of the Black Death in 1348.[27]

The following period, from about 1450 to 1550, was probably characterized by demographic stagnation, if not decline. Census materials show relatively little change during this century in Béarn and in Navarre.[28] For the French Basque provinces of Labourd and Soule we have no information.

After about 1600, however, the population of the area again began to increase.[29] The growth accelerated during the eighteenth century. Most parishes reached a maximum sometime during the first half of the nineteenth century, after which decline set in. The decline has continued to the present. Villages in Spain and France alike followed this pattern, although population maximums in Spain occurred somewhat later than in France.

The more rapid growth of the seventeenth century and later wrought important changes in the Basque landscape. Making temporary assarts on the common was the usual way of augmenting the arable in times of need.

Farmers exercised their right to cultivate the common more and more frequently in the seventeenth, eighteenth, and early nineteenth centuries. The cleared and enclosed patches of arable on the common were called *labakis* in Basque. In some cases the clearings were formalized to the extent that they became rhythmic incursions of cultivation on the waste, relieved by relatively long periods of fallow when the common again became rough grazing land. Such clearings remind one of neolithic systems of slash-and-burn, or modern swidden in the tropics. The practice was widespread throughout Atlantic Europe. Scots knew it as the 'infield-outfield' system: the infield was the land close by the dwellings, intensively and continuously farmed, and the outfield was the waste lying beyond, farmed in patches and at intervals. The French used more evocative terms to describe the same divisions: *terres chaudes* and *terres froides*. In some Pyrenean villages the farmer had to pay a modest sum to the community for the privilege of farming a piece of the common. He who temporarily enclosed and ploughed the common pasture had no title to the arable he made, though the fruits of this cultivation were his. After farming it for two or three years the peasant was expected to abandon the land to the livestock again. Indeed, assarts were usually not so well manured as the home fields, and were located on poorer soils, so that yields dropped after the second year or so.

As the population grew denser, however, the assarts tended to become permanent arable fields, worked as carefully as the rest. The *labakis* then became the sites for whole new farms. A circular clearing surrounding an isolated farmstead often identifies these assarts today. Population expansion thus led to the dissemination of settlement. Dispersed farmsteads eventually became numerous enough to overshadow the older nucleated villages as the dominant type of settlement in the region. It was generally the dispossessed younger children who moved out of their natal farms to occupy the commons. The family *borda* often provided the nucleus for their new farmstead. Many farms at higher altitudes, or those located in remote places, still bear names including the word *'borda'*, e.g.: 'Bordaberria' (new *borda*), or 'Pikoziakoborda' (the *borda* belonging to the house Pikozia).[30]

The entire Aldudes region was settled in this way. Before about 1600 the area was uninhabited save in summer when herders from three valleys, Erro, Baztán, and Baïgorry, brought their flocks to graze there. The Aldudes basin and its surrounding mountains were a pasture held in common by the three valleys. But beginning in the seventeenth century, settlers (most of them from Baïgorry) began to clear and farm the basin. Punitive expeditions led by the *jurats* rode out periodically from Baïgorry to drive the interlopers out, but with little success.[31] Again the older parts of the valley were forced to incorporate the newly settled areas, a process which in France at least was hastened by the Revolution.[32]

The seventeenth century also saw the advent of a new crop in the Western Pyrenees, one which within about one hundred years would rise to predominance, displacing millet and wheat and engendering fundamental changes in the area's agriculture. This was maize, which was probably first introduced around 1570–5 in Guipúzcoa and spread thence to the Western Pyrenees.[33] In the late sixteenth and seventeenth centuries maize was consumed primarily by humans, not animals. Only later was it used as forage or grain for livestock. For human consumption, the kernels were ground and made into flat cakes (called *talo*, in Basque).

Taloak became a dietary staple, for town-dwellers as well as farmers. In 1673, Louis de Froidour, the Intendant of Louis XIV, wrote: 'The peasants subsist mainly on large millet ["gros millet"–maize] from which they make a kind of bread or cake they call *milasse*[?]. It tastes very good . . . but it lies heavy in one's stomach and one need eat only a little bit to feel full.'[34] The cakes were made until fairly recently. One may still see hanging by Basque hearths the long-handled shallow pans in which they were roasted. In 1698 another Intendant, this time reporting on Béarn and Basse Navarre, again cited maize as human food.[35] The new grain is first mentioned at the market of Pau in 1764, and doubtless by that time it was used to feed livestock in the region.[36]

Maize spread slowly through the area. References to maize become much more common after the mid-seventeenth century, and by 1720 it was in widespread cultivation. By 1644 farmers were growing it in the valley of the Gave de Pau, at Nay and Monein.[37] The early spread of the plant seems to have occurred in the lowlands: in 1669 it was unknown in the mountain valleys of Aspe and Ossau.[38] In 1673 the Intendant Louis de Froidour said maize and wheat were the only cereals commonly grown in Soule.[39] This probably means that maize had displaced millet by then, but that it had not yet risen significantly above wheat in importance. In 1698, however, peasants in Béarn depended on maize, according to the Intendant Guyet.[40] His successor, Intendant Lebret, noted five years later that the plant had been introduced to Béarn only a few years before.[41]

Maize's rise to predominance therefore seems to date from the 1690s, and in fact it was encouraged by several years of disastrous harvests and famine (1690–6) during which, for example, 6,000 persons starved to death in Béarn in two years.[42] Before the introduction of maize the reserve crops in case of failure of the wheat harvest were millet, turnips, and beets. Maize, however, yielded in years when the wheat crop failed—and yielded better. Maize acreage increased greatly in the 1690s, and by the last years of the seventeenth century it had completely replaced millet in the commerce of Bordeaux.[43] In about 1750 half of Béarn's fields grew maize.[44]

As for the Spanish Pyrenees, María Pilar de Torres Luna believes that maize cultivation diffused quite slowly, becoming common only during the eighteenth century.[45] By 1802 maize grew abundantly in the valleys of Anué and Baztán and those further west; it was not listed among the products of the somewhat drier eastern valleys of Esteríbar, Erro, Arce, and

Salazar, although the Roncalese grew a little bit to feed their poultry.[46] This is similar to the situation today.

One reason why maize was slow to diffuse as a field crop throughout the area was that the system of open fields with regulated three-course rotation could not be altered without the assent of an entire village. Innovation was feared because it led to risk beyond experience. In a tradition-bound society, living on the edge of subsistence, the old ways seemed safer: their outcome was at least familiar if not always comfortable. But maize may have been tried in kitchen plots. Or perhaps it was sown occasionally in spring as a last resort after the failure of a crop of winter wheat, and then, its superior yield having been demonstrated, it may have been accepted more readily. Or it may have been sown first on the temporary assarts which lay outside the open fields and which were especially numerous at times of high population densities such as these.

Maize's most attractive quality was that it yielded more grain and insured a more reliable harvest than had millet and wheat. In Spain in 1817, maize yielded from about half as much again to twice as much grain as wheat,[47] and the crop rarely failed. In Béarn during the eighteenth century maize yielded three times as much as wheat. The seeds were planted at intervals of 80 or 100 centimetres, but even earlier, when it was the custom to sow maize like wheat, it still yielded more.[48] Such an increase greatly improved the countrymen's standard of living. Famine, which had haunted the area since the fourteenth century, visited less frequently.

Agricultural practices changed to accomodate maize, once the new crop had entered the fields. The change in rotation was especially notable. Before maize's introduction farmers followed a triennial rotation which began with winter wheat, spelt, or rye (sown in autumn). This was followed by barley, millet, oats, wheat, vetch, or legumes (peas or beans), sown in spring. The cycle ended with a year of fallow.[49] Maize was a crop to be sown in the springtime, usually in May, and harvested in October or November. 'Sen Mark ardiak bortialat, artoriak lurialat', said a Basque proverb: 'on St. Mark's Day (25 April) the sheep to the mountains and the maize seed into the fields'. So at first maize replaced the spring-sown cereals in the three-course rotation. During the eighteenth century it became apparent that the short winter fallow between the winter wheats and the spring sowing of maize gave sufficient rest to the earth, and that the third year of fallow was unnecessary. The shift to a biennial rotation with no fallow was an important event. It increased the potential yield of the fields by half as much again.

Maize demanded more from the soil than millet or wheat. Therefore the abandonment of the fallow year—the reversion to a two-course rotation—went hand in hand with the cultivation of legumes and pulses, to help restore the nitrogen the maize had removed. These forage crops grew intercalated with the maize. Turnips might be planted after the wheat harvest. It is unclear when these practices became common, but Arthur Young noted them as he travelled through the region in 1787. [50] Young also saw fields dressed with ashes obtained by burning straw on them. But most fields were enriched with manure from stables. The manure was a mixture of dung with litter cut from the *touyà* heaths; this use of the heaths led to their enclosure and protection in the eighteenth century. Farmers also periodically marled the acid soils of the region with quicklime obtained by calcining native limestone.[51] This neutralized the soil to make more nutrients available. In the Basque forests one still encounters the large hive-shaped lime-kilns which once produced the quicklime. They consumed great quantities of wood as well as limestone: much deforestation accompanied their operation in some places.[52]

Maize's greatest contribution was to make Pyrenean animal husbandry more productive. The two-course rotation, maize, and the forage crops grown with it provided much more winter fodder than had formerly been available. Transhumance to lowland pastures in winter thus declined and could be replaced by stabling during the late eighteenth century. In addition, the elimination of fallow, the increase in arable, and incursions on the common had diminished lowland grazings: this also encouraged stabling. The stables in the villages then became the sources of the manure with which farmers improved their fields. All in all, the change-over to maize led to more intensive use of the land. To the traditional flocks of sheep and herds of cattle, countrymen were able to add swine in greater numbers than before, and this despite a decrease in the extent of the forests in which swine formerly had grazed on mast.[53] The open fields and common rights on the arable were gradually abandoned. Standards of living improved to such an extent that in 1757 d'Étigny wrote that maize was consumed by Béarnese and Labourdins only in times of scarcity.[54]

The substantial increase in productivity which eighteenth-century Pyrenean farmers achieved made it possible to cope with the growing population. Although some authors have asserted that maize's introduction provoked demographic growth, the facts seem to indicate that the stresses of prior increases in population stimulated agricultural productivity, and encouraged men to switch to maize. Unfortunately we have no information on food prices and wages or land values to show the way in which these developments took place, but the very timing of population growth, coupled with maize's slow diffusion, indicates that this is probably what happened. The beginnings of population increase preceded rather than followed the spread of maize. Throughout the seventeenth century the population grew. The increase was general: other regions of the Pyrenees,[55] as well as France and Europe as a whole, experienced it. Where we have figures, they are dramatic. The Parish of St. Étienne de Baïgorry grew from about 600 or 700 persons in 1603 to 2,500 or 3,000 in 1700, 5,000 in 1764.[56] Maize spread slowly during that century; but not fast enough to improve living conditions.

In fact it was the famine of 1690—6 which prompted the change-over to maize on a large scale.

The agricultural revolution wrought by maize was largely an eighteenth-century phenomenon. It was part of the rise in agricultural productivity which was one of the components of the industrial revolution. By this time, however, the circumstances of Spain and France being very different, contrasts were beginning to appear on the two slopes of the Pyrenees. The Treaty of the Pyrenees, signed in 1659, fixed the boundary between two countries whose governments were achieving that consolidation of power and economy which marks the modern nation-state. The making of the boundary is the subject of the next chapter. The following chapters describe the integration of the Spanish and French portions of the Western Pyrenees with their two nations, and the growing differences between them.

<hr />

1 For an overview, with archival citations, see Cavaillès, *La Vie pastorale*, chap. III; Florencio Idoate, 'La comunidad del Valle de Roncal', *Actas*, V CIEP, III, 141—6; and Angel J. Martín Duque, *La Comunidad del Valle de Salazar; origenes y evolución histórica* (Pamplona: Junta general del Valle de Salazar, 1963).

2 Unfortunately there are no detailed studies of the medieval economy of the region. P. Tucoo-Chala, the historian of Béarn, believes that the area was isolated enough to be only slightly affected by the currents which swept through the rest of Europe. (P. Tucoo-Chala, *Histoire du Béarn* (Paris: Presses Universitaires de France, 1962), and id., 'Forêts et landes en Béarn au XIVᵉ siècle', *Actas*, II CIEP, VI. 161—73.) Much of the documentary evidence for both Béarn and Navarre—at least that which is quantitative, such as census materials—dates only from the fourteenth century, a period when Europe was suffering a general decline in prosperity and population. (For example: José Javier Uranga, 'Fuegos de la Merindad de las Montañas en 1350', *Principe de Viana*, XV (1954), 251—94.) We have no long-term series of data. However it would be difficult to argue that the Western Pyrenees was an unvisited backwater, except in certain valleys, if only because the well-travelled pilgrim road to Santiago de Compostela passed through the region. The route was taken by Europeans from all parts of the continent, especially during the twelfth and thirteenth centuries. Emigrants from Gascony also travelled southward through the region on their way to northern Spain, where the king was encouraging them to settle lands recently taken from the Moors. (Marc Bloch, *French rural history; an essay on its basic characteristics* (Berkeley: University of California Press, 1970), pp. 13—14; José María Lacarra, 'À propos de la colonisation "franca" en Navarre et Aragon', *Annales du Midi*, LVX (1953), 331—42.)

3 Tucoo-Chala, *Histoire du Béarn*, p. 34.

4 Viers, *Les Pyrénées*, pp. 66—7, 87.

5 Assart = défrichement temporaire, roture (French); rotura, roturación (Spanish); labakis (Basque); treitin (Béarnais). Temporary assarts are a variant of the infield-outfield system. Assarting is discussed on pp. 34—5, below.

6 Before the eighteenth century, open fields seem to have been widespread, though probably not universal. See Jean Caput, 'La formation des paysages agraires béarnais; observations et problèmes', *RGPSO* XXVII (1956), 219—42, and id., 'Les anciennes coutumes agraires dans la vallée du Gave d'Oloron', *Bulletin de la Société des sciences, lettres et arts de Pau*, 3ᵉ série, XVII (1954), 62—70.

7 The best account of open field systems in general is: C. S. and C. S. Orwin, *The open fields* (2nd. ed.; Oxford: Clarendon Press, 1954).

8 Although there was not necessarily a correspondence between the actual number of fields around a village and the type of rotation it practiced.

9 The wheat was generally spelt. A few villages grew rye. Oats were sown only after the fourteenth century, according to Lefebvre (*Les Pyrénées atlantiques*, p. 202 n.), which may mean that the three-course rotation was not widespread until then. See also Lefebvre, pp. 407—10. I have been unable to find other evidence for three-field rotation.

10That is, meadows which are sown and tended, not 'natural' meadows which may be grazed or mown but which are not the object of careful cultivation. These are *prados artificiales* (Spanish), *Prairies artificielles* (French).

11The aftermath, by Pyrenean definition, is the grass which may grow between All Saints' Day (1 November) and Lady Day (25 March).

12Henri Cavaillès (*La Vie pastorale*) gives a good summary of this development.

13Justin Edouard Mathieu Cénac-Moncaut, *Histoire des peuples et des États Pyrénéens (France et Espagne) depuis l'époque celtibérienne jusqu'à nos jours* (2nd ed.; Paris: Amyot, 1860), V. 424—6.

14Cavaillès, *La Vie pastorale*, pp. 77—9; P. Tucoo-Chala, *Histoire du Béarn*, pp. 22—3. See also below, Chapter VI, for more information on the Navarrese *fueros*.

15Between 2 and 7 per cent of all the land in Béarn was owned by noblemen under the *ancien régime*. (Foursans-Bourdete, p. 27). The figure was probably much lower in the mountainous parts of Béarn, and lower still in the Basque country.

16Some nobles collected the tax known as the 'dîme', the tithe or tenth part of the peasants' production. For more information on social classes before the French Revolution, see: Jean Etcheverry-Aïnchart, 'Une vallée de Navarre au XVIIIᵉ siècle, Baïgorry; II—Les Gens,' *Eusko-Jakintza*, II (1948), 65—95. On the economy of the area, see: Foursans-Bourdette, op. cit. Some nobles, of course, pretended to more privilege. In the eighteenth century, for example, the viscountess of Echaux in Baïgorry tried to assume control of the valley's council, but she was unsuccessful. See: Etcheverry-Aïnchart, 'Une vallée de Navarre au XVIIIᵉ siècle, Baïgorry; III—Les Institutions', *Eusko-Jakintza*, II (1948), 209—28; and Georges Viers, 'La vallée de Baïgorry; les paysages, la vie rurale' (unpublished typescript; Université de Bordeaux. Faculté des Lettres. Mémoire pour le diplôme d'etudes supérieurs de géographie. Bordeaux: 1950), pp. 113—17, 176—7. In Spain, the valley of Baztán resisted similar noble pretensions in the sixteenth and seventeenth centuries: see Alfredo Floristán Samanes & María Pilar de Torres Luna, 'Influencias pastoriles en el paisaje rural del valle de Baztán', *Pirineos*, vol. XXVI, no. 95 (1970), pp. 12—13.

17Julio Caro-Baroja, *Los Vascos* (2nd ed.; Madrid: Minotauro, 1958), p. 78.

18The traditional architecture of the Basque country varies slightly from district to district. For a summary, see: *Pays basque français et espagnol* ('Les Guides bleus illustrés', Paris: Hachete, 1963), pp. 81—5, or the illustrations in Violant y Simorra, *El Pirineo español*. See also: J. de Yrizar, *Las casas vascas* (San Sebastian: Librería Internacional, 1929); Leoncio Urabayen, *La Casa navarra* (Madrid: Espasa Calpe, 1929); L. Colas, *L'Habitation basque* (Paris: Massin, 1925); Ch. Higounet, 'L'habitat rural dans les Basses-Pyrénées', *Bulletin pyrénéen*, no. 215 (1935), pp. 17—21; and on the folk architecture of the Béarnese area and the Central Pyrenees, see: Maurice Moreau, 'L'habitat rural dans la vallée d'Ossau', *Bulletin pyrénéen*, no. 241 (1946—7), 30—42; Fritz Krüger, *Die Hochpyrenäen. A. Landschaften, Haus und Hof* (2 vols.; Hansische Universität Hamburg; Abhandlungen aus dem Gebiet der Auslandskunde. Band 44 (1936) and Band 47 (1939). (Reihe B: Völkerkunde, Kulturgeschichte und Sprachen; Band 23 and Band 26) Hamburg: Friederichsen, de Gruyter, and Co. m.b.H., 1936 and 1939).

19As in Connor's Place, Flannery's Place, etc. See Conrad Arensberg, *The Irish Countryman* (Cambridge, Mass., Harvard University Press, 1938).

20The churchyard of Ste. Engrâce is a good place to see these. On the role of the sepulchre in Basque culture see: William A. Douglass, *Death in Murélaga* (American Ethnological Society, Monograph 49; Seattle: University of Washington Press, 1969). Toponyms are important in the Basque country. Indeed, no countryside seems more crowded with names. Not only each farm, but even each field and meadow goes by a name. Old trees, crossroads, hill-slopes, cols, hollows and spurs on the mountainsides, bends in a stream, outcrops of rock, paths, barns and sheds, all have names like those elsewhere bestowed on rivers, summits, and towns. These names are very ancient (say the Basque etymologists) reflecting long occupancy. Many names describe former characteristics of a place and may thus be useful historical evidence. Caro-Baroja, in *Los Vascos* (pp. 152—8), discusses house names more extensively. He distinguishes four categories: 1. names which are derived from the original owner's name (Anxonea, Anthony's place; Arosteguia, the carpenter's house); 2. names indicating former functions (Tolareta, the press house (a wine or cider press in the Basque country); Anxonekoborda, the shepherd's summer cabin belonging to the house Anxonea (the suffix -ko makes a noun possessive)); 3. names referring to the qualities of the site (Errekartea, the house between the streams); 4. names describing the house itself or its relation to others (Cortaberria, new hut; Etchebeltza, black house).

21The writings of some social anthropologists examine Basque family life and social structure in far greater detail than is possible or appropriate here. Julio Caro-Baroja, nephew of the novelist Pío

Baroja, has written three important books: *La vida rural en Vera de Bidasoa* (Biblioteca de Tradiciones Populares; Madrid: Consejo Superior de Investigaciones Científicas; Instituto Antonio de Nebrija, 1944); *Vasconiana, de historia y etnología* (Madrid: Minotauro, 1957); and *Los Vascos*; José Miguel de Barandiarán has written several articles on individual Basque villages, most of which appear in volume III (1923) of *Anuario de Eusko-Folklore*; see also Philippe Veyrin, *Les Basques* (2nd ed.; Paris: Arthaud, 1955), and William A. Douglass, 'Opportunity, choice-making, and rural depopulation in two Spanish Basque villages', Ph.D. dissertation, University of Chicago, 1967.

22On primogeniture and the development of oligarchic valley societies, see Cavaillès, *La Vie pastorale*, pp. 86–91.

23María de Bolós i Capdevila, personal communication, 20 September 1971.

24Florencio Idoate, 'Poblados y despoblados o desolados en Navarra (en 1534 y 1800)', *Príncipe de Viana*, nos. 108–9 (1967), pp. 309–38.

25The *fors* (charters) granting autonomous government to the three valleys date from 1221 (Ossau), 1222 (Aspe), and 1247 (Barétous).

26P. Tucoo-Chala, 'Forêts et landes en Béarn', pp. 161–73.

27Tucoo-Chala, 'Notes sur la Peste Noire de 1348 en Béarn', *Revue régionaliste des Pyrénées*, XXXIV (1951).

28P. Tucoo-Chala, *Histoire du Béarn*, p. 35; Florencio Idoate, 'Notas para el estudio de la economia Navarra y su contribución a la Real Hacienda (1500–1650)', *Príncipe de Viana*, nos. 78–81 (1960), pp. 77–129, 275–318.

29But the evidence for this is far from clear. Rural unrest, the persecution of non-Basques living in their midst, and witchcraft terrors punctuated the early sixteenth century in the region, especially in Labourd. Some economic historians attribute such manifestations to the stress of dense populations. (The *cascarots* were gypsy-like immigrants from central Spain who setled in parts of the Basque country after the end of the fifteenth century. They often maintained distinct communities. Another non-Basque group, the *cagots*, also lived in segregated clusters in the region. Basques, who considered the *cagots* untouchable, claimed they were descended from lepers. They lived in hamlets set apart from the village. Mitchélénia in Baïgorry, and Bozate in Arizcun are supposed to have been *cagots'* hamlets once. Their houses were required to have only the smallest of windows. They had to use a separate doorway and balcony in the church. No trace of any such distinctive group remains, however.)

30For example, see Julio Caro-Baroja, *La vida rural en Vera de Bidasoa*, pp. 237–44.

31See Viers, 'La vallée de Baïgorry', pp. 136–145; id., 'Le pays des Aldudes', *RGPSO* XXII (1951), 260–83; and Etcheverry-Aïnchart, 'Les Aldudes autrefois', in *Traditions des Aldudes* (Bayonne: Gure Herria, n.d. but *c.* 1964), pp. 57–64. On similar tendencies in the valley of Baztán, see Floristán Samanes & Torres Luna, *Pirineos*, vol. XXVI, no. 95, pp. 11–12.

32It was the Napoleonic cadaster which "legitimized' many such holdings in the last years of the eighteenth and the first years of the nineteenth century. By recognizing *de facto* occupancy and thereby establishing a man's title to the land, the cadaster put the new farms (some of these 'new farms' were two hundred years old by then!) on the same legal footing as the old. The same process took place in Spain, although at a later date. The Navarrese cadaster was extended to the mountains in the 1890s.

33According to M. Larramendi, *Corografía o descripción general de la muy noble y muy leal provincia de Guipúzcoa* (Barcelona: 1882), it was an inhabitant of Hernani, by the name of Percaiztegui, who introduced maize to the Basque country. In 1952, René Cuzacq ('Origine de la culture du maïs en Gascogne', *Bulletin de la Société archéologique, historique, littéraire, et scientifique du Gers* (1952), pp. 79–97, and 246–60) asserted that maize was first mentioned in a municipal ordinance of Bayonne in 1523, and his findings were repeated by Maurice Bordes, 'Les anciennes céréales et les origines de la culture du maïs en Gascogne', *Séances de l'Association Marc Bloch de Toulouse*, 1951–2 and 1953, p. 7; and Foursans-Bourdette (p. 35). Cuzacq was mistaken, however. The word used by the ordinance in 1523 was 'artho mayro', which has since been shown to be not maize but *Sorghum bicolor* Moench. I am indebted to Prof. Jean Sermet for bringing Cuzacq's error to my attention (personal communication, 1 March 1972).

34H. de Coincy, *Louis de Froidour en Pays basque* (Bayonne: Imp. du Courrier, 1929), p. 18.

35Lefebvre, *Les Pyrénées atlantiques*, p. 205, n. 4.

36Archives des Basses-Pyrénées, B 4564.

37Pierre Cuzacq, 'Introduction du maïs dans les Basses-Pyrénées et les Landes', *Bulletin de la Société des sciences et lettres de Bayonne* (1902), 196.

38Foursans-Bourdete, p. 35, n. 43.

39de Coincy, *Louis de Froidour*, p. 15.

40Lefebvre, *Les Pyrénées atlantiques*, p. 205, n. 4.

41Foursans-Bourdete, p. 36.

42Foursans-Bourdette, p. 35.

43Henri Enjalabert, 'Le commerce de Bordeaux et la vie économique dans le bas Aquitain au XVII siècle', *Annales du Midi*, LXII (1950), 29, 32, 34.

44Foursans-Bourdette, p. 37.

45María Pilar de Torres Luna, *La Navarra húmeda del noroeste* (Madrid: Consejo Superior de Investigaciones Científicas, 1971), p. 62. This is her doctoral thesis at Pamplona.

46Real Academia de la Historia, *Diccionario geográfico-histórico de España ... comprehende el Reyno de Navarra, Señorío de Vizcaya, y Provincias de Alava y Guipúzcoa* (2 vols.; Madrid: en la Imprenta de la viuda de D. Joaquin Ibarra, 1802), articles under each valley.

47Archivo General de Navarra. Informes sobre la riqueza territorial, comercial e industrial. Año 1817. Legajos 33, 39; cited by María Pílar de Torres Luna, p. 62, n. 95.

48Foursans-Bourdette, p. 37.

49See Bloch, *French rural history*, p. 31.

50Arthur Young, *Travels during the years 1787, 1788, and 1789 ...* (2 vols.; Dublin: for R. Cross *et al.*, 1793), II. 146–7. See Bibliography for complete citation.

51Cf. C. Juste and P. Dutil, 'Les sols d'altitude du pays basque', *Bulletin de la Fédération française d'économie montagnarde*, nouvelle série, no. 17 (1966–7), pp. 355–64.

52See also Arthur Young, *Travels during the years 1787, 1788, and 1789 ...* (2 vols., 2nd ed.; Bury St. Edmonds: for W. Richardson, 1794), II. 82, 134; and J. M. Barandiarán, 'Bosquejo etnográfico de Sara, II', *Anuario de Eusko-Folklore*, XVIII (1961), 152–4. In some valleys, furze and broom traditionally were reserved to fuel the lime-kilns (Viers, 'La vallée de Baïgorry', p. 120).

53Foursans-Bourdette, p. 46.

54Archives du Gers, C. 10, fº 47, cited by Bordes, *Séances de l'Association Marc Bloch de Toulouse*, 1951–2 and 1953, p. 8. Bordes does not agree with this interpretation, believing instead that maize became human food only later.

55M. Chevalier, *Les Pyrénées ariégeoises*, 132–3.

56G. Viers, *RGPSO* XXII. 269.

CHAPTER V
Statesmen and Shepherds:
The Making of the Boundary

The boundary between France and Spain has been one of the most stable divisions in Europe.[1] The line has lasted more than three hundred years since it was established in 1659.[2] On the seventh of November of that year, Don Luis de Haro, acting for Philip IV of Spain, and Cardinal Mazarin, prime minister of France, signed the Treaty of the Pyrenees in a splendid Baroque pavilion erected especially for the negotiations on a small island in the middle of the Bidasoa River. The Bidasoa separates France from Spain for about 13 kilometres before flowing into the Atlantic between Hendaye and Irun. The Island of Pheasants, as the meeting place was called, lay exactly astride the international boundary, and the pavilion and the negotiating table were constructed so that the line bisected both.[3] Thus the two ministers could meet without either having to submit to the humiliation of leaving his own country to treat on foreign soil.[4]

Although it is true that the Treaty of the Pyrenees contains the first formal agreement on the limits of the two sovereignties, it was primarily intended to end the hostilities between France and Spain, resolving the Spanish War which had begun as part of the Thirty Years' War (1618–48). It also arranged the marriage of Spain's Infanta María Theresa to Louis XIV. To contemporaries, however, the treaty seemed important for other reasons. It clearly established the European hegemony of France and the decline of Spanish power, and it justified Richelieu and his successor Mazarin in their policies of national aggrandizement and the consolidation of the domestic and international power of the King.

The Treaty of the Pyrenees thus embodied one of the outstanding themes of seventeenth-century history, the rise and establishment of the modern nation-state. Under the kings following Henry IV, and especially during the ministries of Richelieu and Mazarin and the reign of Louis XIV, France had grown from a collection of feudal baronies, held together by bonds of allegiance which were respected only whenever it was convenient to respect them, to a unified dominion ruled by a single sovereign government. Since the marriage of Ferdinand II of Aragon and Isabella of Castile in 1469, Spain had followed a similar course. By 1659 it too was a recognizable state, though one whose power had waned during the seventeenth century, while that of France had grown. To the legal prerogatives of sovereignty formulated by the beginning of the century, the policies of France were adding the concepts of territorial sovereignty and integrity. The tangible expression of this dominion was the boundary. Many of the treaties of the time contained clauses which assigned territories to one state or another, and perhaps thus established boundaries.[5]

The articles of the Treaty of the Pyrenees which concerned the boundaries of the two signatories were relatively few. Several articles dealt with towns and districts in the Low Countries and in Italy, both areas under Habsburg dominion which had been theatres of war. In the Pyrenees, the treaty was specific about the boundary between France and Spain near the Mediterranean, in Catalonia and Rousillon, an area which had also been one of the seats of war. Two annexes signed in 1660 settled the partition of the Cerdagne region of Catalonia by assigning thirty-three villages of the Cerdagne (from the Carol valley to the Capcir) to France, incidentally producing the anomalous situation of Llivia (a Spanish enclave in France which, because it was a city not a village, was later declared to be an exception to the treaty).[6] But the greater part of the Pyrenean boundary was not specifically delimited by the treaty of 1659. This is the degree of precision with which the negotiators fixed the boundary of the Pyrenees, according to Article 42: '. . . the Pyrenees mountains, which formerly divided Gaul from Spain, shall continue henceforth to separate the same two kingdoms. . .'[7]

The exact course of the boundary was nowhere described. Even in Catalonia, in the east, where some villages had been assigned to one country or the other, no line was mentioned. What the treaty established therefore was not a boundary line but a notion of sovereignty which apparently was precise enough for the time. Since the inhabitants of a village presumably knew the extent of their lands, the ambassadors doubtless assumed that to attach a village to a country would be clear enough. But even this degree of precision was seemingly lacking in the Central and Western Pyrenees. There the uncertainty occasionally caused confusion or quarrel—although not nearly so often as one might expect—until the matter was resolved two centuries later by the Treaty of Bayonne.

It may seem remarkable that a line proclaimed in the middle of the seventeenth century should have waited until the nineteenth to be determined exactly. But in only one small area, the Pays Quint in the Aldudes, did a significant jurisdictional question ever arise. Everywhere else villagers apparently knew to which country they belonged, although there were minor disputes over small pieces of land, especially in the Cerdagne. Indeed, when one thinks about the conditions of negotiation in 1659, it is clear that the line was even then fairly well known, at least locally, for the negotiators themselves had been able to meet at it.

The line was known locally—precisely enough for practical purposes— because it was in effect much older than its legal foundations, as it were, being the product not of statesmen but of centuries of adjustment by the inhabitants of the Pyrenees, especially the shepherds. The modern boundary originated with the medieval Pyrenean communities. Its origins gave it certain peculiarities of usage and status, legal transgressions of the usual concepts of sovereignty which for the most part were preserved in the nineteenth-century treaties of delimitation.

The shepherd's boundary was embodied in the twelfth- and thirteenth-century *traités de lies et passeries*. These treaties resolved quarrels over the use of pastures located along the crests between adjacent valleys, usually by arranging means of sharing the valuable borderlands. There were numerous such treaties in the Pyrenees, not only between valleys which later became separated by the international boundary, but also between adjacent valleys on the same slope.[8] In the Western Pyrenees, every valley along the international boundary made agreements with its neighbours (see Fig. 3).[9]

The pastoral treaties varied from place to place, but most established zones of compascuity along the boundary where livestock from either side might graze together. The agreements usually specified the kinds of animals which could use the shared pastures, and they might enumerate many other privileges, such as the right to gather furze or gorse, or to mow bracken for bedding, or even (as in the Echalar-Sare treaty) to remove limestone from quarries on the common. In a few cases the animals could only visit foreign territory during daylight hours (*de sol à sol*). Usually, however, flocks could range freely in the whole area of the *facería*.[10] Sometimes the privileges were not reciprocal, that is, the herders from one valley used the pastures of the other but not vice versa. In such cases a grazing fee had to be paid, although fees might also be required even in cases of reciprocal privilege. The agreements usually named guards to enforce the provisions of the treaty, and set penalties for infractions—often the confiscation of the offending livestock.

The pastoral agreements, in replacing bloodshed with compromise, also became commercial and political instruments. To further trade within the mountains the treaties also protected the free circulation of persons and goods. They enjoined the inhabitants of each valley to come to their neighbours' aid in case of emergency. The treaties were also treaties of peace. The valleys concluded them independently of the central powers. After the fifteenth century, despite continued French and Spanish wars, many treaties pledged their valleys to eternal peace, whatever the quarrels of their titular sovereigns.[11] Villagers even promised to warn their neighbours of approaching soldiery, and there were instances in which citizens of these valleys refused to bear arms in the service of Spain or France, citing their obligations to the medieval *facerías*. During the War of Spanish Succession (1701–13) both the Spanish and French armies were frequently thwarted in the Pyrenees by the inhabitants' refusal to fight or even contribute to the military effort.[12] Even during Napoleon's Peninsular Campaign (1812) both sides resisted participation and collaborated to keep their mountains peaceful. For three centuries the frequent wars between France and Spain rarely troubled the trans-Pyrenean harmony.[13]

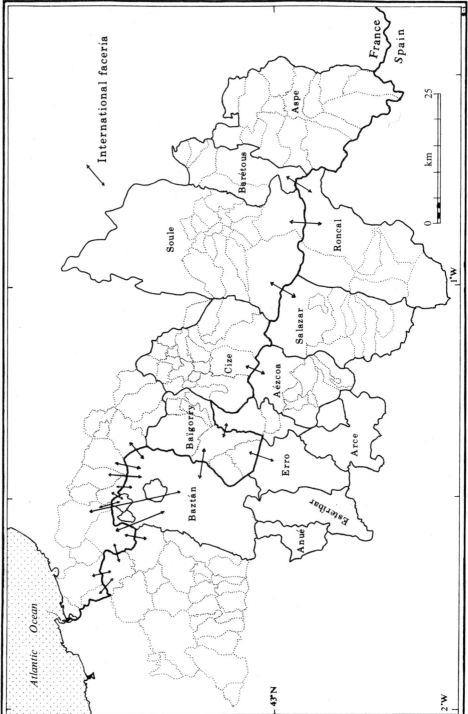

Fig. 3 Major pastoral groupings and international grazing agreements (1965).

The medieval *traités de lies et passeries* welded the Pyrenees into an alliance of nearly autonomous republics linked by custom, transaction, and pastoral necessity, which the modern nation-state displaced only slowly. Within this peaceful confederation the future international boundary could be traced along the zone where valleys met: it was given its peculiar form by the practical requirements of transhumance. In places there was no boundary as we understand it, but rather an upland shared by both sides. Elsewhere the treaties recognized a line separating two valleys' jurisdictions, but made it permeable by allowing herders and others to cross it freely. In Baztán the zone foreign livestock could graze was either 2 or 5 kilometres wide. Other treaties allowed grazing anywhere on the commons of either valley.

The treaties delimited the boundary quite precisely. The agreement between Roncal and Barétous in 1375 ran in part:

We, as arbiters, have demarcated [the boundary], by hammering and chiselling various crosses at the base and on the sides of the stone of Saint Martin [still a prominent marker] on solid rock. And from there we erected various crosses and other markers on a line running to the first hill from which the lowland can be seen . . .[14]

Several of the 'modern' boundary stones in the Pyrenees have been recognized for more than five hundred years. Every patch of grass, tree, or stream was thereby assigned to a particular community, or to several to share.[15]

It is curious that although many *traités de lies et passeries* were in force during the seventeenth century when the Treaty of the Pyrenees was signed, there was no clause in that document which attempted to repudiate these important expressions of local independence. For the next two centuries, also, most administrators in the region wisely allowed the valley communities a large degree of autonomy. During the War of the Spanish Succession, for example, commerce between French and Spanish valleys continued without interruption. In 1712, Barillion, Intendant of Béarn, familiar with local ways, wrote to his superiors asking leave to allow the Béarnese to sell their cattle at the fair of Saint Christina in Aragon, as was their custom:

. . . certainly these mountain people, accustomed to this commerce, would never consent to sell their cattle in the [French] lowlands, and I doubt even that we could prevent them from going to this fair no matter how forcibly we tried: all the passes are open at this time of year; it would be impossible to guard them, and you know how difficult it is to prevent people—especially people as fiercely independent as these—from following their old customs. You also are aware that the inhabitants of the French and Spanish mountains will do anything to conserve their union, which has never been interrupted even by the bitterest of wars. Besides the money they realize from these sales [of cattle] they bring back grain [from Spain] which they need . . .[16]

Barillion's attitude was not rare—other administrators wrote similar letters, although perhaps their 'tolerance' was really acknowledgement that it was impracticable to enforce French territorial integrity in the mountains. The free trade in cattle, grains, cloth, oil, and other necessities continued uninterrupted until the nineteenth century. When at last the governments of Spain and France attempted to regulate it, the inhabitants of the mountains turned unhesitatingly to smuggling.

Although France and Spain were frequently at war, the Pyrenean boundary itself never became a strategic issue after 1659. Boundary questions in this area were never as politically important to France and Spain as they had been to communities which solved them in the Middle Ages, so the medieval settlements endured. During the search for 'natural' boundaries at the time of the French Revolution the Pyrenees escaped close scrutiny: indeed they were considered an archetype of 'natural' boundary, though of course examined in detail they would have shown only partial coincidence between watershed and boundary.[17]

The lack of an unequivocal boundary rarely troubled Madrid and Paris as long as the Pyrenean valleys remained economically as well as physically peripheral to their states. What was adequate in 1659, however, by the nineteenth century no longer sufficed. The greater involvement of the Pyrenees in the circumstances of France and Spain—the result of expanding metropolitan economies—and the occasional disputes over the usufruct of pasture and timber in the boundary zone eventually made it desirable to mark the line on the ground. Two hundred years after the Treaty of the Pyrenees, a series of three treaties (1856, 1862, 1866) and their annexes described the location of the stone monuments which were erected to demarcate the boundary between the two countries.[18]

In the middle of the nineteenth century relations between France's Napoleon III and Spain's Isabella II were very cordial. The Empress Eugénie was Andalusian, and Napoleon III knew the Pyrenees at first hand for he and the Empress often vacationed there. Desiring to settle definitely the discord which had occasionally troubled the borderland (especially in the Aldudes region), in 1853 the two sovereigns established a *Commission des Limites* to locate and mark the entire boundary and to 'eliminate uncertainty about the ownership of certain territories and the enjoyment of certain privileges',[19] The commissioners were asked to do more than draw a line: the desired end being a peaceful boundary, they were explicitly instructed to ascertain and respect the rights, traditions, and needs of the inhabitants of the borderland. The commissioners themselves, who worked together for fifteen years, were few and apparently friendly: two plenipotentiaries (the French one was changed three times; the Spaniard remained during the whole period); and two engineers, a Frenchman and a Spaniard, who did all the field-work for the Commission. Proceeding methodically from the Atlantic to the Mediterranean, the commissioners gathered evidence in Pyrenean villages and incorporated their findings in three treaties and various annexes.[20] The division they established followed the ancient ways not only in its location but also in its recognition of the traditional pastoral rights of the Pyrenean communities.

Along its entire length, the boundary was drawn along the old inter-communal lines. Especially in the west, these rarely coincided with drainage divides, reflecting instead peculiarities of local usage. From the Atlantic to a point about 13 kilometres upstream the boundary follows the course of the Bidasoa river.

Both nations share the use of the river. Article 12 of the Treaty of 1856 stipulates that wherever the boundary follows a stream, road, or path (which it does in many places), or wherever it touches a spring or watering place, the waters or tracks shall be held in common by the two countries, to be freely used by the inhabitants or livestock of either side. Article 9 (1856), however, puts the dividing line in the centre of the Bidasoa, so although the stream constitutes a commons, it is not held *pro indiviso*. Fishing, police, and navigation rights in the Bidasoa and in its estuary, the Bay of Higuer, having been disputed at times, were the object of several clauses in the Treaty of Bayonne and subsequent agreements.

The first boundary stone[21] was placed on the right bank of the river where the line rises along a crest dividing Vera de Bidasoa from Biriatou and Urrugne. At the Col d'Ibardin, crossed by the road from Vera to Urrugne, the boundary abandons the watershed and drops into the Inzola ravine, leaving the headwaters of the Berra river in Spain. This is an ancient 'irregularity' in the boundary, and the old Basque name of the slope was *Mugakozubikomalda* ('slope by the boundary stone's bridge'). In fact many of the boundary stones and crosses cited in the annexe of delimitation antedate the treaty, and the Basque word *muga* (boundary stone) appears frequently in toponyms along the modern line. From Inzola the boundary proceeds eastward, bisecting the ruins of a hermitage build on the summit of Larraún, now on a crest, now deviating from it, then turning southward to encompass the pocket of Sare's basin. The Col de Lizuraga which here lies 200 metres west of the boundary here again illustrates the line's antiquity. This pass on the old pathway between Sare and Vera (once a route taken by prehistoric pack trains from copper mines near Oyarzun, now a forest track frequented by smugglers, soon to be a motorable tourist road) lies in Spain, but the boundary runs through a spring and past a dolmen or table made from three large flat stones. It is an ancient meeting place: here, just below the col, where the old copper road left the open to enter the forest, the *facerías* between Sare and Vera were signed.

In this way, running by the edges of woods, along streams or through springs, by dolmens, menhirs, and medieval boundary stones, the line divides France from Spain with more regard for local history than for landforms. Around Sare and the northern part of the valley of Baztán the line crosses the rolling uplands of the Nivelle's tributaries, leaving the divide between the Nivelle and the Bidasoa far to the south, in Spain. Here, and in the Aldudes

region, around Valcarlos, and in the Irati forest, it is easy to cross
accidentally from one country to the other without being aware of the fact;
even Land Rovers or Jeeps can do it in many places.[22] Indeed, the boundary
follows high and difficult crests only between Baztán and the valley of
Baïgorry (from the Col d'Iparla to Beorzubuztán), and, in the east, from the
summit of Orhy to Errayzekolepoa. But even in these heights there are
several deviations to accommodate traditional sheep-walks—two between
Baztán and Baïgorry, and three between Roncal and Soule.[23]

It is not the location of the boundary itself, however, but other
concessions to pastoral traditions which make the Treaty of Bayonne truly
remarkable. It legitimized, rather than abrogated, the old *facerías*. Article 14
allowed communities to continue to make arrangements for reciprocal
grazing privileges, provided they renewed them every five years.[24] Although
some *facerías* have been abandoned in recent years, most survive. Thus
unrestricted boundary crossings by shepherds and cowherds continue to this
day, and mayors still meet in the mountains to sign ancient pastoral
agreements, pay the traditional rents, nominate wardens (who may exercise
legal authority in foreign territory),[25] settle grievances, and even swear
eternal peace. For certain purposes the customs boundary is in effect pushed
back to exclude the common pastures. Other provisions of the treaty
allowed inhabitants of the boundary zone to cross the line without
passports, and, if their property were divided by the boundary (in the west,
this occurs mainly around Arnéguy), to carry agricultural produce freely
back and forth. The treaty also gave the duty of maintaining the boundary
monuments to the frontier villagers. Mayors from each side are supposed to
meet at the line and inspect the monuments each August.

Apart from quinquennial pastoral agreements permitted in general by the
Treaty, a few extraordinary grazing privileges received specific recognition.
These are the singular case of the perpetual French grazings in Spain's
Quinto Real; the compascuity in the southern portion of the Quinto; the
right of transit across the valley of Baïgorry enjoyed by livestock travelling
between Baztán and Valcarlos; and the perpetual *facerías* between Aezcoa
and Cize and between Roncal and Barétous.

The most unusual of these is the case of the grazings in the Quinto Real, a
zone of about 25 square kilometres, consisting of the headwaters of the Nive
des Aldudes.[26] The Quinto Real, or Pays Quint, lies entirely in the Spanish
valleys of Erro and Baztán, just south of their boundary with the French
communes of Aldudes and Urepel. The whole basin of the Aldudes, of which
the Quinto Real is a part, has a long history of pastoral disputes. It was
originally uninhabited, a vast common pasture shared *pro indiviso* by the
valleys of Baztán, Erro, and Baïgorry. Numerous sixteenth- and seventeenth-
century sentences and agreements concerned these commons; in essence they
established the right of Baïgorry and Erro to the Aldudes' pastures, woods,
waters, and subsoil. Assarts were allowed, provided they were temporary, as

were *bordas*, but permanent settlement was forbidden. Baztán's livestock could graze in the Aldudes during the day (*de sol à sol*); Baztán, Baïgorry, Erro, and Valcarlos might send cattle to graze on the pastures belonging to the monastery of Roncesvalles; and Valcarlos and Baïgorry allowed each other grazing rights on the pastures that separated them.[27] Most of these agreements probably originated before 1512 when this whole area was part of Navarre. (See Fig. 4).

The demographic expansion of the seventeenth and eighteenth centuries, however, brought setlers to the Aldudes, primarily Baïgorriards turning *bordas* into permanent homes. Resisted but ultimately successful, the new settlements not only usurped former pasture, but also increased French pressure on the grazings that remained. Disputes were frequent and violent.

Various other treaties relating to the Aldudes preceded that of 1856, the most important being the Treaty of Elizondo (also known as the Caro and d'Ornano treaty from the names of the two negotiators) of 1785, which attempted to eliminate the discord and confusion over the use of this zone by simply drawing a geometrical line to divide the area between Spain and France. All *facerías* were declared invalid.[28] The restrictions of the 1785 treaty, which severely compromised Baïgorry's pastoral economy, were evaded by the Baïgorriards. The Treaty of Elizondo had only a short effective life: it was ignored after the French Revolution and the war with

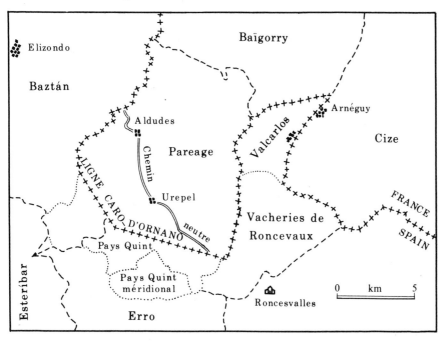

Fig. 4 The Pays Quint and the pastures of the Aldudes
Sources: G. Viers, 'Le pays des Aldudes', p. 264; and 1:50,000 Spanish topographic survey.

Spain. In 1839 the Prefect of Basses-Pyrénées reported that all Caro and d'Ornano's stone markers had somehow disappeared.[29] Conflict and doubt continued until 1856.

The Treaty of Bayonne preserved the Caro and d'Ornano line, but gave exclusive and perpetual use of the Quinto Real's pastures to Baïgorry, in return for a fixed annual rent paid by France to Spain.[30] Frenchmen and their livestock might enter and leave the Quinto Real freely, and the few farms of French citizens that were there in 1856 were recognized as legitimate French property. But otherwise the French rights extended only to the Quinto Real's pastures, nothing else (except wood and water for local domestic use). Neither were the Spaniards allowed to alter the landscape in any way (as by building or logging). The result of these restrictions has been a stalemate in the development of the region, although natural regeneration of the forest has prevailed in the western part, whereas the woods have receded in favour of grazing in the central part of the Quinto Real. Spain's sovereignty there is largely theoretical, since she has little effective jurisdiction. Neither Spanish nor French police and customsmen enter the Quinto Real, which is policed by wardens from Baïgorry, though it is subject to Spanish law. That the area is virtually French territory is illustrated by the extension of the French cadastral survey to it in 1840, and by its partial inclusion in the 1900 edition of the French *Carte d'État Major* (Type 1889, sheet 238, 1:80,000) which everywhere else stops at the boundary. A fence (erected by Baïgorry) even separates the area from the rest of Spain. The three dozen inhabitants of the Quinto Real are French citizens, and send their children to school in Urepel, although they pay taxes to Spain.[31] Smuggling is rife.

The southern slope of the Quinto Real, belonging to the valley of Erro and formerly part of the undivided Aldudes pastures, also includes an area grazed by cattle from Baïgorry and Erro and is the subject of a separate accord.[32] French cattle using these pastures must be marked with a 'B' (for Baïgorry) before entering, and this gives rise to an annual ceremony in Urepel at which French and Spanish officials oversee the branding. Another remnant of the former status of the Aldudes is preserved in Article 17 of the Treaty of Bayonne: the right of Baztán's herds to pass freely across the French valley on their way to pastures in Valcarlos or Roncesvalles. The path they take is marked on the map of the Aldudes' pastures (Fig. 4).

Besides the special status of the Quinto Real, the Treaty of Bayonne also recognized two perpetual *facerías*: between Aezcoa and Cize (providing for reciprocal grazing rights), and between Roncal and Barétous.[33] The Roncal/Barétous *facería* comprises a zone of pasturage (straddling the boundary) which the Barétous herders use exclusively for twenty-eight days before July 10, and the Roncalese use thereafter. This *facería* can be traced back to at least 1375. The Treaty of Bayonne also perpetuates an ancient payment of three cows by Barétous to Roncal; perhaps as rent, but thought by some to be originally a tribute to expiate a murder committed by shepherds from Barétous in the fourteenth century.[34] Accordingly, on the thirteenth of July every year the officials of Barétous and Roncal meet at the stone of Saint Martin on the boundary to sign a new treaty, and to transfer the three cows which, the treaty stipulates, must be 2 years old and unblemished. At the end of the ceremony the representatives from the two valleys, dressed in their seventeenth-century robes of office, place their hands one over the other atop the boundary monument and with the words 'Patz abant' swear eternal peace.[35] With the opening of a motorable road over the pass in 1973 the ceremony will doubtless become an important tourist attraction; the site itself makes a magnificent backdrop, for here the Pyrenees rise lofty above the timber-line: only five kilometres to the south-east the Pic d'Anie, still snow-covered, marks the beginning of the high and continuous crest of the Central Pyrenees.

[1] See the map in S. O. Gilfillan, 'European political boundaries', *Political Science Quarterly*, XXXIX (1924), 458–84.

[2] Of course it has a longer history than that. For Roman subdivisions and the medieval units see: Paul Raymond, *Dictionnaire topographique du département des Basses-Pyrénées, comprenant les noms de lieu anciens et modernes* ('Dictionnaire topographique de la France'; Paris: Comité des travaux historiques et scientifiques, 1863). On the history of the boundary, see: Antonio Ubieto Arteta, 'Las fronteras de Navarra', *Principe de Viana*, XIV (1953), 61–96; and R. Plandé, 'La formation politique de la frontière des Pyrénées', *RGPSO* IX (1938), 221–42. The Hundred Years' War (1337–1453) also divided the Western Pyrenees: two of the 'French' Basque provinces, Labourd and Soule, were part of Gascony and the Duchy of Aquitaine and belonged to the English kings during most of the period. Basse Navarre was part of the kingdom of Navarre, and Béarn belonged to the counts of Foix.

[3] The island is now jointly owned, *pro indiviso*, by Spain and France.

[4] Jean Sermet, 'Île des Faisans, .le de la Conférence', *Annales du Midi*, LXXIII (1961), 325–45, id., *Le Tricentenaire de la paix des Pyrénées 1659–1959* (Saragossa: Instituto de Estudios Pirenaicos, 1960).

[5] Sir George Clark, *The seventeenth century* (2nd ed.; New York: Oxford University Press, 1961), chap. 10.

[6] Treaty of St. Jean de Luz, 31 May 1660; Treaty of Llivia, 12 November 1660. See Josep M. Guilera, *Unitat històrica del Pirineu* (Barcelona: Aedos, 1964), pp. 164–70.

[7] 'XLII. (1) Et pour ce qui concerne les Pays & Places que les Armes de France ont occupez en cette Guerre, du costé d'Espagne: Comme l'on auroit convenu en la negociation commencée à Madrid en l'année 1656. sur laquelle est fondé le present Traitteé, que les Monts Pyrénées, qui avoient anciennement divisé les Gaules des Espagnes, seront aussi dorenavant la division des deux mêmes Royaumes ...' [This is followed by the division of the Cerdagne]'. Cited by Jean Dumont, Baron de Carels Croon, *Corps universel diplomatique ...* (8 vols.; Amsterdam: P. Brunel, R. et G. Wetstein, etc., 1726–31), vol. VI, pt. 2, p. 269.

[8] Alfredo Floristán Samanes and María Pilar de Torres Luna have described at least twenty-eight in the Navarrese Pyrenees which are not international. Many survive. 'Distribución geográfica de las facerías navarras', in *Miscelanea ofrecida al Ilmo. Sr. D. José María Lacarra y de Miguel* (Saragossa: Universidad de Zaragoza, 1968), pp. 223–47.

[9] See: E. Zudaire, 'Facerías de la cuenca Baztán-Bidasoa', *Principe de Viana*, nos. 106, 107 (reprint dated 1967), pp. 61–96, 161–241. Victor Fairén Guillén, *Facerías internacionales pirenaicas* (Madrid: Instituto de Estudios Políticos, 1956).

[10] Both the pastoral agreements themselves and (more loosely) the common grazing zones they delimit are called *facerías*.

[11] For an example, see: Manuel Lucas Alvarez and María Rosario Miralbés, 'Una carta de paz entre los valles de Tena y Ossau (1646)', *Pirineos*, VIII (1952), 253–95.

12 Bernard Druène, 'Les lies et passeries, spécialement pendant la Guerre de Succession d'Espagne', *Actes* II CIEP, VII. 5—37.

13 Henri Cavaillès, 'Une fédération pyrénéenne sous l'ancien régime—les traités de lies et de passeries', *Revue historique*, CV (1910), 1—34, 241—76.

14 Archives des Basses-Pyrénées, E 2186. Cited by Cavaillès, *Revue historique*, CV. 12.

15 See also Jacques Descheemaeker, 'La frontière dans les Pyrénées basques (organisation, antiquité, fédéralisme)', *Eusko-Jakintza*, IV (1950), 141—2.

16 A. de Boislisle, *Correspondance*, t. III, no. 1121; cited by Cavaillès, *Revue historique*, CV. 258.

17 Jacques Ancel, *Géographie des frontières*, pp. 75—6, 88—9. Diderot seems to have been the first to apply the 'laws of nature' to France's territorial limits. N. J. G. Pounds, 'France and "les limites naturelles" from the seventeenth to the twentieth centuries', *Annals of the Association of American Geographers*, XLIV (1954), 51—62; and id., 'The origins of the idea of natural frontiers in France', ibid., XLI—XLII (1951—2), 146—57.

18 Plandé, *RGPSO* IX. 221—42. Jean Sermet, 'Le Centenaire des traités des limites et la Commission Internationale des Pyrénées,'*Revue de Comminges*, LXXXIII (1970), 234—55. The treaties are reproduced in *Acuerdos fronterizos con Francia y Portugal* (Madrid: Ministerio de Hacienda, 1969). For a legist's point of view on the development of the boundary, see the thesis of Jacques Descheemaeker, 'La frontière pyrénéenne de l'Océan à l'Aragon' (2 vols.; (unpublished) Thèse (droit), Université de Paris, 1945). Turgid with legal minutiae and obscurities, exhaustive in its exploration of hypothetical litigation, the thesis was never published except as a series of articles (listed in the Bibliography). Descheemaeker, primarily interested in law, tended to overlook the line's pastoral origins. He also erred in his interpretation of the legal status of the valley of Baztán, but otherwise his studies of the complex juridical foundations of the boundary are not likely to be surpassed.

19 From the charge to the Commission, quoted by Sermet, *Revue de Comminges*, LXXXIII. 245.

20 Collectively known as the Treaty of Bayonne. The stages were as follows. 1856: treaty delimiting the boundary from the Atlantic to the Table des Trois Rois (where France, Navarre, and Aragon meet); 1858: five annexes to the 1856 treaty; 1862: treaty delimiting the boundary from Navarre to Andorra; 1863: three annexes to the 1862 treaty; 1866: treaty delimiting the boundary from Andorra to the Mediterranean; 1866: additions to and amendment of the 1862 treaty; 1868: amendment to the 1856 treaty; 1868: final treaty statement and five annexes. Andorra's boundaries have never been delimited in a modern international treaty. Strictly speaking, this would be difficult to do, since Andorra is not legally a sovereign state, but a co-principality paying homage to both the President of France and the Bishop of Seo de Urgel.

21 There are 602 from the Atlantic to the Mediterranean (plus some subsidiary markers). Nearly half of these—272—are in the Atlantic Pyrenees, where the boundary coincides least often with prominent natural features or watersheds.

22 Of course the deliberate crossings are more common than the accidental ones in these places. This is smuggler's country, and contraband is not only a respected way of life for villagers, but a significant component of the local economy.

23 It also follows a watershed from Lindus peak to Mendimotxa between Baïgorry and Valcarlos. This divide separates two tributaries of the Nive.

24 Grazing privileges are the main purpose of the modern *facerías*, but Article 14 gives the Pyrenean communities broad competence: they have the right to conclude '. . . all pastoral or other agreements which may tend to be in their best interests or promote good relations between neighbours'. See also Victor Fairén Guillén, 'Notas sobre la actualidad de las facerías internacionales pirenaicas', *Actes* II CIEP, VI, 215—45.

25 1858, annexe 4 to Treaty of 1856.

26 See: A. Ospital et G. Eppherre, 'Les Aldudes, un fleuron du Pays basque', in *Traditions des Aldunes* (Bayonne: Gure Herria, n.d. but *c.* 1964), pp. 5—21; R. Vignau, 'Aspect historique et juridique du Pays Quint', ibid., pp. 65—87; Jean Sermet, 'Problèmes pastoraux frontaliers du Pays Quint', *Actas*, III CIEP, Resumen, pp. 64—5; Jacques Descheemaeker, 'Une frontière féodale au XXe siècle', *Pyrénées*, no. 12 (1952), pp. 289—97; id., 'Le statut du Pays-Quint', *Eusko-Jakintza*, I (1947), 213—29. The figure of 12 square km used by Descheemaeker and Fairén Guillén is incorrect, as is the map opposite p. 206 in José María Cordero Torres, *Fronteras hispanicas; geografía e historia, diplomacia y administración* (Madrid: Instituto de Estudios Políticos, 1960). The figure of 25 square km was measured on the Spanish topographic map at 1:50,000 (Valcarlos, No. 91), using the watershed as the southern limit of the Quinto Real, as specified in Article 15 of the Treaty of Bayonne.

27 Viers, *RGPSO* XXII. 265.

28Michel Etcheverry, 'Une page d'histoire frontalière', *Eusko-Jakintza*, II (1948), 633—47.

29Sermet, *Revue de Comminges*, LXXXIII. 245.

30The amount of the rent has been renegotiated several times. It is not paid by the valley of Baïgorry but by the French government to Spain. The Spanish treasury hands it over to Erro and Baztán.

31See Christian Bombédiac, 'Les quarante Français du Pays Quint', *Sud-Ouest* (16 July 1967), p. 11.

32Annexe 2 of 1858, Treaty of Bayonne, and subsequent local agreements.

33And perhaps a third, which is mentioned only in the Annexe of delimitation (monument 234), between Salazar and Soule.

34For an exhaustive legal discussion, see Jacques Descheemaeker, 'Le tribut de la vallée de Barétous', *Eusko-Jakintza* III (1949), 399—428. Also: Victor Fairén Guillén, 'Contribución al estudio de la facería internacional de los valles de Roncal y Barétous', *Principe de Viana*, VII (1946), 4—28.

35Even the German occupation during World War II did not interrupt the ceremony.

CHAPTER VI
The Infra-structures of Change

The rise of the modern nation-state in seventeenth-century Europe, and the meeting of French and Spanish ambassadors on the Isle of Pheasants in 1659, properly marks the moment at which the Pyrenees became a borderland, at least in the modern sense. From that time on, two disparate administrations met in the mountains, their influences differently moulding the landscapes over which each was sovereign. What before might have seemed one region, autonomous and relatively homogeneous in its isolation, gradually became two: one French, the other Spanish. Of course it was not the mere contrast in sovereignty which brought about this disparity, but rather an increasing involvement in the wider world, the fruit of the great economic and social transformation of the eighteenth, nineteenth, and twentieth centuries. In the Pyrenees, the way to the wider world led either through Paris or Madrid, and as the circumstances and fortunes of the two capitals varied, so eventually did those of their provinces.

The breakdown of the Pyrenees' isolation from the rest of France and Spain best explains this emergence of two distinctive borderland communities. It is a more important fact than the creation of the boundary *per se*: a division which in this case has always been fairly permeable. The Pyrenees were never utterly isolated from the countries to the north and south, but it happened that most of their links to metropolitan economies were forged after 1659, and so reflected national differences. The links were the infra-structure of economic development in the region: roads, railways, postal services, and communications of all sorts; banks; schools; the distribution of services such as electricity; agricultural extension pro-grammes; the cadaster; and many others. All these were directly or indirectly fostered by the governments of France and Spain, and generally extended no farther than the national territory. As they developed, the bordering regions became increasingly involved in the affairs of their nations, and so drew apart from one another. Government itself was both the agent of this development and part of the infra-structure. Policy and law—local and national—determined many differences across the border.

LOCAL GOVERNMENT

The structure of government in the French Pyrenees was very different from that in the Spanish Western Pyrenees. The French communes were linked hierarchically to the strong and centralist government in Paris. The Spanish municipios were part of Navarre, which was originally a kingdom, and is now a Spanish province—but one which has preserved a large measure of local particularisms, autonomy, and special privilege. The nature of local and national government differed, too. The civil rights that Frenchmen have enjoyed for the last century and a half have been only sporadically available to Spaniards.[1] These differences in what one might call the civil climate may also be important sources of differences in prosperity across the boundary.

There are two themes which run through the story of local administration in the French Western Pyrenees. The first is the pastoral theme: the story of the valleys' continuing struggle to preserve their grazings and the right to manage them. This pastoral authority was important because it was the key to the agricultural economy of the area, and the *raison d'être* of the valley communities. The second theme concerns the development of modern municipal administration and local political power. It had a briefer history. Both are considered here.

Threats to the Pyrenean valleys' 'autonomy' and pastoral authority were directed at the vast common lands they controlled. In France, Colbert's famous forest ordinance of 1669 allowed communities to let unused portions of the common for terms of 1 to 3 years.[2] The edict was ignored in the Pyrenees; most villagers preferring to maintain the traditional integrity of the commons.[3] But during the eighteenth century stronger and stronger pressure to eliminate the commons as an anachronism and an impediment to progress came from the few but vocal agronomists whose passion for 'improvement' spurred the agricultural revolution of the late 1700s.[4]

The agitation for modernization in France, which wealthy country proprietors and agricultural writers led during the eighteenth century, was conducted through an almost endless stream of tracts, manuals, and periodicals. These extolled the benefits of the new methods of agriculture which English gentry had been among the first to implement. The prescriptions of English propagandists such as Arthur Young, Jethro Tull, or H. Pattullo, were paraphrased by a series of French authors (Duhamel du Monceau, Rozier, d'Essuiles, etc.). The practices they urged upon their countrymen included better manuring, new crops (turnips and mangels, for example), new races of sheep or cattle, different and more 'scientific' schemes of rotation, and in general a more intensive and rational use of the land. Marc Bloch has referred to this movement as the struggle for agrarian individualism.[5] The old communal ways were regarded as impediments to reform by progressive farmers striving for higher yields.

Of course there was more talk of new agricultural methods than there was implementation. The changes in the countryside came much more slowly than the reformers wished, and were restricted at first to the fields of wealthy landowners who could afford to risk experimentation.[6] Yet maize did spread throughout the Western Pyrenees, albeit slowly, and the old common rights on the arable gradually gave way to private control. In many cases, however, the French agricultural writers seized upon the outward manifestations of the English agricultural revolution (e.g. enclosure) and advocated them as if they would themselves insure greater productivity. Landowners were exhorted to build fences and hedgerows, and to rid their communities of the dead hand of the open field system and its rights of pasture on the stubble.

Passing through France in 1787, Arthur Young noted with pleasure that in several regions neat enclosures appeared to be the norm, but added 'the marvellous folly is, that, in nine-tenths of all the inclosures of France, the system of management is precisely the same as in the open fields.[7]

Two important targets for the French reformers became the elimination of rights of common which prevented landowners from managing their property freely, and the alienation or 'disentailment' of the common lands (because they supposedly were not utilized intensively enough and would be better managed as private property). Agronomists pointed to England's agricultural prosperity, saying that only the enclosure of the commons had made it possible.[8] After about 1766 (when a lengthy study on the subject appeared in the *Journal de l'Agriculture*), the pressure intensified. In 1770 the count d'Essuiles published his influential *Traité politique et économique des communes*. Although d'Essuiles urged the partition of the commons, nevertheless he pointed out the futility of expecting high productivity from commons such as those found in mountains which were more suited to pastoralism. Further, d'Essuiles advocated the equal division of the commons amongst the inhabitants, recognizing thus the role they already played in assuring some measure of security to the landless peasantry. As a result of the agronomists' efforts, bureaucrats, such as H. L. Bertin, Minister of State for Agriculture (1763–80), attempted to legislate for agricultural reforms, but regional peculiarities precluded making laws for the whole of France, so a series of local edicts was promulgated instead. On 2 December 1767 an edict authorized all enclosures in Béarn, but it was so hobbled by restrictive amendments by the Parliament of Pau that the government at Paris sent forth a second edict (February 1770) authorizing the enclosure of freehold inheritances, and abolishing reciprocal grazing privileges (*droits de parcours*) between communities. This edict was duly registered by the Parliament of Pau, but widely ignored in the countryside. Indeed, protests from the mountain communities were strong enough to produce another edict in 1773 exempting them from the provisions of the 1770 law.[9] Another Arrêt du Conseil (28 October 1771) authorized communities in the *généralités* of Auch and Pau to divide their commons in equal shares amongst all their households. An amendment (9 May 1773) extended the concept to include lands held in common by several villages (as was the case in the Pyrenean valleys). However, the division could be carried out only with the consent of a majority of the community's households.[10] This provision prevented the alienation of the commons in the valleys, although many villages in the plains and foothills lost most of their commons in the next few years.[11]

The agronomists' fervour continued during the French Revolution.

Indeed, the commons were often regarded as but another instance of the anachronisms which subjugated the country and which must be swept away along with the *ancien régime*. Thus a law of 1791 allowed owners to enclose their land (to protect it from graziers) and abolished the right to graze on the aftermath of artificial meadows.[12] A decree of the Convention (10 June 1793) did not merely permit but required the commons to be divided. In the Pyrenees these measures again went unheeded, although many valleys felt their effects in the loss of their winter grazings in the lowlands.[13]

Although the edicts of the 1770s and later may have been ineffectual, there probably was a progression towards 'agrarian individualism' in the French valleys of the Western Pyrenees during the eighteenth century. The right to assart had always been recognized, and some of the assarts became fully fledged farms. There were also simple usurpations of the commons which the valleys were unable to prevent. There must have been a shift away from the open field and its attendant rights as the new crops (maize, root crops, legumes, and artificial meadows) spread through the region, although these crops may have been somewhat late coming to the mountains.[14] Arthur Young recognized that most of the Western Pyrenean enclosures were not transformations of the open field but the result of assarting the common.[15] Daniel Faucher has made a similar point.[16] In the French Pyrenees, the definitive abandonment of the open field and the rights to graze it probably occurred in the last years of the eighteenth century and the first years of the nineteenth.[17]

Other increases in productivity during the eighteenth century compensated for the loss of these lowland grazings. The fields of maize and legumes (haricot beans, mostly), and, later, forage crops such as red clover, alfalfa, and sainfoin which made the new artificial meadows, meant that animals could be fed from the arable for the first time. These crops allowed winter stabling and themselves freed the open field from the restrictions of common rights on the rowen.

But the common grazing lands in the mountains remained largely intact. With the Revolution, however, came another, much more serious threat to this keystone of the valley economy: the reorganization of the structure of local government. *Départements* replaced provinces. The new *départements* were divided into *districts* (later *arrondissements*), *cantons*, and *communes*. The Département des Basses-Pyrénées[18] was created in 1790 by the *Assemblée nationale* from Béarn, Soule, lower Navarre, Labourd, Bayonne, and part of the generality of Bordeaux. There were 6 districts, 52 cantons, and 663 communes.[19] Subsequent fusions reduced these to 3 arrondissements, 41 cantons, and 560 communes in 1968.

The communes were generally the church parishes of the *ancien régime* under another name. Each corresponded to a village, and in a region where churches were numerous and habitat dispersed, communes pullulated. Many Pyrenean communes included less than one or two hundred inhabitants.

Tiny though they were, they acquired a mayor, council, secretary, constable, village hall, and the responsibilities of local government. As jural entities, they could own and administer property.

The valley communities, however, had included several villages, now several communes. The valleys lost their legal status in the Revolutionary reform. In the new system they corresponded quite closely to cantons. But the arrondissements and cantons were largely groupings of convenience. They were not corporate bodies, unlike the communes (and departments), and thus had neither responsibility for government nor the right to own property. It was therefore decreed that the valleys' common lands must be given to the constituent communes. This arrangement was unsatisfactory because it gave the upstream villages enormous pastures whereas those downstream had none or very little. The threat to the pastoral livelihood seemed intolerable.

Again the Pyrenean communities resisted. They successfully forestalled the implementation of these laws for nearly fifty years. In 1838 (during the July Monarchy) a Royal ordinance sanctioned the communes' subterfuge of transferring their common lands to valley-wide syndicates. Since then these pastoral syndicates have represented the old valley republics of the French Western Pyrenees. They maintain the integrity of the grazings and forests, preserving the commons to this day.

The management of the syndicates resembles that of the medieval communities, with syndics elected from each of the constituent villages. Thus the valley of Baïgorry has become the *Syndicat de la vallée de Baïgorry*, encompassing eight communes. Similarly the *Syndicat de Cize* administers the common land of twenty communes just west of Baïgorry. There are five major pastoral syndicates in the French Western Pyrenees (see Fig. 3), and in addition there are a number of smaller syndicates whose purview is limited to a single forest formerly shared by two or three villages (now communes). The competence of the large pastoral syndicates is fairly broad. In addition to regulating and taxing the use of the pastures, they manage and sell forest products, and control the rights to hunt and fish. They spend most of the money they receive on making improvements to the grazing lands (roads, *bordas*, drinking-troughs, etc.) In short, the modern syndicates have inherited all the 'seigniorial' rights formerly enjoyed by the valleys. Generally it is the syndics who sign the modern *facerías* as legal representatives of their valleys.[20]

Thus the valleys preserved the great pastures upon which their agriculture had depended for centuries. Grazing continued uninterrupted; it even increased in relative importance. The achievement was conservative: it tended to perpetuate the old ways and it minimized change. Maize and meadows and the abandonment of the open field were the most important changes in three hundred years of Pyrenean farming. But even as late as the mid-twentieth century the open field pattern was still visible in some communities.[21]

Except in pastoral matters, however, the medieval isolation and autonomy of the mountains gradually ceded place to control by the central government. Although the local, pastoral authority of the valleys or their syndicates has a history longer than memory, the exercise of modern political power in the French Pyrenees is less than 200 years old. In the seventeenth and eighteenth centuries, the authority of the Intendant—the royal administrator of the *généralité* under the *ancien régime*—figured prominently in the deliberations and litigations of the valley assemblies. The system of generalities and intendants, developed during the seventeenth century, effectively placed the Pyrenean communities under the tutelage of the monarchy: decisions made by the assemblies might require the approval of the Intendant, who could modify or annul them as he saw fit.[22] The power of the King, represented by the intendants, was somewhat—but not much—diluted by the Parliament of Pau, whose jurisdiction covered Béarn and Basse-Navarre. This region or *gouvernement* was one of the *Pays d'États*—generalities whose traditional assemblies were allowed to keep some restricted measure of power, mostly relating to finances.[23]

After the French Revolution, the centralism of the *ancien régime* was abandoned briefly in favour of local powers. The Constituent Assembly in 1790 authorized municipal and departmental councils. The councils' powers were considerable, although their finances were nearly non-existent. They were elected rather than appointed; but only property owners might vote. The reform was short-lived. In 1800, the basic law on local government of the year VIII brought centralism back again. The departmental councils' powers were reduced to insignificance, and mayors, communal assemblies, prefects (in charge of departments), and sub-prefects (in charge of arrondissements) all served at the pleasure of the central government—Napoleon's, at that time.

The Bourbon restoration maintained centralism and a limited franchise. The July Monarchy (1830—48) made departmental and municipal councils (and later the mayors) elected officials once again, though the suffrage was still restricted.[24] Nevertheless the tutelage of the prefect, who has always been a creature of the government in Paris, insured that decentralization was largely theoretical during the Monarchy, the Second Republic, and the Second Empire. Even the implementation of 'universal suffrage' (except for women, who did not vote in France until the Fourth Republic, after World War II) by the Provisional Government of 1848 did not change this. Throughout most of the nineteenth century national elections were commonly manipulated by the Ministry of the Interior, acting through the prefect. In fact vote-getting and election-rigging in national elections were often the prefects' most important duties. Local elections were freer.

The bases for the modern structure of departmental and communal government were the laws of 10 August 1871 and 5 April 1884 (during the Third Republic). At the local level most authority was given to the elected municipal council and the mayor (whom it elected). The department also received a large degree of autonomous power and fiscal responsibility as a result of the decentralization of 1871, and is governed by a departmental assembly (and its commission). The prefect is still the representative of the executive power of the state at the departmental level. The municipal councils, mayors, departmental assembly, and other governmental authorities remain under his tutelage; although with the important exception of his direct control of the police, the activities of the prefect have become much less authoritarian.

In the Spanish Western Pyrenees, local government had a different history. From the Table of the Three Kings (of France, Aragon, and Navarre) in the east to Vera de Bidasoa in the west these mountains belong to Navarre. Navarre, not Spain: even today the Navarros say their province is different from the rest. Before Spain was unified under Ferdinand and Isabella, the Kingdom of Navarre was at one time one of the peninsula's most prestigious dominions: in the early eleventh century the empire of Sancho el Mayor dominated much of northern Iberia.

After 1234, the Kings of Navarre were 'Frenchmen';[25] indeed, many fiefs of the kingdom were located in what is now France—even as far north as Champagne and Brie (1234–1328). But in 1512, Ferdinand of Aragon conquered Navarre, which then belonged to Jean d'Albret (who nevertheless kept the title of King of Navarre; from him it passed to the French monarchs). Navarre swore allegiance to Ferdinand in 1513 and thus joined Spain.

The longest-lasting of the 'French' territories of Navarre—they were then called 'ultra-puertos' (beyond the passes)—was Lower Navarre, today part of France. The district had belonged to Navarre at certain periods before, but was joined to Navarre for the final time in 1207. It remained one of Navarre's half-dozen *merindades* (provinces) until it was lost in 1524, after the war between Carlos I (the first Habsburg king of Spain, the emperor Charles V) and François I of France. Lower Navarre (with Béarn and other properties) passed to the French crown at the end of the sixteenth century with the accession of Henry IV.[26]

Like other towns and valleys in northern Spain, many of those in Navarre were governed by collections of regional customary laws. The documents and the privileges that they accorded to the citizens are known as *fueros*. Between Pamplona and the Pyrenees the towns' *fueros* may have been extensions of the charter granted to Jaca in 1063 by Sancho Ramírez of Aragon. Essentially the privileges were those pertaining to freemen, although we are not certain that they applied to all inhabitants.[27] In the thirteenth century there appeared a general *fuero*, applicable to all of Navarra. There was also a *cortes* or parliament of Navarre, to which certain municipalities sent representatives.[28]

Even after the capture of Navarre by Aragon the *cortes* and the municipalities continued to enjoy their privileged status; the *fueros* were maintained fervently, and for two hundred years they checked the power of the Habsburg kings of Spain. In the eighteenth century Philip V (of the house of Bourbon) succeeded in subjugating the privileged institutions of Catalonia, Valencia, and Aragon, but allowed the foral provinces (the Basque provinces of Vizcaya, Guipúzcoa, Alava, and Navarre) to keep their privileges. During the nineteenth century, however, the *fueros* were dismantled by a succession of liberal governments.[29] In part this was an expression of the liberals' desire for a unified and centralized Spain, but in part it was also punishment for the Basques' support of the reactionary Carlist cause in the two Carlist Wars. Until the first of these wars (1833–40) the foral provinces had managed to keep most of their privileges: exemption from Spanish taxes, tariffs, and conscription; the right to maintain their own mint, parliament (which had to approve Spanish laws before they were effective in Navarre), and militia. Indeed, the Spanish customs boundary ran to the south of the Basque provinces. In 1839 these *fueros* were revoked, although many foral privileges were retained by the *Ley Paccionada* which replaced the *fueros* in 1841. It was still difficult for Spain to raise taxes or soldiers in the region, but after the failure of the Second Carlist War (1870–5) the *fueros* effectively disappeared, though the provinces managed to salvage a large degree of administrative autonomy and were granted a *concierto económico*. This agreement allowed the Basques to collect their own taxes, from which they paid a certain sum to the Spanish treasury in Madrid. Only Navarre and Alava kept these privileges after the Civil War of 1936–9. More conservative than the other Basque provinces, they had supported Franco while Vizcaya and Guipúzcoa fought for the Republic or for their own autonomy.

Today the *Diputación foral de Navarra* finances and manages its own highway programme, departments of agriculture and industry, forestry service, cadaster, and so on. Navarre is better administered and more abundantly supplied with municipal services of all kinds than most other Spanish provinces. The *Diputación foral* still collects its own taxes, and the province has relatively more money to spend locally. There is a great contrast between Navarre's relatively dense and well-maintained network of roads and those of the rest of Spain, for example.

The Navarrese *municipios*' common lands and *facerías* were not threatened so persistently as were their French counterparts. This was not only because the municipios (or valleys) were protected by the foral rights of the province, but also because the influence of the eighteenth-century physiocrats or agronomists produced less legislation in Spain than it did in France.[30] The agrarian reformers of Carlos III's reign saw under-

employment on the great estates of southern Spain as the main impediment
to Spanish progress. The settlements on the road over the Sierra Morena
represented one effort to correct this.[31] In 1795 Gaspar Melchor de
Jovellanos, in his *Informe* ... [sobre la] ... *Ley Agraria*, discussed the
problems of land reform in terms that would have been familiar to a French
minister, but his recommendations (including disentailment, and the sale of
church and common lands) were not enacted until the middle of the
nineteenth century.

The Constitution of Cadiz (1812) called for the establishment of the right
to enclose land, disentailment, and the sale of monastic and common land;[32]
but it went unheeded. In 1855, however, Liberals acting on the advice of
Pascual Madoz passed a law requiring the sale of common lands, which did
result in a significant redistribution of Spanish land, especially in Andalucia
and Estremadura.[33] The *Diputación foral* of Navarre, still fighting for its lost
fueros, protested vigorously against the law (in 1859), and eventually a royal
order (6 June 1861) allowed the province itself to supervise the sale of the
commons.[34] Very little land was sold. In the whole province only about
30,000 hectares of the commons changed hands.[35] Most of the sales took
place in the lowlands and the Ebro valley; Pyrenean municipios lost only
1,450 hectares. Only the large valleys of Esteríbar and Arce sold more than
100 hectares each;[36] an insignificant fraction of their whole commons. In
many Pyrenean communities the sales served mainly to clear up irregularities
in the arrangement of the common, as by selling a small remnant of land to
the farmer whose private holdings surrounded it. Many villages also sold their
communal mills at this time. The Spanish valleys were thus as successful in
keeping their common land as their French counterparts.[37] Common land in
Navarre, however, is held differently than in France. Instead of syndicates,
valleys and municipios manage their commons much as they did centuries
ago.[38] The valleys themselves were never split into 'artificial'
municipalities—thus municipios in the Spanish Pyrenees generally are much
larger than communes across the boundary. In the study area the mean size
of Spanish municipios is 4,320 hectares against 2,660 hectares for French
communes. There are Spanish valleys composed of several municipios, but in
these the interdependent organization of the valley has always been based on
interlocking *facerías* (between municipios) and a valley-wide council.

There are various forms of common-land ownership.[39] Valleys may own
their common entirely, as in France, where village commons are rare. Where
the valley is a single municipio (e.g. Baztán) this is obviously the simplest
form of tenure. Other municipios comprising an entire valley, however, are
subdivided further into *concejos*—each corresponding to a village—and
although the *concejos* are not civil divisions (have no legal status as
corporations, and no powers of government) each has a definite territory and
each may have a distinctive and exclusive common (e.g. Bertizarana). In
some cases (e.g. Anué—see Fig. 5) there is yet another common, shared by all

the *concejos* of the valley. Where several municipios constitute a valley, the valley-wide commons may be held *pro indiviso* (as a '*facería*') and managed by a junta of the component municipios (e.g. the Montes de Bidasoa[40]); or each municipio may own separate commons; or the two systems may coexist (as in Roncal). Where municipios or *concejos* comprising a valley own separate commons there may be a system of *facerías* allowing valley-wide grazing. In essence Navarre has preserved local peculiarities in these arrangements, while France has destroyed them.[41]

Furthermore, there are six state forests in the Navarrese Pyrenees (see Fig. 6). All originally belonged to the Crown of Navarre. One of these forests (Aézcoa) is subject to the rights of pasture and wood-gathering still enjoyed by the inhabitants of the valley of Aézcoa. The other five forests (Quinto Real, Erreguerena, Legua Acotada, La Cuestión, and Changoa) are free of servitudes. After the loss of the *fueros* in 1839 the status of these forests provoked no end of disputes between the Spanish government, the villages, and the *Diputación foral de Navarra*. In 1930 a royal decree gave control of the forests which were subject to local rights of usage to the *Diputación foral* (which has its own forestry service), while those free of servitudes were given to Spain (thus the Spanish forestry service also has jurisdiction in Navarre). There is nothing similar in the French Western Pyrenees, where the major forests are part of the valley syndicates' common lands (although their exploitation is subject to approval by the French *Office national des forêts*); that is, there are no national forests (*forêts domaniales*) in the area.[42]

The common lands of Navarre are also subject to different rights of usage from those of the French commons. In the French syndical lands every householder of the valley enjoys the same rights (except that sites of *cayolars* (herders' cabins) are rented to individuals) on the common. In Navarre some families or neighbourhoods (*auzalán*)[43] have acquired exclusive rights to some portions of the common. Thus a farmer or a neighbourhood may have the right to mow the bracken of a certain slope, gather firewood from a certain grove or the chestnuts from certain trees, or to make temporary assarts in certain areas. Furthermore, a single piece of land may be subject to a congeries of rights: as when one family is entitled to the fruits of the trees, another to the bracken harvest, and a third to the pasturage. If a family's exclusive right on the common (such as the right to mow bracken) goes unused for a certain period (five years in Baztán) it reverts to the valley as a whole. Common of pasture, that is, the right of all to graze on the aftermath or stubble of private fields after the harvest, is still practised in some Spanish valleys, such as Roncal.[44] Inhabitants of the Navarrese Pyrenees also still enjoy the right to make temporary assarts on the common, although some municipios (e.g. Baztán) discourage the practice.

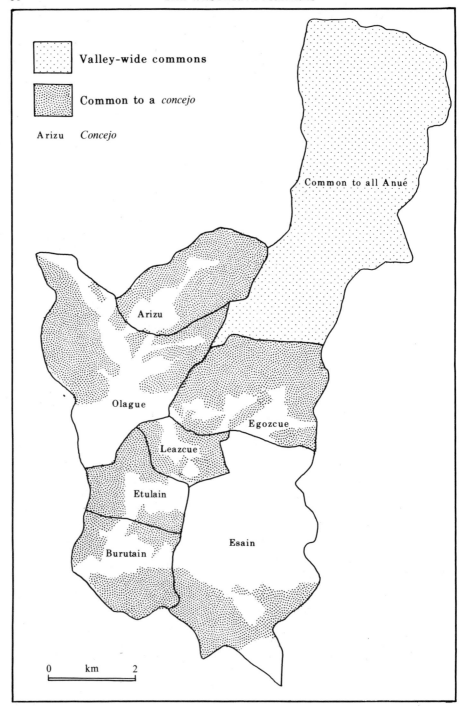

Fig. 5 Common land in Anue and its *concejos*
Source: Torres Luna, *La Navarra húmeda*, p. 31.

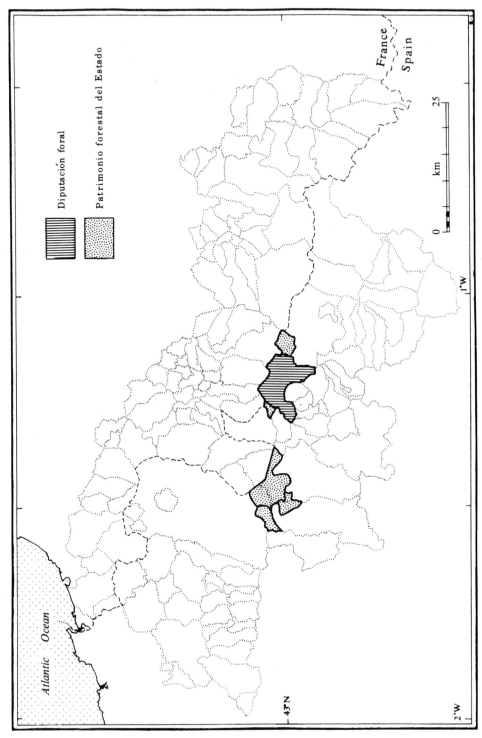

Fig. 6 State-owned forest districts in Navarre.

COMMUNICATIONS

The infra-structure of an economy or of a nation is concerned primarily with communication. Clearly economic activity depends upon communication, for the movement or transfer of goods, services, people, or ideas is the essence of transaction. And the growth of a nation, to be effective, must be accompanied by the development of inter-regional communications. It seems a reasonable hypothesis that as the ability to communicate grew, so did the involvement of the Western Pyrenees in the fortunes of their nations.

Means of communication are largely created by governments. In the Western Pyrenees there were substantial differences between France and Spain in the rate at which communications developed, and these clearly are important in explaining differences in economy.

Before electronic means of communicating existed, the most important ways were by road, later by rail.[45] The early roads of the mountains were lanes or tracks: impassable by wheeled traffic. Maps show Roman 'roads' between Dax and Pamplona (via Roncesvalles) and from Beneharnum (perhaps modern Lescar, just west of Pau) over the Puerto del Palo to Jaca. But these were footpaths, or at best tracks for horsemen or muleteers, not for carriages.[46] Roman vehicles could cross the Pyrenees only at the Perthus pass in the east.[47]

During the Middle Ages Pyrenean roads acquired fame as pilgrimage routes. Through the Western Pyrenees ran the two most important routes to the shrine of Saint James the Greater in Compostela. From the tenth century on the Jacobean roads drew pilgrims from all over Europe: the pilgrimage ranked equally with those to Rome and Jerusalem. Today, the many Romanesque churches in the area recall the popularity of the pilgrim roads, and the currents of ideas that were drawn along them. In the mountains, however, the medieval roads were inaccessible to vehicles. They were tracks along which pilgrims walked or rode on horseback.[48]

In the Middle Ages the lack of carriageable roads in the Pyrenees did not differ markedly from conditions elsewhere in Europe. Whereas in the modern period villages inaccessible to vehicles are quite isolated, much medieval overland trade moved by pack horse. Thus at that time the Pyrenees were not especially disadvantaged. Commerce, albeit local by modern standards, did link the valleys. To a certain extent the economies of the northern and southern slopes complemented one another: wine, olive oil, and livestock moved from south to north, and cloth went southward.[49]

There was also some commercial activity linking the mountains with the plains. The Romans had prized Pyrenean lard and hams; the trade in these commodities passed through Toulouse. Other products of Pyrenean agriculture, such as leather, and textiles woven from wool or flax, enjoyed wide markets then and afterwards. Occasionally these productions became small industries, especially as adjuncts to religious establishments. There was a hospice at Elizondo which produced woollens and linens for commerce.[50]

Most towns had tanners, who used the tannin from chestnut and from the common oak and the Pyrenean oak.[51] The trade was never very large, but muleteers from Pamplona regularly carried salt, wine, oil, and small manufactured articles into the Spanish valleys, for example, and returned to town with wool, hides, cloth, and cheese.[52]

Most traffic was local, however, and the region remained relatively isolated until recently. The first carriageable roads date from the eighteenth century. In Spain programmes of public works under the Bourbons were initiated by Philip V and Carlos III and by ministers such as Floridablanca, Jovellanos, and Alcudia.[53] A network of vehicular roads for the peninsula and the development of regular coach services resulted. The centralist tendencies of the Bourbons meant that the most carefully kept roads were those radiating from Madrid. A map constructed in 1758 showed many towns in the peninsula linked to the capital by 'caminos de ruedas'. In the Spanish Western Pyrenees, however, there were no carriageable roads north of Pamplona.[54] Between 1765 and 1772 the famous royal highway from Madrid through Burgos to Irún was built. A road from Pamplona (via the Azpiroz pass) joined it at Tolosa in 1815.[55] Not until the very end of the eighteenth century did Spain acquire a bureaucracy concerned specifically with roads. The first comprehensive highway law was published in 1794; the Inspectorate General of Highways dates from 1799; and the first school for civil engineers opened in 1802.[56]

Road building in the foral provinces, however, was also a provincial prerogative. In Navarre it still is. In the Western Pyrenees the relatively wealthy Basque cities saw the need for roads to further their economic development. Local 'scientific and literary' societies, such as the influential *Real Sociedad Vascongada de Amigos del País*, founded in 1765 by the Count of Peñaflorida, advocated road construction. By about 1840 Pamplona had a direct link over the mountains to France which was passable by vehicles. This was the road which led northward over the Velate pass and through the valley of Baztán to Aïnhoa. (The much more famous route which led to St. Jean Pied-de-Port over the Ibañeta pass could not be used by vehicles until 1881.)[57] The road over the Velate pass remained the Spanish Western Pyrenees' only carriageable road until the 1850s, and even then it was only irregularly maintained. (Fig. 7a shows roads in 1850.) In 1841 a traveller called it bad and only occasionally passable, but five years later another traveller praised its commodiousness.[58] By 1847 a branch from the Baztán valley ran along the Bidasoa river as far as Vera; by 1866 this road had been extended to Behobia where it joined the Irún highway.[59] Lefebvre stated that the road from Pamplona to Lumbier existed in 1850, and that the Aoiz—Burguete road (in the valley of Arce) joined it in 1853. Another road linked Burguete with Garralda in 1860. It is not clear, however, whether or not these were carriageable at those dates.[60] In the mid-nineteenth century, no other routes in the Navarrese Pyrenees could carry

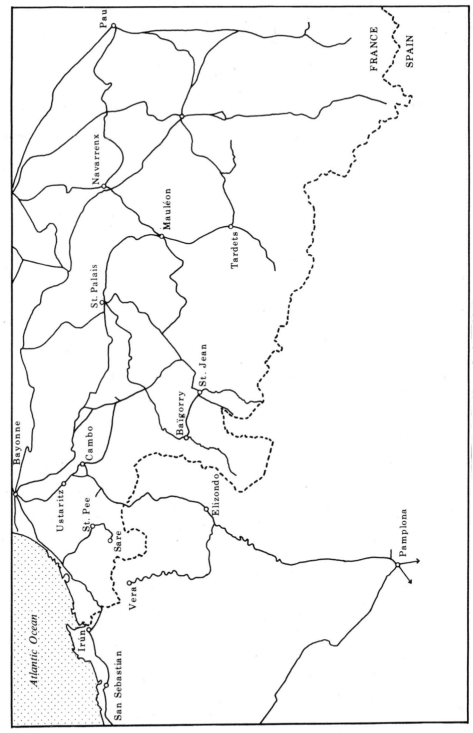

Fig. 7a Carriageable roads about 1850.

Sources: 1858 Guide Ioanne; Ford's *Handbook for Spain* (1847); Sermet, 'Communications pyrénéennes'.

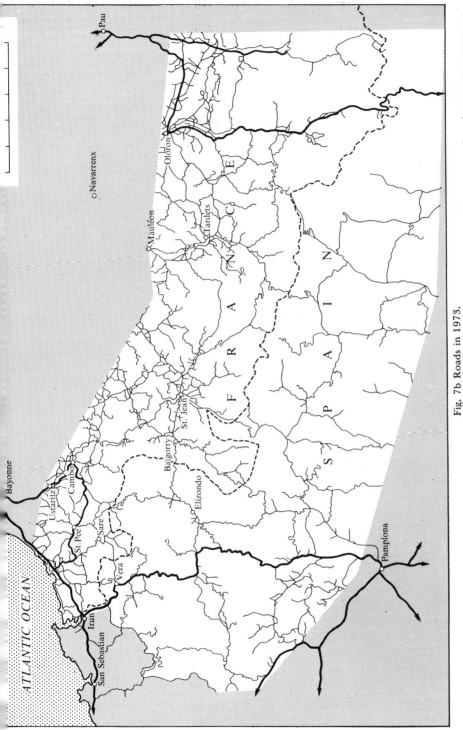

Fig. 7b Roads in 1973.

Sources: Michelin et Cie. *Carte au 200.000ème* no. 85, 1972 ed.; Diputación foral de Navarra, *Provincia de Navarra* [map] 1:200.000, 1962 ed.; Official French and Spanish topographic surveys; Field observations by author, 1973.

wheeled traffic. Entire valleys were inaccessible to vehicles, and even in those valleys where there were roads, many settlements remained isolated, several kilometres from the highway.

Other trans-Pyrenean links were forged during the last half of the nineteenth century. The roads to the Ibardin,[61] Lizarrieta, and Ispéguy passes were completed in Spain by 1885. The Ispéguy pass route, however, remained incomplete for twenty-eight years until the French built their sector in 1913. To the west, the Spanish section of the road over the Somport pass was opened in 1877—the French had finished their side in 1863.[62]

Both the French and the Spanish military authorities were loathe to construct trans-Pyrenean roads. This is one reason why connections were slow to develop. To the military, a carriageable road was one over which enemy cannon could travel; the frontier was better left impenetrable. The attitude faded in France during the last years of the nineteenth century, but persisted even as late as the 1950s in Spain. The *Diputación foral* of Navarre would probably have constructed mountain roads at a faster pace had it not required the approval of military authorities for projects in the boundary region. In 1885, for example, as the *Diputación foral* was making the road to the Ispéguy pass, Spanish army engineers briefly arrested the civilian engineers in charge of what was supposedly an officially sanctioned project.[63]   Even today the Pyrenean approaches to Spain are guarded by numerous concealed forts and pillboxes.

By 1910, however—the date a road in the Aézcoa valley was built—most Navarrese valleys had roads.[64]   The roads linking the valley heads with one another were built much later. Still, some villages remain isolated.

In France, Colbert, minister of Louis XIV, created the administration of highways, the *Ponts et Chaussées*, in the 1660s.[65]   Thereafter the French government consistently supported a programme of highway construction and maintenance, although progress at first was limited largely to the Paris region. Relatively little was done in the Western Pyrenees during the seventeenth century. The eighteenth century, however, saw much more activity, both nationally and in the French Pyrenees. Regional inspectorates and engineering divisions, and a school for engineers, date from the first half of the eighteenth century. In 1738 a special tax for roads, the infamous *corvée*, was instituted. It was paid in labour by the peasants through whose communities the roads passed. Although the *corvée* lasted only fifty years (to 1787), it secured the independence of the *Ponts et Chaussées* from the rather precarious royal finances of the period, and perhaps permitted more roads to be built than might have been otherwise, despite the dilatoriness of workers forcibly recruited. It was immensely unpopular, and has been cited as one of the irritations provoking the French Revolution.

Originally, the *corvée* applied only to the *pays d'élection*. The Western Pyrenees were *pays d'état*. But the presence in Béarn and Auch of the

KEY TO FINDER MAP

43°30′

A   B   C   D

ATLANTIC OCEAN

Bayonne

Biarritz

1

San Sebastian

St.Jean-de-Luz

Urrugne

St. Pée-sur-Nivelle

Cambo-les-bains

Hendaye

Biriatou

Ascain

Souraïde

Espelette

Irún

COL D' IBARDIN

Oyarzún

Sare

Ainhoa

Itxassou

Macaye

St

Vera de Bidasoa

LARRAÚN

PTO. DE LIZURAGA

Dancharia

Louhossoa

Zugarramurdi

Urdax

ARTZAMENDI

Bidarray

Lesaca

PTO. DE LIZARRIETA

PTO. DE OTSONDO

Irissary

Ossès

2

Echalar

IPARLA

St. Martin d'Arossa

Suhescun

Yanci

Maya-del-Baztán

CIZE

Jaxu

Ainhice

Arano

Sumbilla

Errazu

St. Etienne de Baigorry

Bustince-Iriberry

Gamarth

Goizueta

Aranaz

Arizcun

COL D' ISPÉGUY

Irouléguy

Ispoure

Lacarre

St. Jean le Vieux

Anhaux

Ascarat

St. J.-P.-P.

Bussunarits-S.

Elgorriaga

Santesteban

Elizondo

Banca

Caro

Ainhice

Ahaxe

H

Ituren

Navarte

Irurita

Lasse

Lecumberri

Zubieta

Donamaria

St. Michel

Mendive

Béhor

Leiza

Ezcurra

Saldias

Oiz

Urroz de S.

BEORZUBUZTÁN

Arnéguy

Estérençuby

Areso

Erasun

Beinza Labayen

Almándoz

HAYRA

Aldudes

Valcarlos

PTO. DÉ VELATE

Quinto Real (Pays Quint)

IZTERBÉGUY

Urepel

PTO. DE IBAÑETA

Fábrica de Orbaiceta

IRATY

43°

COL DE LINDUS

Roncesvalles

Fábrica de Olaberri

Eugui

Burguete

AEZCOA

Viscarret

Espinal

Orbaiceta

Olagüe

Orbara

Aria

Villanueva de Aezcoa

Garralda

Zubiri

Erro

Arive

Oc

Urdániz

Garayoa

Larrasoaña

Abaurrea Baja

Abaurrea Alta

Esc

Oroz-Betelu

Jaurrieta

Oro

Zuriáin

Uriz

Espa

Sar

SALAZAR

Nagore

Güe

4

Pamplona

Gallu

0   5   10   15   20   25 km

5

2°

A   B   C   D

E   F   G   H   0°

43° 30

Orthez

1

Sauveterre de Béarn

PONT-LONG

Navarrenx

Pau

2

Mauléon - Licharre

SOULE

Oloron - Ste. Marie

Féas

ucq

Saugufs - St.E

Ossas-S

Trois-Villes

Ance

Lourdes

Alos-S.-A.

Tardets-

Sorholus

Lanne

Aramits

3

iou-C.

A.-S.

Lichans-S.

Montory

Arette

Issor

y-

Laguinge-R.

Escot

Etchebar

Haux

BARETOUS

Licq-

Lourdios-Ichère

Sarrance

Athery

rrau

Ste. Engrâce

ISSAUX

Bedous

43°

E LARRAU

COL DE LA PIERRE

Osse-en-Aspe

Aydius

COL D' AUBISQUE

ST. MARTIN

ARLAS Lées-Athas

Accous

Eaux-Bonnes

ERRAYZEKOLEPOA

ANIE Lescun

Cette- Eygun

Eaux-Chaudes

4

TABLE DES
TROIS ROIS

Borce

Etsaut

OSSAU VALLEY

Isaba

Urdos

FRANCE

Urzainqui

SPAIN

cal

Garde

COL DU SOMPORT

5

E   F   G   H   0°

energetic and forceful intendant, Antoine Mégret d'Étigny (1751–67) saw the application of at least a modified form of the *corvée*; and under d'Étigny's personal direction, several important roads were constructed. These were the highways between Bayonne and Pau, Pau and Mont de Marsan (to the North), Pau and Toulouse, and—especially important for the Pyrenees—the road from Pau up the Aspe valley nearly to the Somport pass.[66] This carriage road, which by 1837 had become impassable beyond Urdos,[67] was rebuilt by Napoleon III in 1861–3. The Spanish link was completed in 1877.[68]

In 1763 d'Étigny opened a carriageable road to one of the Pyrenean spas: Bagnères-de-Luchon. Hot springs were becoming an important economic asset for the mountains. French (and later, English) aristocrats 'discovered' the Pyrenean springs as early as the sixteenth century, but the real heyday of the spas came after the 1760s when roads were built to them, and after they had been provided with the hotels, baths, parks, and casinos necessary to attract a large clientèle.[69] Most of the spas were in the Central Pyrenees, though a few, Eaux Bonnes, Eaux Chaudes, St. Christau, and Cambo, were in the study area.

Speaking of the Pyrenees in general in 1847, Richard Ford noted the contrast between France and Spain, a contrast he implied was due to the greater development of tourism in the French Pyrenees and to the relatively remote situation of the Spanish slope.

> The finest portions of the Pyrenees lie in Aragon, and have yet to be investigated by geologists, botanists, artists, and sportsmen; while the French slope is full of summer watering-places and sensual, the Spanish side is rude, savage, and Iberian, the lair of the smuggler, and wild bird and beast. All who venture into the recesses must attend to the provend, and take a local guide.[70]

Ford's prose was probably more hyperbolic than that which an unbiased observer would have written, but it points nevertheless to fairly early differences between the two parts of the borderland.

The road built by d'Étigny in 1763 from Montréjeau to Bagnères-de-Luchon—supposedly to accommodate the Duc de Richelieu, who enjoyed taking the waters there—was soon supplemented by other roads linking the various spas.[71] These became the famous 'route thermale', or 'route des Pyrénées', running east and west from valley to valley in the French Pyrenees. Thus d'Étigny built the road from Bagnères-de-Luchon to Bagnères-de-Bigorre over the Peyresourde and Aspin passes. Later, under Napoleon III, the road was continued over the spectacular Tourmalet, Aubisque, and Soulor passes to Eaux-Bonnes. D'Étigny also began the road to Eaux-Chaudes (finished in 1774) and to Eaux-Bonnes from the north. By the end of the eighteenth century the French Pyrenees were beginning to be linked to the rest of the country. The outlines of the modern road network were evident, especially in the west, where the sheets of the Cassini topographic survey of 1770—80 (revised in 1803—12) show several major roads (from St. Jean Pied-de-Port to St. Palais and to Bayonne, from Mauléon to Tardets and thence by way of the Barétous to Oloron, and from Mauléon to Navarrenx (and Pau?)), plus a profusion of less important roads.[72]

Trans-Pyrenean connections, however, were tenuous. The Spanish royal road from Madrid to Irún met a rougher road at the boundary (passable with difficulty by vehicles). The carriage road to Bayonne was unfinished until the very end of the eighteenth century. No carriageable French road joined Navarre's route over the Velate Pass until the nineteenth century; nor was there a Spanish road from Jaca to the Somport Pass before 1877.

On the whole, the French Pyrenees by 1800 were much better equipped with carriageable roads than the Spanish Pyrenees, although Navarre's relatively privileged position made differences somewhat less pronounced in the west. Even though it refers to the Mediterranean Pyrenees, Arthur Young's comparison of French and Spanish roads at the time is instructive. He was crossing the Pyrenees at the Perthus pass in 1787:

> Here take leave of Spain and re-enter France: the contrast is striking. When one crosses the sea from Dover to Calais, the preparation and circumstance of a naval passage lead the mind by some gradation to a change: but here, without going through a town, a barrier, or even wall, you enter a new world. From the natural and miserable roads of Catalonia, you tread at once on a noble causeway, made with all the solidity and magnificence that distinguish the highways of France. Instead of beds of torrents you have well built bridges; and from a country wild, desert, and poor, we found ourselves in the midst of cultivation and improvement. Every other circumstance spoke the same language, and told us by signs not to be mistaken, that some great and operating cause worked an effect too clear to be misunderstood. The more one sees, the more I believe we shall be led to think, that there is but one all-powerful cause that instigates mankind, and that is GOVERNMENT! —Others form exceptions, and give shades of difference and distinction, but this acts with permanent and universal force. The present instance is remarkable; for Roussillon is in fact a part of Spain; the inhabitants are Spaniards in language and customs; but they are under a French government.[73]

Young was not noted for understatement.

The modern system of highway classification and administration owes much to Napoleonic legislation of the early 1800s.[74] In Napoleon's plan for a French national road system, one first-class route (no. 11, now no. 10), the Paris—Madrid road, ran through the study area, linking Bayonne with Irún. Two third-class trans-Pyrenean routes were projected in the area: that from St. Palais and St. Jean Pied-de-Port to Roncesvalles (completed to the boundary at Arnéguy by 1837; the Spanish link to Pamplona was finished in 1881); and the Somport Pass road (opened in 1877). Although Napoleon's achievements were more legislative than concrete, during the entire nineteenth and twentieth centuries road building proceeded faster in the French than in the Spanish Pyrenees.

At present, eight roads link Navarre and the Pyrénées-Atlantiques, and two more may be opened soon: these out of a total of nineteen boundary crossings in the whole range (1974). Yet most commercial traffic crosses the boundary at only two or three points. Besides serving a trickle of local traffic, the primary function of many trans-Pyrenean roads has become tourism. Having its own budget has allowed Navarre to invest in more such roads than other Spanish provinces. In general, however, there are more French roads to the boundary than are met by Spanish counterparts.

Modern maps showing the network of vehicular roads demonstrate clearly the superior development of communications in France throughout the period. And as a function of the greater development of France, traffic is denser there.[75] (Fig. 7b.)

The construction of all-weather local roads serving each community's dispersed farmsteads only became general in the 1960s. Again, the French communes led the Spanish municipios—such roads are built and maintained at communal expense—although some of the wealthier Spanish municipios began constructing farm lanes in the late 1960s. Thus Baztán opened more roads in 1967 and 1968 than it had in the previous forty years, and by 1970 had a fairly good network of local roads.[76] Providing such services is of course much more onerous for communities where most farms are dispersed rather than nucleated. The percentage of persons living in agglomerations (villages rather than dispersed farmsteads) is higher in the Spanish Western Pyrenees than in the French (see Fig. 8). Nevertheless, in 1968 only two or three farms in the valley of Baïgorry (France) could not be reached by vehicles, whereas in Baztán (Spain), with a less dispersed settlement pattern, there were several dozen isolated farms even in 1970.

Railways are also better developed on the French side than on the Spanish side of the boundary. The first line to be built was that from Paris to Madrid, via Hendaye. It was finished in 1864.[77] The local French line from Bayonne to St. Jean Pied-de-Port was built in the 1890s and the spur to Baïgorry in 1899. Later, the railway from Puyôo (on the Bayonne—Pau line) to St. Palais and to Mauléon was built. The second trans-Pyrenean railway in the west was that under the Somport pass, begun in 1882 and finished in 1928.[78] In Navarre, the only railway lines in the mountains were two narrow gauge (1 metre) tracks, built by private concerns in about 1920 from Pamplona to San Sebastian via Leiza, and from Elizondo to Irún (built after the first). Both functioned for only a few years before being abandoned for lack of custom in the early 1950s.[79] The French lines to Baïgorry, St. Jean Pied-de-Port, and Mauléon, however, also attract relatively little traffic. The *Société Nationale des Chemins de Fer français* is gradually replacing passenger runs on them with bus services.

Other forms of communication, such as newspapers, postal services, and telephones, exist in both countries. Postal services are ubiquitous, although

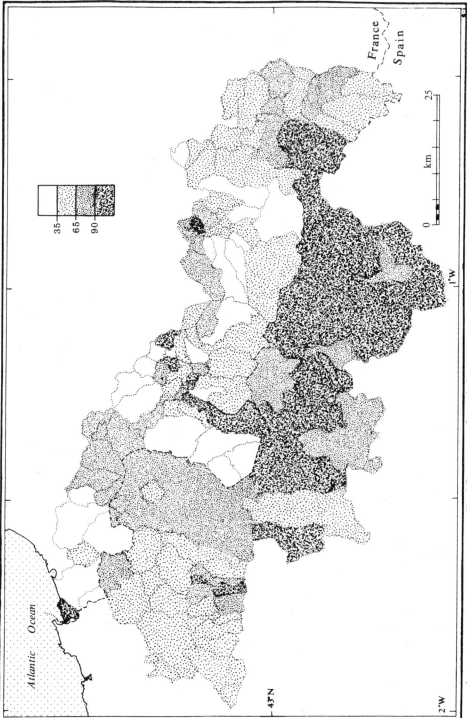

Fig. 8 Percentage of population living in agglomerated settlements

rural delivery is more widespread in France than in Spain. It was not possible to obtain information on newspaper circulation. Telephones, which in both countries are operated by a central administration (the *Ministère des Postes et Télécommunications* in France, and the *Compañia Telefónica Nacional* in Spain) are found in almost every community.[80] Telephones might provide a useful index of 'development' or prosperity, except that in both France and Spain supply and demand are not in equilibrium. The waiting list for subscribers to telephone services is long. In the Basses-Pyrénées in 1967, for example, 2,305 new subscribers were added, whereas at the end of the year 5,292 requests for telephone services were still outstanding, which suggests an average wait of more than two years for an installation.[81] Telephones are not widespread, even in small towns, and they are extremely rare in the countryside. Almost no farmer has a telephone; few persons besides storekeepers and professional persons would even think of using a telephone more than occasionally. There are, however, more telephones available to Frenchmen than to Spaniards. In 1968 there were 2,291 telephones in the 81 French communes in the study area, an average of one telephone for every 12 persons. The 59 Spanish municipios had 1,979 telephones, one for every 22 inhabitants. Public telephone booths are included in these counts—there are many communities where these are the only installations. But it is difficult to compare or interpret these data, since the availability of telephones does not depend only on desire or need for service, but also upon the telephone companies' tariffs and policies regarding installation and service.[82]

ENERGY

Electric power is another component of the infra-structure upon which economic development depends. The Pyrenees both supply and consume power. The region as a whole is a net exporter of electricity. Late in the nineteenth century the Pyrenees began to yield hydro-electricity, and today the mountains supply considerable amounts of power to the grids of France and Spain.[83] In fact, the Pyrenees are Spain's most important source of hydro-electricity. Most of the generating potential and capacity is located in the higher Central Pyrenees. A sprinkling of many small stations in the Western Pyrenees (in both France and Spain) provides power for 'local' consumption.

Although large hydro-electric projects are far more important in the economy of the Central Pyrenees than in that of the Atlantic Pyrenees, the big generating stations actually provide relatively little work for local inhabitants, being largely automated. Derived industries, such as electro-chemical and electro-metallurgical industries, which may use the power, are usually located in the lowlands near the Pyrenees rather than in the mountains. An exception is the paper industries, using both Pyrenean timber and hydro-electricity, which occupy some valleys in the Central Pyrenees. Paper companies built several of the early generating stations. The early electrification of the Basses-Pyrénées involved a large number of very small generators installed by diminutive local industries: grain mills, leather works, textile weaving, and sandal-making. In the French Pyrenees many early hydro-electric projects were also initiated by the predecessors of the *Société Nationale des Chemins de Fer français* (SNCF) to provide power for electric traction railway lines.[84] These stations today are tied into the power grids of France's public utility, *Électricité de France*, created after World War II. The ÉDF controls the distribution of most electricity in France.[85]

Rural electrification in the French Western Pyrenees is complete. Since World War II every single rural dwelling, even the most isolated farmsteads, has received electric service. The government (through the *Génie Rural*), not the consumer, pays for the long lines to rural farms. The capacity of the low tension lines to the farmhouses is between three and four kilowatts.[86]

The situation in the Spanish Pyrenees and in Navarre is very different. Hydro-electric generating stations came much later to the Navarrese Pyrenees. In the 1920s only four Navarrese municipios in the mountains had generating stations, while they were quite common along the rivers of the French Western Pyrenees.[87] There is still no single public electric utility in Spain, but a number of small private companies and a few large enterprises. Territories may overlap. Since all these companies try to make a profit, and since the state does not subsidize the distribution of electricity to rural areas, many distant villages, and all isolated farmsteads, go without adequate electric power, often with no power at all. *Fuerzas Electricas de Navarra*, the largest supplier in the province, links only the large towns. Many Pyrenean villages draw their power from an anarchic profusion of small, often antique, generating stations. In many cases their capacity is limited to providing energy for two or three incandescent bulbs in each house.[88]

In Baztán, one of the more progressive Spanish valleys, the inadequate output of two small privately-owned generating stations hamstrung the community's efforts at industrialization, albeit small scale. In 1968 fluorescent lights, sensitive to voltage fluctuations, sometimes would not light up, television screens would not fill up, and it was not possible to use electric motors extensively in the valley. Baztán was at that time negotiating the construction of a high-tension line by *Iberduero* (another Spanish electric utility) to replace the local generators.[89] Nevertheless, without some form of subsidy, dispersed farmsteads and the smaller, remote villages of the Spanish Pyrenees are not likely to be supplied with power as their French counterparts are.

Other commercial energy sources besides electricity (and petrol for automobiles) are relatively unimportant in the Western Pyrenees. Households, especially in France, use bottled propane for cooking and for heating water, if they do not burn wood. The natural gas fields at Lacq, near Pau, provide both energy and raw materials for petro-chemical industries, but the

Lacq industrial complex is twenty-five kilometres north or the Pyrenean front, outside the study area. No results have come from searches for oil and gas in the Western Pyrenees themselves.[90]

EDUCATION

No less than roads, schools link a community with the wider world. Not only does education increase awareness of the world, it also is the medium by which innovation and perhaps better economic opportunity may enter an area. If opportunity seems limited at home, education may stimulate and facilitate emigration. In the Western Pyrenees, schooling has had both these effects. In addition, the schools have fostered the sense of 'French-ness' or 'Spanish-ness' in the borderland, primarily by teaching Basques to speak French or Spanish, and have thus been instrumental in widening the cultural and social gap the border now represents. In the predominantly agricultural, rural milieu of the mountains, such cultural changes may be among the schools' most important effects. They are difficult to measure, however. Indeed most indexes of education are quite crude; even these are not available for the whole of the study area.

In Spain, compulsory primary education was required by law after 1857. In actual practice, however, primary education in Spain was available only to a few children. Illiteracy remained high. The 1860 census showed 77 per cent of the population of the Spanish Western Pyrenees to be unable to read.[91] The figure changed slowly during the next century. Even as late as 1940 23 per cent of the area's total population remained illiterate.

The reasons for the discrepancy between policy and practice were that the state was poor, and unable to finance education for the masses, and that responsibility for primary education was in the hands of municipal committees, who were in fact free to do as they wished. Teachers' salaries, paid by municipalities, were utterly inadequate. Priests and religious orders had a strong influence upon primary education: not only did they provide much of the teaching staff, they also influenced the content of the secular curriculum in many communities.[92] In 1923, according to figures quoted by Salvador de Madariaga, 50 per cent of Spanish children did not attend school, 25 per cent attended a church-run school, and 25 per cent a state-run school.[93] In Spain as a whole, during the 1930s, *adult* illiteracy was 25 per cent.[94]

The second Spanish Republic (1931–9) attempted to introduce mass education and take control away from the church, but its efforts were cut short by the Spanish Civil War (1936–9), after which Franco put the control of primary education into the hands of the church more firmly than ever. The Spanish church controls the secular as well as the religious curriculum in primary schools. The State, however, pays for education. After the Civil War and during the 1940s Spain lacked money to improve and expand schools. By the late 1950s the situation had improved and most communities had primary schools. In 1962 it was estimated that two-thirds of Spanish adults had completed primary schooling.[95]

In the Spanish portion of the study area, census figures for literacy show that in only one community in 1860 could more than half of the population read. But this was Roncesvalles, dominated by its monastery. Elsewhere between 50 and 97 per cent of the inhabitants were illiterate. The distribution of illiteracy in the mountains is fascinating, even though we possess no comparable data for France. The least literate municipios were those on the north slope, in the humid Basque country; the most literate were the high valleys of Salazar and Roncal in the east (see Fig. 9). The west to east 'literacy gradient', corresponding also to a cultural gradient (Basque to non-Basque) and a physiographic gradient (from the humid, low mountains of the north slope to the drier, higher mountains of the south slope), persisted in 1900 and 1940 (Figs. 10, 11).

There might be several reasons for the east—west contrast. First, the rates are not corrected for the age-structure of the population. Thus the Basques' greater illiteracy might be explained by the fact that they have more children (if indeed they do[96])—but in fact the discrepancy is too great to be explained thus. Some of the difference is doubtless due to the Basques' distinctive language. Spanish dialects, not Basque, were spoken in Salazar and Roncal, making literacy in Spanish easier to attain. Another cause of the discrepancy might be differences in the availability of schooling or in the quality of education. According to Pascual Madoz, most municipios in the area had primary schools in the 1840s. This information does not seem to agree well with the low literacy rates given in the 1860 census, but Madoz's observations are usually fairly reliable. Perhaps the quality of instruction was poor. Most local primary schools enrolled both boys and girls, though a few were for boys only. Where Madoz gives attendance figures, it is possible to calculate the percentage of the municipal population attending school in the 1840s, and in doing so, we see that there may be some tendency for higher enrolments in the east than in the west.[97]

But the most likely explanation for the higher illiteracy of the Basque country, especially in view of its persistence for at least eighty years, is the greater dispersion of settlement there (see Fig. 8). Schools, like roads and most municipal services, are much easier to supply to a community which is concentrated in a town. The dispersed farmsteads of the Basque country may be isolated and remote from the market towns, making it difficult to send children to the towns to school. Even today a substantial number of caseríos in the Spanish Basque Pyrenees, without access to roads and far from towns, remains beyond the reach of schools. School bus services are relatively less developed in Spain than in France. It is possible to find couples in the Spanish Pyrenees who speak only Basque and who cannot read, and whose children have never been away from the farm where they were born. Of course illiteracy is more prevalent among the elderly than the

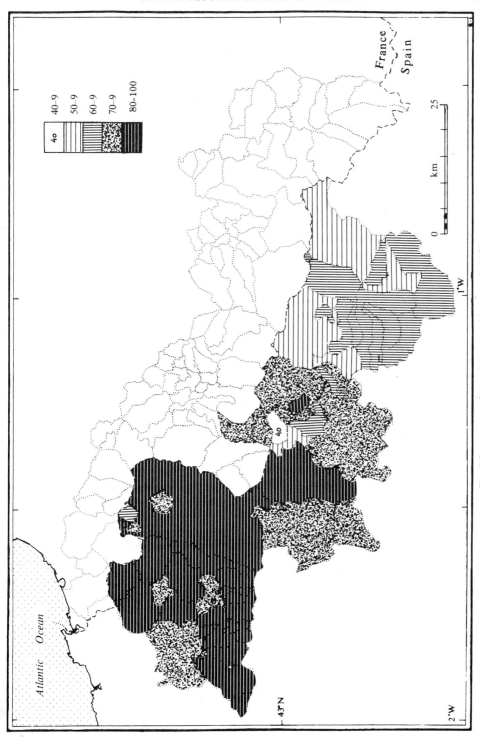

Fig. 9 Percentage of population unable to read, 1860
Source: 1860 Spanish census. Mean = 77 per cent.

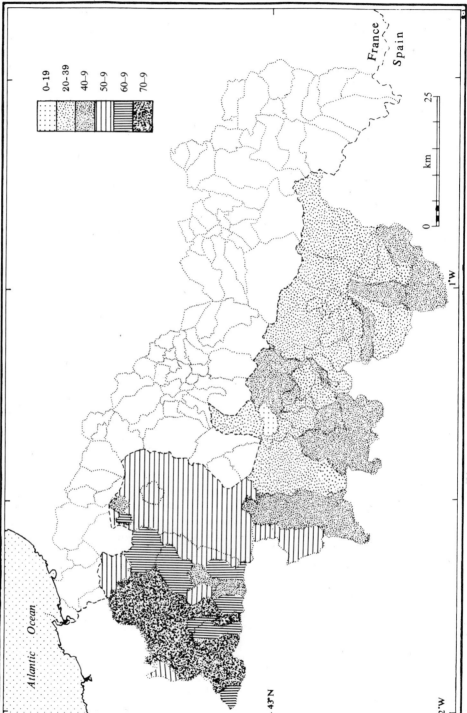

Fig. 10 Percentage of population unable to read, 1900

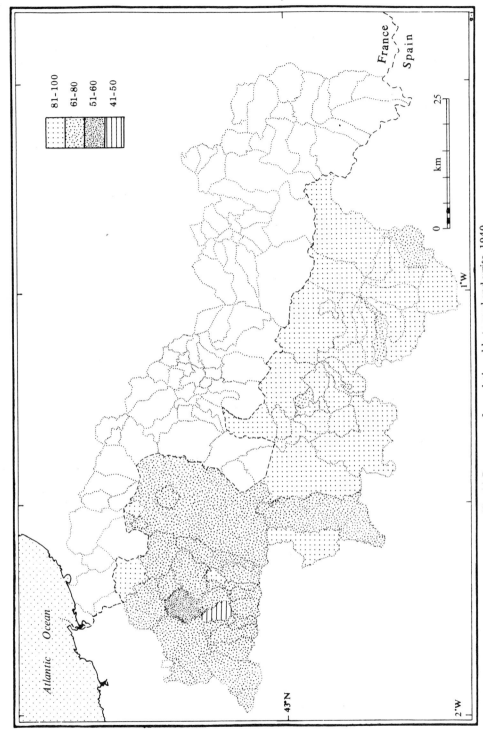

Fig. 11 Percentage of population able to read and write, 1940
Source: 1940 Spanish census. Mean = 79 per cent.

young. In a few localities (around Urdax and Zugarramurdi, for example), children from isolated farms in Spain walk across the boundary to attend school in France.

Unfortunately, comparable data on literacy are not available for the French communes of the study area.[98] It is a pity, because they might throw light on several topics, such as differential rates of emigration during the last 150 years, or the correlation of dispersed settlement with low education (dispersion is even greater in the French portion of the study area.)

In general, education was better developed in nineteenth-century France than in Spain. In 1816 a Restoration decree ordered that each commune in France must have at least one primary school, thus filling a gap in Napoleon's 1802 law outlining the French educational system. The Napoleonic law left the responsibility for primary education to either the communes or the religious orders. The result was a long political struggle between clerical and secular forces for the control of education in France. The conflict lasted at least a hundred years, but gradually secular education predominated—a development which Spain enjoyed only briefly. One of the reasons for the secular triumph was, ironically, the Falloux law (March 1850), which allowed members of church orders to teach even without qualifications, and thus ensured that the lay schools eventually would be of higher quality.

In 1833 the Guizot law established the modern arrangement of primary and secondary schools in France. But even before that date, primary education was spreading rapidly. By 1820 there were 27,000 primary schools in France. More than half (24,000) of France's 44,000 communes had such a school, and literacy figures for 1830 show that these early schools were having an effect.[99] By 1829 there were 31,000 primary schools, and by 1848 63,000, enrolling 3,500,000 pupils.[100] The percentage of the 'school-age' (5 to 14 years) population actually attending school in France in 1850 was 49 per cent. By the mid 1880s the figure had attained its present level of around 85 per cent.[101] After 1850, communes of more than 800 inhabitants (600 after 1867) were required to provide primary schooling for girls as well as boys. In 1881 primary education became free, and in 1882 obligatory, for children aged 6 to 13.[102]

Illiteracy in France fell accordingly. In 1861, 36·5 per cent of newly-weds could not write, and neither could 32 per cent of the French army's conscripts. By 1901 the same percentages had dropped to 5 and 5·6.[103]

The Basses-Pyrénées seem to have been fairly close to the average performance for all France during this period. Unfortunately it is not possible to be more precise about the effects of education in the communes of the department. In 1786—90, according to Maggiolo's data, between 40 and 49 per cent of marriage contracts in the department had been signed.

The national average was 37 per cent. In 1871–5, when the average for France was 72 per cent, the average in the Basses-Pyrénées stood at between 60 and 69 per cent.[104] These figures suggest at least that education advanced more quickly through the French portion of the borderland than the Spanish.

At present the French Western Pyrenees are somewhat better endowed with primary and secondary schools than the Navarrese mountains. Every commune has at least one primary school, and virtually all children attend school. School buses serve isolated families. The buses are usually 'free', but in some places the family pays 10 per cent of the cost. Secondary schools exist in the larger towns.[105] In addition, since at least 1929, there have been several agricultural schools in the region, and a corps of itinerant agricultural extension agents.[106] The Navarrese farmer must travel to Pamplona for an agronomist's advice.

There are many other components of the Western Pyrenees' infrastructure besides administration, communications, energy, and education, but in general they follow a similar pattern: the French side of the borderland developed earlier and more completely than the Spanish. The French cadastral survey, for example, covered the mountains by the 1830s, whereas that of Navarre did not reach the Pyrenees until the 1890s. The provision of social services: health care, welfare, and pensions, is much more widespread in France than in Spain. Subsidized credit is now available to farmers on both sides of the boundary, but it has been available longer in France. There are a few exceptions: the forestry service in Navarre has been more effective in protecting forests there than has the French forestry service in Basses-Pyrénées. Some of these topics will be dealt with in the following chapter, which describes the emergence of two distinctive regions in the borderland.

1 Before the reforms of the Third Republic, however, *national* elections were commonly rigged, and the franchise was very restricted in France.

2 Edict of August 1669, title XXV, art. 7.

3 Foursans-Bourdette, p. 29.

4 The eighteenth-century agrarian movement itself is beyond the scope of this study. There is an excellent and comprehensive study by André J. Bourde, *Agronomie et agronomes en France au XVIIIe siècle* (3 vols.; Paris: École pratique des hautes études, 1967). On the limited effects of the agrarian movement in France see Michel Morineau, 'Y-a-t-il eu une révolution agricole en France au XVIIIe siècle? ' *Revue historique*, CCXXXIX (1968), 299–326.

5 Marc Bloch, 'La lutte pour l'individualisme agraire dans la France du XVIIIe siècle', *Annales d'Histoire économique et sociale*, II (1930), 329–83; 511–56.

6 See B. H. Slicher van Bath, *The agrarian history of Western Europe, 500–1850* (London: Arnold, 1963), pp. 239 ff.

7 Young (1793 ed.), II. 227–8.

8 See Bourde, p. 557, for citations. Bourde's exposition is the source of much of the material which follows here.

9 Bourde, pp. 1158–1159.

10Bourde, pp. 1183–1184.

11Foursans-Bourdette, pp. 29–30. It was mostly the smallholders who profited, however, so that the social dislocation of these edicts seems to have been minimal in Béarn.

12Lefebvre, *Les Pyrénées atlantiques*, p. 228.

13Cavaillès, *La Vie pastorale*, p. 148.

14See: Jean Caput, *RGPSO* XXVII. 231 ff; Cavaillès, *La Vie pastorale*, pp. 150 ff.

15Young (1793 ed.), II. 87.

16Daniel Faucher, 'Le Bocage pyrénéen', *RGPSO* II (1931), 362–5.

17This is a question which ought to find a solution in an examination of the villages' Napoleonic cadasters. See also: de Castarède, *Du progrès agricole dans le département des Basses-Pyrénées* (Pau, 1865) and Orcurto-Joany, *Recueil des usages locaux constatés dans le département des Basses-Pyrénées* (Pau, 1868), both cited by Caput, *RGPSO* XXVII. 233–4.

18The name was changed in 1969 to Pyrénées Atlantiques.

19Raymond, *Dictionnaire*, p. x.

20Interviews with various syndics in the area (1968).

21Caput, *RGPSO* XXVII. 219–42.

22See Jean Etcheverry-Aïnchart, *Eusko-Jakintza*, II, 209–28.

23Actually, the situation in the Western Pyrenees was far more complex than this; so complex in fact that authors disagree over the arrangement of the various kinds of civil divisions. Labourd was for most of the period part of the *généralité d'Auch* (not a *Pays d'État*). At other periods the whole of the Western Pyrenees (Labourd, Basse Navarre, Soule, Béarn) was part of the single generality of Bayonne and Pau—a *Pays d'État*. Sometimes, however, Soule and Labourd depended upon the Parliament of Bordeaux. The generalities (and the other subdivisions of the *ancien régime*, which rarely coincided) altered with the passage of time, and it would be pointless and probably impossible to chronicle the changing boundaries of these internal units. See Paul Raymond, *Dictionnaire*. See also plates 146–8 of William R. Shepherd, *Historical Atlas* (7th ed.; New York: Henry Holt, 1929).

24See Hervé Detton, *L'Administration régionale et locale de la France* (Paris: Presses Universitaires de France, 1964), for a brief summary.

25Except from 1419 to 1434, when Navarre was allied to Aragon by the marriage of Blanche d'Evreux.

26On the evolution of the territory that was Navarre, see the historical maps in Antonio Ubieto Arteta, 'Las fronteras de Navarra', *Principe de Viana*, XIV (1953), 61–96.

27See José María Lacarra, 'Notas para la formcaión de las familias de fueros de Navarra', *Anuario de historia del derecho español*, X (1933), 203–272; and Ralph E. Giesey, *'If not, not;' the oath of the Aragonese and the legendary laws of Sobrarbe* (Princeton, New Jersey: Princeton University Press, 1968).

28In the Pyrenees these were Goizueta, Lesaca, Echalar, Santesteban, Larrasoaña, St. Jean Pied-de-Port (now in France), and the monasteries of Urdax and Roncesvalles.

29See Raymond Carr, *Spain 1808–1939* (Oxford: Clarendon Press, 1966), pp. 62–3, 220–1, 269, 556–8; and Rodrigo Rodriguez Garraza, *Navarra de reino a provincia (1828–1841)* (Pamplona: Universidad de Navarra, 1968).

30See Jean Sarrailh, *L'Espagne éclairée de la seconde moitié du XVIIIe siècle* (Paris: Imprimerie nationale, 1954).

31See Marcelin Defourneaux, *Pablo de Olavide ou l'Afrancesado (1725–1803)*, (Paris: Presses Universitaires de France, 1959), 175–245.

32Carr, pp. 99–100.

33Carr, 255–6, 272–4. Carr is not well-informed on what happened in Navarre (p. 274). A law passed earlier in the century had already resulted in the sale of church lands throughout most of Spain, but in Navarre lands belonging to the church were given to the municipalities, thus enlarging the commons.

34Navarre is one of the few regions for which detailed studies of the effects of the 1855 law have been made. See: Alfredo Floristán Samanes, 'La desamortización de bienes pertenecientes a corporaciones civiles y al estado en Navarra', in *Homenaje al Excmo. D. Amando Melon y Ruiz de Gordejuela* (Saragossa: Instituto de Estudios Pirenaicos, 1966), 109–16; and Rafael Gómez-Chaparro, *La Desamortización civil en Navarra* (Pamplona: Ediciones Universidad de Navarra, 1967).

35Navarre comprises about 1,000,000 hectares, of which approximately 500,000 are common land.

36Floristán Samanes, 'La desamortización',

37Gómez-Chaparro, 110–11. See the itemized list of sales, pp. 175–236.

38Their right to do so was reaffirmed by articles 6 and 10 of the *Ley Paccionada* of 1841.

[39] See: María Pilar de Torres Luna, *La Navarra húmeda del noroeste* (Madrid: Consejo superior de investigaciones científicas, 1971), chap. I; and Alfredo Floristán Samanes, 'Los Comunes en Navarra', *Actes*, IV CIEP, IV. 74–86.

[40] Actually, the Montes de Bidasoa are shared by three municipios and one *concejo* from a fourth municipio.

[41] For details see: Florencio Idoate, 'La comunidad del valle de Roncal,' *Actas*, V CIEP, III. 141–6; and Felipe de Arin y Dorronsoro, *Problemas Agrarios; estudio jurídico-social de las corralizas, servidumbres, montes y comunidades de Navarra* (Segovia: 'Heraldo Segoviano', 1930).

[42] Interviews with French, Spanish and Navarrese forestry officials, 1968. Archives of *Patrimonio Forestal del Estado*, Pamplona.

[43] In the dispersed habitat of the Basque country the *auzalán* is the isolated neighbourhood made up of a few *caseríos* (farms). It is an important social entity. See also Art. 573, *Reglamento de Administración Municipal de Navarra*, which equates the *auzalán* with a form of statute labour.

[44] Private lands must be ceded voluntarily to this custom. The Spanish law of 1817–18 abolishing the privileges of the Mesta also established the right of property owners to enclose their fields. This was also recognized by the Parliament of Navarre. Nevertheless the ordinances of the valley of Baztán still recognized common of pasture in 1832. Floristán Samanes & Torres Luna, *Pirineos*, vol. XXVI, no. 95, p. 18.

[45] Or water; but this was unimportant in the Western Pyrenees except for exporting logs.

[46] See: Henri Cavaillès, *La Route française: son histoire, sa fonction: étude de géographie humaine* (Paris: A. Colin, 1946), p. 17. Also: id., 'Les chemins de la vallée d'Aure', *Bulletin pyrénéen*, no. 215 (1935), pp. 6–16.

[47] Jean Sermet, 'Communications pyrénéennes et transpyrénéennes', *Actes*, II CIEP, VII. 97–8. This is the best local history.

[48] The passage through the Basque mountains was arduous at best; harrowing, if one is to believe Amery Picaud, author of the twelfth-century guidebook to the pilgrimage: 'Hec est gens barbara, omnibus gentibus dissimilis ritibus et essentia, omni malicia pena ... prava, perversa, perfida ...' (Jeanne Vielliard, *Le Guide du pèlerin de Saint-Jacques-de-Compostelle* (Mâcon, 1938), cited by Sermet, II CIEP. 99.) In the same study Sermet supplies a map of Jacobean roads. The literature on the pilgrimage is vast. The following publications deal only with the routes in the study area: J.-B. Daranatz, 'La chapelle de Saint Sauveur ou de Charlemagne, à Ibañeta', *Bulletin du Musée Basque*, I–II (1935), 149–60; Bernard Duhourcau, 'Sur les chemins de Saint-Jacques de St. Palais à Roncevaux', *Sanctuaires et Pèlerinages*, X (1964) (offprint); *El Camino de Santiago a través de Navarra* (Pamplona: Diputación foral de Navarra, 1954); Charles Higounet, 'Un mapa de las relaciones monásticas transpirenaicas en la Edad Media', *Pirineos*, VII (1951), 543–53; José María Lacarra, 'Rutas de peregrinación: Los pasos del Pirineo y el camino de Santa Cristina a Puente la Reina', *Pirineos*, I (1945), 5–27; Elié Lambert, 'Le livre de Saint Jacques et les routes du pélerinage de Compostelle', *RGPSO* XIV (1943), 5–34; id., 'Le pélerinage de Compostelle et le pays basque français', *Pirineos*, XI (1955), 135–47; Claude Urrutibéhéty, *Voies d'accès en Navarre et carrefour des chemins de Saint Jacques* (Bayonne: Imprimerie S. Sordes, n.d.); P. Germán, 'El camino de peregrinación jacobea Bayona-Urdax-Velate-Pamplona', *Principe de Viana*, XXV (1964), 213–33.

[49] Elié Lambert, 'Les routes des Pyrénées atlantiques et leur emploi au cours des âges', *Actas*, I CIEP, VI. 121–64.

[50] Real Academia de la Historia, *Diccionario*, I. 244.

[51] Lefebvre, *Les Pyrénées atlantiques*, p. 238.

[52] Violant y Simorra, *El Pirineo español*, pp. 137–40.

[53] Pablo de Alzola y Minondo, *Las obras publicas en España; estudio historico* (Bilbao: Casa de la Misericordia, 1899), 295–410.

[54] Gonzalo Menendez Pidal, *Los caminos en la historia de España* (Madrid: Ediciones Cultura Hispánica, 1951), 115–30. The map is that of José Matias Escribano and is reproduced at the end of the volume. The Pyrenees could be crossed by the Perthus route, which had been improved after having fallen into disrepair during the Middle Ages.

[55] Jean Sermet, *Les Routes transpyrénéennes* (Toulouse: Société d'Histoire des Communications dans le Midi de la France, 1965), p. 22.

[56] Alzola y Minondo, pp. 368–75.

[57] Sermet, *Actas*, II CIEP, VII. 105. The map drawn by Santiago Lopez in 1812 (reproduced by Menendez Pidal) errs in this respect. On the French side of the Ibañeta pass, however, there was a track which vehicles could negotiate: the crest road from St. Jean Pied-de-Port to Bentartea, via Château Pignon, which Napoleon's engineers had improved.

58Sermet, *Actes*, II CIEP, VII. 105.

59Sermet, *Actes*, II CIEP, VII. 105; and Richard Ford, *A Handbook for Travellers in Spain* (2nd ed.; London: John Murray, 1847), p. 62.

60Lefebvre, *Les Pyrénées atlantiques*, p. 292.

61Sermet has found a reference to this road in 1815, but it is not mentioned in later accounts. Sermet, *Les Routes transpyrénéennes*, p. 37; and id., *Actes*, II CIEP, VII. 110—11.

62Sermet, *Les Routes transpyrénéennes*, pp. 37—8.

63Sermet, *Actes*, II CIEP, VII. 109.

64Anué, Esteribar, Arce, Aézcoa, Salazar, Roncal, Baztán, Cinco Villas; but not Erro or Urraúl.

65Cavaillès, *La Route française*, chap. III.

66Cavaillès, *La Route française*, pp. 98—9.

67France. Ministère des travaux publics, de l'agriculture et du commerce. Direction générale des ponts et chaussées et des mines, *Recueil de documents statistiques* (Paris: Imprimerie Royale, 1837), pp. 304—5.

68Sermet, *Les Routes transpyrénéennes*, p. 38.

69There is a substantial literature concerning Pyrenean thermalism (which actually has Roman beginnings). Many guidebooks and brochures for the clientèle were published, beginning even in the seventeenth century. M. Dralet, who cited some of these, devoted a section of his book to discussing the properties of various springs (Dralet, *Déscription des Pyrénées*, (2 vols.; Paris: A. Bertrand, 1813) II. 166—75). Most authors of books on the Pyrenees did the same. See also: Georges Cazes, *Le Tourisme à Luchon et dans le Luchonnais* (Toulouse: Institut de Géographie de la Faculté des Lettres et Sciences Humaines, 1964), pp. 29—42; Jean Fourcassié, 'Luxe et misère aux Pyrénées, il y a cent ans', *Annales de la Fédération pyrénéenne d'économie montagnarde*, XI (1944—5), 42—5; id., 'Comment on voyageait aux Pyrénées a l'époque romantique', (Pau: 1936 (extrait du *Bulletin pyrénéen*, 1936)); and Joseph Duloum, *Les Anglais dans les Pyrénées et les débuts du tourisme pyrénéen (1739—1896)* (Lourdes: Les amis du Musée pyrénéen, 1970).

70Ford, *Handbook*, p. 579.

71Sermet, *Actes*, II CIEP, VII. 100—1.

72'Carte géométrique de la France au 1/86, 400, dite de l'Académie ou de Cassini', sheets 108, 139, 140. The Cassini maps were made between 1750 and 1815; those of the Western Pyrenees appeared in the 1770s. There were revisions made in 1803—12, especially of the road network. On the history of the survey and on its reliability see: Henri Marie Auguste Berthaut, *La Carte de France 1750—1898; étude historique* (2 vols.; Paris: Imprimerie du Service géographique de l'Armée, 1898), I. 54—61.

73Young, *Travels* (Dublin ed. of 1793), I. 59—60.

74Cavaillès, *La Route française*, pp. 183—97.

75Michelin et Cie., *Carte Michelin de la France*, 1:200,000, no. 85: St. Sébastien—Tarbes (edition of c. 1925); Diputación foral de Navarra, Servicio de caminos, *Mapa de Navarra*, 1:200,000, formado por el Teniente Coronel del Cuerpo de Estado Mayor D. Frederico Montaner Canét (año 1926); Michelin, *Carte au 200,000ème*, no. 85: Biarritz—Luchon (edition of 1970); Diputación foral de Navarra, *Provincia de Navarra*, [map] 1:200,000 (1962); France, Ministère des travaux publiques, des transports et du tourisme, 'Recensement de la circulation sur les routes nationales en 1965', (MS. map in Bayonne office of 'Ponts et Chaussées'); Spain, Ministerio de obras públicas, Dirección general de carreteras, Traffic census for Navarre in 1967 (ozalid map with MS. notations; 1:400,000).

76Interview with the mayor of Baztán, 12 August 1968, and field notes.

77For the range as a whole, see Luis Solé Sabarís, *Los Pirineos* (Barcelona: Alberto Martín, 1951), pp. 422—5. Trans-Pyrenean railway links involve a change in gauge, from the 1·435 metres (4'8·5'') of France to the 1·674 metres (6 Castillian feet) of Spain, and therefore a change of trains at the border.

78See Sermet, *Actes*, II CIEP, VII. 135—7. The Somport line required, besides the 6·73 kilometre tunnel under the pass, fourteen tunnels in France—one in the form of a helix—and many roofs to protect it from avalanches. Built at great cost, the line's steep gradients and tight curves limit traffic-flow rates and make it uneconomical to operate. The line has been out of service since the collapse of one of the French bridges in 1970.

79Lefebvre, *Les Pyrénées atlantiques*, p. 296; Leoncio Urabayen, *Una geografía de Navarra* (Pamplona: Libe, 1959), p. 305.

80In 1968 one Spanish municipio (Elgorriaga) had no telephone service, and five French communes lacked it (Hosta, Laguinge-Restou, Bussunarits-Sarrasquette, Lichans-Sunhar, and Haux).

81Chambre de commerce et d'industrie de Pau, *Rapport sur la situation économique et perspectives d'avenir* (Janvier, 1968), p. 83.

82The number of telephones is that listed in the 1968 telephone directories. The French ratio is computed on the basis of the 1960 census. Since the municipios are losing population, the true ratio in Spain may be closer to nineteen or twenty. But these are means for the whole area. They may be misleading. For example, the means for communities vary widely: from over 1,000 to 7 persons per telephone. The median number of persons per telephone in communes and municipios is 50. That is, half the communities have more than 50 persons per telephone and half have fewer than 50. Slightly more than half the French communes (43) have more than 50 inhabitants per telephone. Slightly more than half of the Spanish municipios (32) have fewer than 50 persons per telephone. That is to say, the data seem to yield no significant differences between the two countries. Compañia Telefonica Nacional de España, *Guía telefonica: Pamplona y Provincia de Navarra, Julio 1968*; France, Ministère des Postes et Télécommunications, *Annuaire officiel des abonnés au téléphone: Basses-Pyrénées, 7 mars 1968*.

83The French and Spanish grids are interconnected by trans-Pyrenean high-voltage transmission lines. In 1967 France imported 1,600 million kWh from Spain and exported 200 million kWh to Spain. *Revue française de l'électricité* (Paris) XLI (1968), no. 221, p. 30.

84Henri Cavaillès, 'La houille blanche dans les Pyrénées françaises', *Annales de Géographie*, XXVIII (1919), 425—68. On hydro-electricity in the Pyrenees, among many articles and books, the most useful surveys are: Gérard Jaulerry, *L'Électrification de la région pyrénéenne* (Paris: Girard, 1933); Max Daumas, 'L'équipement hydroélectrique des Pyrénées espagnoles,' *RGPSO* XXXIII (1962), 73—106; plus the notes on current projects which appear in the *Revue géographique des Pyrénées et du Sud-Ouest* at various times.

85Other producers in France are: large electro-chemical and electro-metallurgical industries, paper industries, and refineries; *Charbonnages de France*, and the *Compagnie Nationale du Rhône*.

86Interviews with M. Barboutan, Engineer in Charge, *Électricité de France* (Bayonne), 21 and 31 Oct. 1968.

87Lefebvre, *Les Pyrénées atlantiques*, plate XIII.

88Interview, Engineer at *Fuerzas Electricas de Navarra*, 12 Nov. 1968.

89Interview, mayor of Baztán, 12 August 1968.

90In the past, iron forges and foundries were sprinkled over the area. They consumed great quantities of charcoal and entire watersheds were deforested to supply them with fuel. This topic is considered in the next chapter.

91The percentage is that of the total population. It includes babies.

92Carr, *Spain*, pp. 472—91.

93Salvador de Madariaga, *Spain* (New York: Scribner's, 1930), p. 228.

94Stanely G. Payne, *Franco's Spain* (New York: Crowell, 1967), p. 100.

95Payne, pp. 89, 100–1.

96Information on the age-structure of the municipios is available in the census but was not gathered for this study.

97Pascual Madoz, *Diccionario geográfico-estadístico-histórico de España* (16 vols.; Madrid: Imprenta del Diccionario, 1848—50), *passim*.

98In fact, the only series of statistics on literacy in France are: a study made in 1877—9 by Louis Maggiolo, who gathered parish data on the proportion of newly-weds able to sign their marriage contracts at various periods (1686—1876); and military statistics on the proportion of recruits unable to write (for the years 1832—1935). See J.-C. Toutain, 'La population de la France de 1700 à 1959', Supplément no. 133 aux *Cahiers de l'Institut de science économique appliquée* (1963). Toutain also gives figures on newly-weds' ability to write for 1856—1931.

99Antoine Léon, *Histoire de l'enseignement en France* (Paris: Presses Universitaires de France, 1967), p. 79; Toutain, p. 220.

100Léon, p. 80.

101Toutain, tables 158 and 160. The percentage is not higher because the age group 5—14 years at census time does not correspond exactly with the age group of children required to go to school.

102Toutain, p. 221. Since 1959 the school-leaving age has been 16.

103Toutain, table 156.

104There were great differences between the sexes, however; much greater than those obtaining nationally. In 1786—90, 47 per cent of Frenchmen and 27 per cent of women signed their contracts, but it was 70—79 per cent (men) and 0—9 per cent (women) in Basses-Pyrénées. In 1871—5, the percentage of men signing in Basses-Pyrénées conformed to the national average, while women were about ten percentage points lower. See: M. Fleury et P. Valmary, 'Les progrès de l'instruction élémentaire de Louis XIV à Napoléon III d'après l'enquête de Louis Maggiolo (1877–9)', *Population*, XII (1957), 71–92, ref. to maps 5, 6, 9, 10, 11, 12.

[105] *Enquête Montagne*, I. 127–34; II. 92–3 bis.

[106] France, Ministère de l'Agriculture, *Statistique agricole de la France, annexe à l'enquête de 1929; Monographie agricole du département des Basses-Pyrénées* (Pau: 1937), pp. 446–7; and France, Ministère de l'Agriculture, *Monographies agricoles départementales: 64—Les Basses-Pyrénées* (1953), (Paris: La documentation française, 1961), pp. 57–62.

CHAPTER VII

The Nineteenth and Twentieth Centuries

At some time during the nineteenth century or afterwards the economy of the Western Pyrenees underwent a profound, though not instantaneous, change. This was essentially the progression from a relatively closed and self-sufficient economy to a more commercialized one, open to the currents of enlarged markets and wider opportunities.

It happened as increasingly efficient communications and improvements in education bound the Pyrenees more and more closely to the fortunes of France and Spain. In the new contexts of national (or supra-national) markets the Pyrenees played a very different role than they traditionally had done when subsistence polyculture and circumscribed, local networks of transaction occupied the valleys. In the nineteenth and twentieth centuries, activities which fit into the larger metropolitan economies came to predominate, such as extensive livestock husbandry, forestry, tourism, and hydro-electric power production.[1] Similarly, differences between the French and Spanish portions of the Western Pyrenees emerged more and more clearly during the nineteenth and twentieth centuries.[2]

Because the infrastructure of change developed earlier and more rapidly in the French Pyrenees than in the Navarrese, the French borderland participated in the growing metropolitan economy sooner. It was the French Western Pyrenees which first showed the characteristic changes in demography, land use, and economy. In this way the two parts of the borderland came to differ. The differences, of course, arose not from the dissynchrony itself, but from differences between the two nations' circumstances: France enjoyed greater prosperity than Spain during this period.

It is indeed prosperity which marks the greatest difference between the two parts of the borderland today. Changes in demography, economy, and land use are the concern of this chapter. Most of the evidence brought forth points to the developing disparities in the standard of living across the boundary.

POPULATION

The population of the Pyrenees, which had been growing since at least the sixteenth century, attained its greatest density in the early nineteenth century. Evidence (most of it from France) points to a surge in population growth towards the end of the eighteenth century, continuing until just before the middle of the nineteenth, when in some areas the resultant high densities provoked a crisis. Why growth rates suddenly increased is not clear. For Ariège, Michel Chevalier proposed that the early eighteenth-century adoption of the potato may have permitted demographic expansion.[3] In the

west, maize, and changes in pastoral techniques and in the cultivation of the
arable, certainly gave greater yields, and may have allowed more rapid
population growth.

Writing in 1813 of the range as a whole, Dralet was struck by the shortage
of arable which accompanied the dense populations of the Pyrenees. Buyers
clamoured for any piece of land which might be offered for sale, and land
prices were high. Men who could, usurped patches of the common, and so
bit by bit they extended the arable up the slopes.[4] These marginal lands
were the least productive.[5] That people cultivated them at all was a symptom
of the mountains' isolation and closed economy, as well as of their
over-population, as it had been in the late Middle Ages; but the nineteenth-
century expansion seems to have been pushed farther than any previous one.

Both growth and subsequent decline were more marked in the east than in
the west, however. In the first half of the nineteenth century, the Western
Pyrenean population certainly grew, but it did not grow explosively. In the
Navarrese Pyrenees, 41,528 persons in 1802 became 53,469 in 1857, an
increase of 29 per cent in 55 years.[6] Basses-Pyrénées (figures for separate
communes of the study area in 1801 are lacking) grew at a similar rate from
1801 to 1846.

By the third or fourth decade of the nineteenth century, settlement in the
Western Pyrenees reached its maximum extent. At that time there was
approximately 8·5 per cent of the French communes' lands under
cultivation. If the amount seems small, it underlines the region's limited
arable resources and its dependence upon grazing. More than half (52·5 per
cent) of the land was in pasture, and an amount equal to the arable (8·6 per
cent) was used for meadows.[7] We know that the land was intensively used,
that farmers built plots on hillsides by terracing, and that they intercalated
crops whenever possible.[8] Further, the fields provided not only food for the
livestock and the people, but also clothing for the family. The plot of flax
was ubiquitous. With its linen, and with sheep's wool, women made cloth.
Skins, and tannin from oaks, gave leather. The forests provided wood for
tools, utensils, and shelter, as well as browse and mast for livestock, and
chestnuts to feed people through the lean winters. Self-sufficient in most
things, few farmers engaged in commerce outside their villages. Both the
French and the Spanish Atlantic Pyrenees were similar in these ways.

Change came with the roads and the schools. The coming of the roads
opened up the Pyrenees to outside influences, and people learned that
conditions were easier elsewhere. The roads also led to wider markets, which
made the traditional ways seem less remunerative than either the new, less
intensive forms of mountain economy, or the alternative opportunities
available outside. The resultant exodus of people became such a flood that in
many communities population actually dropped. A shift in economy
accompanied the population decline; both were the result of improvements
in communications. The flight to areas of greater opportunity led the

Pyrenees' inhabitants not only to urban areas in Spain and France, but also abroad: to African colonies and especially to the Americas. Few returned.

Over all, the population of the French Pyrenees declined by 56 per cent in the hundred years after 1856. Depopulation was more drastic in the Eastern and Central Pyrenees than in the west. The department of Ariège lost 54 per cent of its rural population between 1876 and 1954. The population of its canton of Massat in 1968 had shrunk to about one-seventh of the 1876 figure. In Lacarat (Ariège), where emigration had left an aged population behind, there were 17 deaths between 1950 and 1958, but not a single birth.[9]

Emigration and depopulation occurred throughout the range, and everywhere it changed the Pyrenean landscape. The most recently settled, most marginal lands were generally the first to be abandoned. Today one can walk through beech forests on the slopes above villages and trace the remnants of old fields now reverted to woods. In some places, hundred-year-old trees grow on hillsides that once were carefully walled and terraced. Remote farmhouses stand vacant.

As a response to its economic and social milieu, demographic history is a sensitive indicator of the changing fortunes of the Pyrenean borderland. Population decline, despite the European context of growth in which it occurred, represented an adjustment to the social and economic conditions of the nations which the Pyrenees 'joined' during the nineteenth century. Broadly, in both Spain and France the Pyrenees became an economically 'peripheral' area, both distant from the large urban markets and relatively unsuited to intensive exploitation.[10] The progress of decline thus reflected the degree to which the region adjusted to the new conditions, as well as the peculiarities of the region itself.[11]

In the Western Pyrenees population declined on both sides of the boundary, but there were differing temporal and spatial patterns of this movement. These reflected cross-boundary contrasts in the infrastructure's development and in the economic conditions of the two countries. Of course there was also local variation in the rate of depopulation. Other things being equal, the more remote and smaller the village, the more people it eventually lost, although its exodus might be late to begin.[12] Some cases were dramatic. In the Aspe valley, in France, 924 persons lived in Aydius in 1831, but only 88 in 1968. The greatest loss in the Navarrese Pyrenees was sustained by Arce, which dwindled from 1,852 inhabitants in 1857 to 643 in 1960, a loss of 65 per cent.

In both the Spanish and the French Western Pyrenees, demographic reversal occurred around the mid-nineteenth century. The French part has declined ever since. However, most Spanish municipios stopped losing people after 1887 and then oscillated or remained static until the 1950s, when their decline became precipitous. In both areas the decline was due to emigration. During the whole period there was an excess of births over deaths. This was

true even though in many places birth rates declined and death rates rose as
younger people emigrated, leaving an older population behind. Thus, over
all, the natural growth of the population remained positive, despite its
ageing.

The French part of the borderland reached its maximum density around
1850,[13] and has declined since then except for a slight gain during the late
1920s.[14]   Indeed the whole department of Basses-Pyrénées lost population
from about 1846 until the early years of this century.[15] In Basses-Pyrénées
the death rate stayed below the birth rate for as long as we have records.[16]
The rate of natural increase was highest during the first half of the
nineteenth century. The death rate had fallen but the birth rate was still
moderately high. Using the quinquennial censuses as a rough basis for
calculation, the mean natural growth rate during 1801–50 appears to have
been about 5·5/1,000 per year. Then, with a declining birth rate, the natural
growth rate dropped, although it remained positive. In 1851–1901 it
averaged about 3·1/1,000 per year, and in 1901–54 about 1·3/1,000 per
year. After 1846, when the population of the department reached its peak of
457,832, massive emigration offset the natural increase, and the population
diminished. During the whole period 147,000 persons left the department.
Table 1 shows natural growth, real growth, and migration in the Basses-
Pyrénées.

Table 1
Population Growth in Basses-Pyrénées
1801–1954

Period	Natural growth (excess of births over deaths) (thousands)	Real growth (change from census) (thousands)	Net migration (thousands)
1801–1850	+114	+91	− 23
1851–1900	+ 68	−20	− 88
1901–1953	+ 30	− 6	− 36
TOTAL	+212	+65	−147

Source: Institut national de la statistique et des études économiques. Direction régionale de Bordeaux.

Figure 12 shows population growth in the two sectors of the borderland
and in Spain and France.[17] Several trends appear. The first is the steady loss
of population from the French Western Pyrenees. From a high of around
70,000 in the late 1840s the communes lost 29 per cent of their population
by 1962. But except for decline between 1857 (perhaps earlier; we lack
data) and 1887, the population of the Navarrese Pyrenees held steady until
after 1950, then dropped precipitously in the next decades.

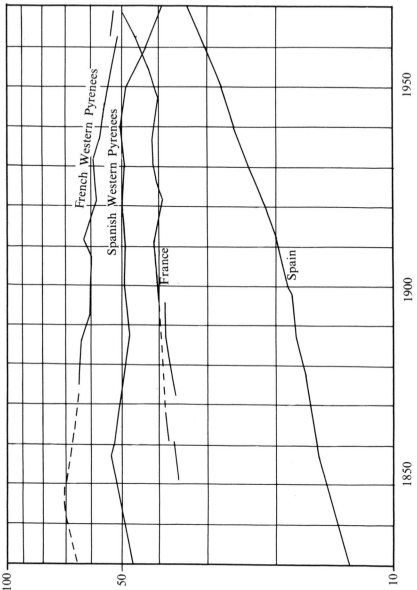

Fig. 12 Population: thousands (study area); millions (nations).

The province of Navarre as a whole never declined in population, but grew from 297,422 in 1857 to 402,042 in 1960, an increase of 35 per cent.[18] The rate of natural increase in Navarre was generally higher than in Basses-Pyrénées. We lack adequate data on nineteenth-century vital rates, but the evidence suggests high and fluctuating birth and death rates in the Navarrese Pyrenees during most of the nineteenth century, with only a modest rate of natural increase. During this period the population in the study area rose to a peak around mid-century, then was drained by emigration until 1887, at which time the death rate began to fall, increasing natural growth and offsetting emigration from the borderland. After 1900–10 the difference between births and deaths in Navarre grew to around 10/1,000 per year (much greater than the Basses-Pyrénées), where it remained until the 1950s. During the period 1900 to 1950, 113,000 Navarrese emigrated, but the rapid natural increase stabilized the borderland's population. This evolution, characteristic of a society influenced by the modern world (primarily by its means of death control) but not yet participating fully in it, contrasts markedly with the situation in the Basses-Pyrénées, where both birth and death rates fell much earlier to produce lower rates of natural increase. The sharp population decline of the 1950s and 1960s reflects opportunities offered to emigrants by the explosive growth of Spain's urban economy during those decades, as well as a falling birth rate in the area.[19]

After 1876 we have comparable series of census data from the communes and municipios of the borderland with which to trace the distribution of depopulation.[20] Fig. 13 shows population growth between 1876 and 1962 (in France) or 1877 and 1960 (in Spain).[21] Very few areas grew. In France the market towns did, although only Hendaye grew more than 1 per cent per year. In Spain, some small, isolated municipios grew, as well as the market towns of Vera de Bidasoa, Lesaca, and Santesteban.[22] But what stands out on this map is the persistence of decline. The much greater decline of the French communes shows clearly, even in the west, where the contrast is less.

Looking at Fig. 14, which shows population changes during the decade 1876–86 (France), 1877–87 (Spain), we see several Spanish municipios still in decline, including four in the Bidasoa valley (fairly well endowed with roads at this time), whereas the isolated Roncal valley continued its increase. In France, where roads were general, the eastern communes were the most rapidly decreasing. Then, from 1886 to the turn of the century, the pattern changed. The Navarrese municipios started to recoup the losses of the past twenty-five years, while rapid decline became more widespread in France (Fig. 15). Maps for the decades from 1900 to 1940 show inconclusive patterns, mostly because there is no discernible trend in the Spanish borderland. During the period as a whole, however, the mean growth rate for Spanish municipios was −0·15 per cent per year whereas that for French communes was −0·53 per cent per year (both are losses).[23] The maps for the two decades since World War II are revealing (Figs. 16, 17). The first, for

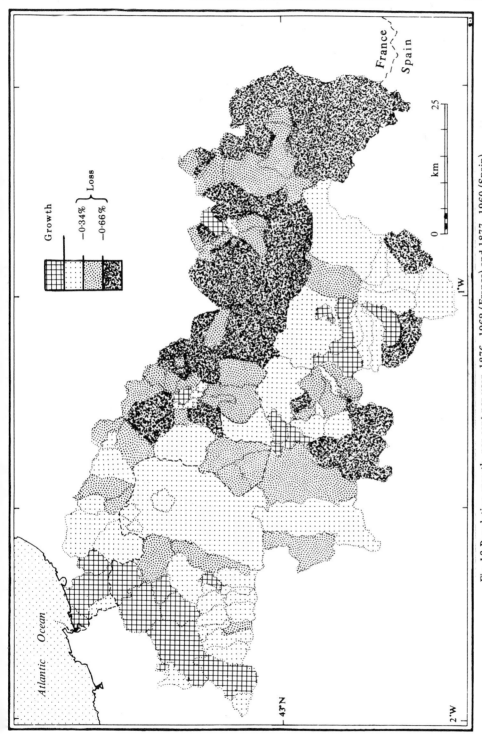

Fig. 13 Population growth, per cent per year, 1876–1962 (France) and 1877–1960 (Spain)
Source: Official censuses.

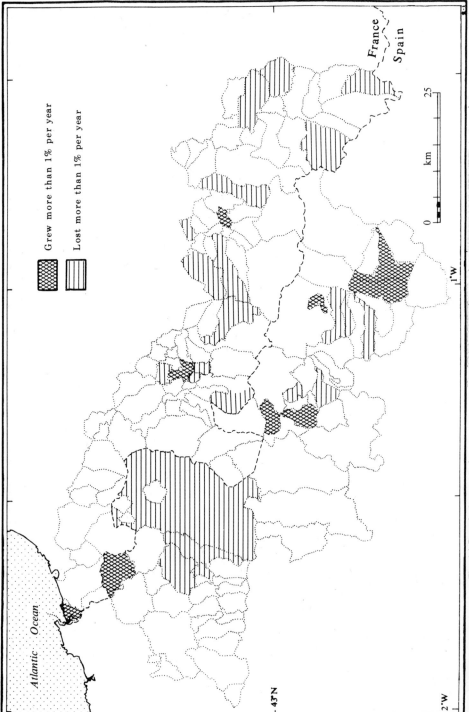

Fig. 14 Population growth, per cent per year, 1876–1886 (France) and 1877–1887 (Spain)

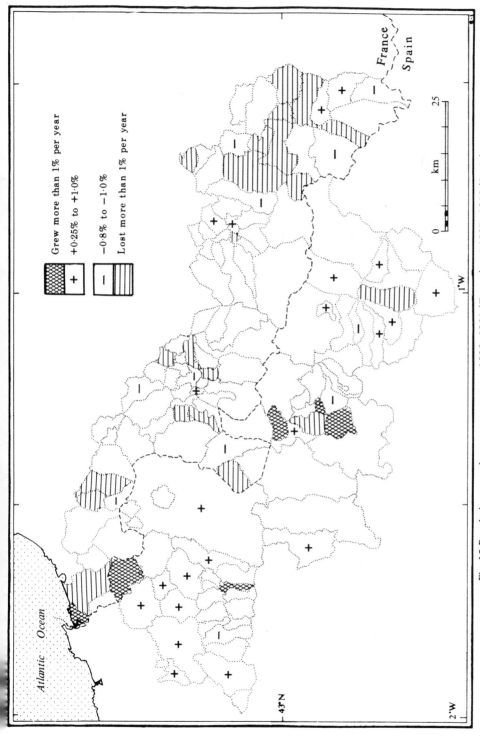

Fig. 15 Population growth, per cent per year, 1886–1901 (France) and 1887–1900 (Spain)
Source: Official censuses.

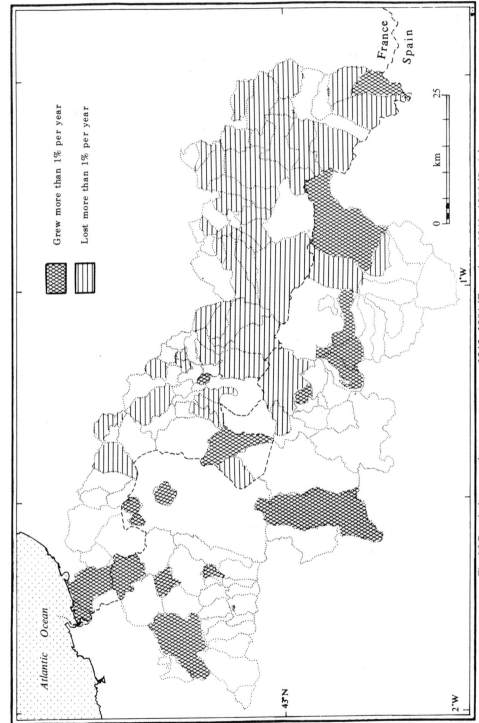

Fig. 16 Population growth, per cent per year, 1946–1954 (France) and 1940–1950 (Spain)
Source: Official censuses.

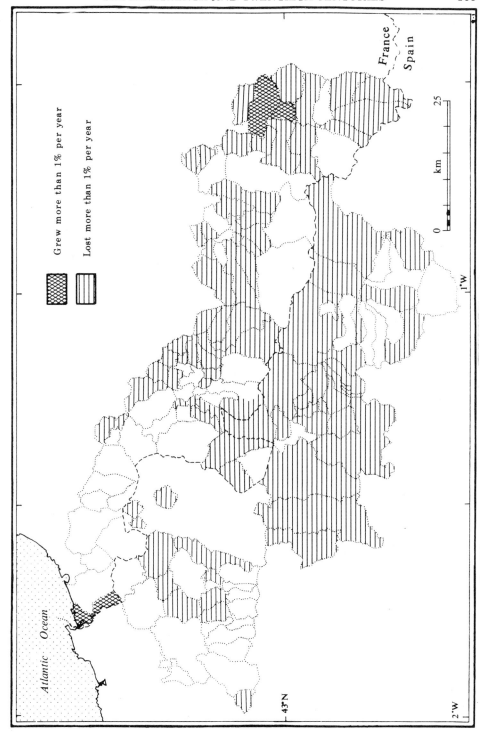

Fig. 17 Population growth, per cent per year, 1954–1962 (France) and 1950–1960 (Spain)
Source: Official censuses.

1946–54 (France) and 1940–50 (Spain), shows decline continuing in French communes, but rare in Spain, which on the contrary shows several municipios growing faster than 1 per cent per year. The second map, however, shows the dramatic change in the Navarrese municipios during the decade of the 1950s, as decline for the first time became general in the borderland.

Despite the regional differences in decline and their apparent correlation with differences in the development of the infra-structure, we cannot be certain (for lack of precise data on births and deaths in each community) whether emigration from the borderland was greater in France than Spain. It would be tempting to think that more emigrants left the French communes since their links with the outside world had been forged earlier, and since they might better be able to afford the journey, but such an interpretation awaits more information. Both parts of the borderland clearly ran counter to their national growth rates. However there was a very important difference between the two, one which certainly asserts the precocity of the French Western Pyrenees' development. That is, Spaniards commonly emigrated to the French Western Pyrenees during this period, but extremely few Frenchmen left to settle in neighbouring Navarrese villages.

There had long been periodic migrations of Pyrenean folk. Before the nineteenth century, in fact, French peasants are mentioned as seasonal workers on Spanish farms, especially at harvest time. In 1673 Louis de Froidour, the intendant, observed, 'the inhabitants of Soule go to work in Spanish fields, vineyards, gardens, and orchards; they make hay, scythe wheat, gather grapes and olives; (and also are employed clearing and ploughing, or cleaning ditches).'[24] Probably most Frenchmen worked on large farms in the Ebro valley south of the Pyrenees, and people from the Navarrese Pyrenees went to seek work there too. Some Frenchmen left the thickly settled Pyrenean valleys to stay permanently in Spain. But after the early nineteenth century the current reversed. Seasonal workers from the Spanish Pyrenees came to work as woodcutters, charcoal burners, shepherds and agricultural labourers in the French Pyrenees. Until about 1900 women from Baztán sought employment cultivating (weeding) grainfields across the boundary. They were called 'yorrariak' (Basque: weeders) and they spent all April weeding during the day and spinning flax or wool in the evening. In December men from Spain (the Aezcoans were famous for it) worked with *layas* (two-pronged digging forks) preparing new fields in the French Pyrenees before heavy ploughs were widespread. The sandal factories of Mauléon gave winter jobs to Spaniards, too.[25]

Permanent emigration also brought many persons from the Spanish to the French Pyrenees. French censuses obscure the real importance of this movement, but Georges Viers calculated that the Spanish Pyrenees had supplied almost a third of the population of the town of Mauléon, for example, in the 1950s. Most of the permanent immigration took place after about 1876, seasonal migration having predominated before then.[26] The cross-boundary migration, a sensitive indicator of the two sectors' varying fortunes, continues today. In the mountains one encounters Navarrese working for Frenchmen as shepherds or woodcutters. The resorts and hotels in the French Basque country employ Spanish women.[27]

Perhaps the most significant movement is that of Spanish Basque brides who leave their villages to marry and settle in France. Many French girls, aware of the harshness of life on mountain farms compared with working as a clerk or typist in Pau or Bayonne, will not stay in the borderland. Although young Frenchmen also leave, emigration affects the girls especially, who usually have stayed at school longer than boys. Their departure creates a real crisis of enforced bachelorhood amongst French farmers in the region. The shortage of women is especially high in the more remote villages, and celibacy amongst French Pyrenean farmers is much more widespread than normal.[28] Some French Basques have found wives in neighbouring villages across the boundary. For Spanish girls the move to a French farmhouse represents economic advancement. In the village of Baïgorry in 1968 more than two-thirds of the marriages united a Frenchman and a Spanish wife.

Apart from trans-montane migration and the movement from the villages to the cities which took place within each country, there was a strong current of transatlantic emigration from the Western Pyrenees. In fact America was the destination of most emigrants from the French sector until about the third decade of the twentieth century.[29] What contemporaries (and some modern authors) called the haemorrhage of the Basques and Béarnais has been much better studied in France than in Spain.[30] It began in France about 1825—perhaps 30 years before it began in Navarre. The first emigrants went to South America, especially to the Plate River area (Uruguay, Argentina). After the late 1840s a few began to go to North America. California was their most common destination until the 1880s. So common was it, in fact, that amongst some Basques the name 'California' still is applied to the whole United States. Many emigrants to South America were farmers or labourers who settled in agricultural colonies promoted by emigration agents in the Pyrenees, but substantial numbers of artisans, merchants, and professionals went as well.[31] Emigration to North America (which was less numerous) provided the western United States with the majority of its shepherds, San Francisco with its gardeners, and Los Angeles with its butchers.[32] The trans-oceanic migration diminished after the 1920s.

Spanish Basques also went to America. Their emigration began later than that from France, probably about the 1850s. It gained strength especially after the second Carlist War. The Bidasoa valley apparently was the most important source of emigrants to America. Relatively few left from the eastern Navarrese valleys of Salazar and Roncal. Recently, the Basque shepherds who come to work in the United States have been Spaniards.[33]

The tens of thousands of Basques and Béarnais left their homes for many reasons. The prospect of economic betterment was the cities' or America's main attraction. But Basque and Béarnais respect for primogeniture and the undivided farm meant also that emigration was virtually the only escape for younger sons (and, later, daughters) in a countryside already crowded with farms. Sometimes the heir would emigrate, planning to return from America with enough money to buy the family farm (if the family were tenants) or to pay off family debts.[34] Some Frenchmen left the country to escape military conscription during the nineteenth century. Whatever the causes of their flight, few *Amerikoak* ever returned, though their emotional ties with the Pyrenees endured.[35]

Emigration in the Basque and Béarnese contexts must have depended somewhat on the degree to which high population densities made it impossible to create new farms, or lowered standards of living. Other things being equal, one would expect emigration to affect the thickly settled villages first. In 1876 the mean density of the borderland was 24·14 persons per square kilometre. But the mean density in 1876 in the French Western Pyrenees was 29·87/km² whereas it was 19·32/km² in the Navarrese Pyrenees (1877). 79 per cent (56) of French communes exceeded the over-all mean density, while 59 per cent (35) of Spanish municipios had lower densities. This suggests that there may have been more compelling reasons for Frenchmen in the borderland to emigrate. With each succeeding census after 1876 the variance in densities decreased. Nevertheless, in 1954/1950 the main density of the borderland was 21·38 persons per square kilometre, 24·29 in the French part, and 18·93 in the Spanish part. 66 per cent (47) of French communes had more than the overall mean density while 56 per cent (33) of Spanish municipios had less. The distribution was almost identical in 1962/1960, although the mean density had dropped to 19·89 persons per square kilometre.

THE FORESTS

A declining population brought a less intensive use of the land. In both the Spanish and the French Western Pyrenees, meadow increased at the expense of arable, and pastures (mostly heaths and mountain grazings) increased slightly as forests diminished (see Fig. 18). This happened as farmers moved in the direction of commercial livestock production and away from unspecialized subsistence farming (although the transition is not yet complete). These changes were broadly similar in both parts of the borderland. The graphs, however, show a striking difference between the two countries' proportions of forest.

To the traditional Pyrenean husbandman, the forest was more an onus than an asset. It harboured danger: the Pyrenees are one of very few places in Europe where wolves and bears still live (though they are extremely rare). It was unimportant in the valleys' economies. In fact it was a hindrance in that the herder must struggle to preserve his grazings from the forest's

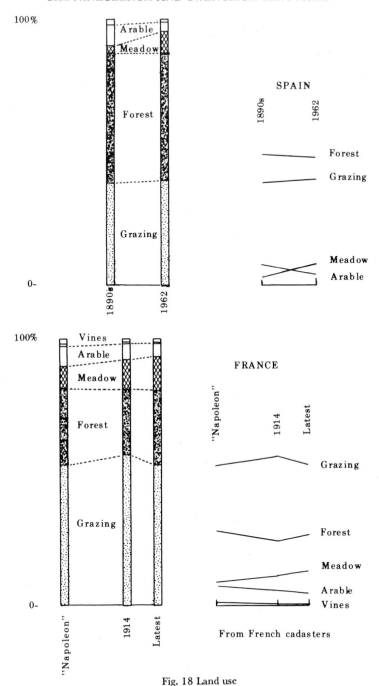

Fig. 18 Land use
Categories as percentages of total area
Sources: 1890s Navarrese cadaster and 1962 Spanish agricultural census (Spain); French cadasters
(France).

growth. *Brûlis*, the firing of the heaths in Spring, was one of his weapons, and of course the effects of grazing itself were another.[36]

Pyrenean forests were not widely exploited before the seventeenth century. The only uses they served before then were the customary rights of the inhabitants to use wood for building houses and making repairs, for utensils and tools, and for firewood, and to cut shoots and small saplings for livestock bedding. On occasion the forests provided game for the Pyrenean table. The forests also contained chestnut trees, walnuts, and oaks, which yielded nuts for human and animal consumption. The chestnuts, before blight killed them after 1860, were an important component of the peasants' diet, especially in winter.[37] These limited demands upon the forest probably had little effect upon the trees' growth. However, in summer, livestock (sheep and cattle as well as pigs) entered the forests to forage and so impeded their regeneration. In some places, to harvest both wood and pasture, the peasants lopped off the trees' branches every few years, producing a massive but thinly-branched trunk (a pollard) beneath which livestock could graze. Pollards yield a supply of branches, but the trunks are not considered good for lumber: they are too gnarled, or so aged that the heart-wood is punk. Much deforestation was thus pastoral: either from the browsing itself or from the pollarding or the annual burnings (against which beech are not very resistant).[38] Farmers no longer cut shoots, saplings, lumber, or even much firewood, but the right to pasturage on the forest still exists in many syndical forests of the French Western Pyrenees, although it is not generally permitted in Spain.[39] Even so, the changes wrought upon the forests in these ways were minimal compared to the modern exploitation. Most cutting took place near the villages. Vast areas of remote forests remained virtually intact, especially in the less populous and more mountainous eastern valleys.[40] And because population densities in the Spanish Pyrenees as a whole were less, Spanish forests probably fared better in these respects than the French.

The earliest commercial use of wood from the Western Pyrenees forests was to fuel iron foundries. These existed in both Spain and France. The area yielded ores of copper and iron even as early as Roman times. They were smelted and cast in numerous small forges in the mountains. In the 1500s, there were at least 70 in north-western Navarre alone.[41] Some were royal establishments, producing cannon, cannon-balls, and arms, such as the Eugui ironworks (established 1496) or those at Olaberri (established much later) and Orbaiceta.

Nearness to wood rather than to ore was the critical factor in a forge's operation, for metallurgy required vast quantities of fuel. The first factories burned wood. Later the 'Catalan forges' used charcoal which charcoal-makers prepared in the forests and then transported to the forges. Cutting fuel for the forges and charcoal kilns ravaged the forests of the mountains and it was exhaustion of the forest resources rather than the mines which extinguished most of the Pyrenean ironworks. At least this was the case in France. There is a fascinating report by an engineer and forge-master at Baïgorry named Muthuon, who inspected the forges of those parts of Navarre and Guipuzcoa occupied by French soldiers in 1793. He described in admiring detail the Spanish method of harvesting wood from large plantations of pollards, rather than logging forests, to supply their forges' charcoal kilns. In this way, he said, the Spanish forges were able to produce steadily while those in France failed when the woods around them were used up.[42] The method was not used for all of Navarre's forges. The requirements of the Olaberri ironworks and armoury, for example, were so great that in 1696 the king of Spain set aside the entire Legua Acotada forest to serve them.[43]

Forges prospered or failed according to the state of the nearby forests. In 1752, the Intendant d'Étigny described the devastated forests of the valley of Baïgorry and the débâcle of its forges: only one was then left.[44] Later the forests grew back and at least three forges resumed production in the valley. Dralet, writing in 1813, listed three active forges in Basses-Pyrénées, and seven which had ceased operations for lack of fuel.[45] In 1828 Dumège noted four Catalan forges in the same area, and one blast furnace.[46] In the valley of Baïgorry the copper smelter at La Fonderie (now the commune of Banca) cut wood in the Hayra forest. From 1823 to 1838, the Société des Forges de Banca made so much charcoal in Hayra (which at the time comprised over 2,000 hectares) that the woods were exhausted again in only fifteen years. The forges at Banca were abandoned in 1838 and never restarted.[47] The last forges in the French Western Pyrenees ceased work in the 1860s and 1870s.[48]

Not only were the woods exhausted during the nineteenth century, but the large mills in Vizcaya and north-eastern France produced iron and steel much more efficiently than the Pyrenean forge-masters could. Nevertheless the later development of communications in north-western Navarre kept forges working there longer than on the other side of the boundary. French troops destroyed the large Navarrese armouries in the early nineteenth century, and, except for the factory at Orbaiceta, they never revived, but Madoz listed fourteen ironworks in north-western Navarre as late as 1847.[49] Charcoal-making and ironworking continued in the Bidasoa valley throughout the nineteenth century.[50] And a few old forges still produced iron in Leiza as late as the 1920s.[51]

Charcoal-making in North-western Navarre lasted much longer than in France.[52] Despite the arduous and lonely conditions of their work, it provided an income to substantial numbers of Navarrese in the mountains south of the Bidasoa river. For lack of English coal during World War I charcoal-making even expanded to meet the demand for an alternative fuel. The two narrow-gauge railways in the area used charcoal for fuel even after the war, and large quantities of charcoal were exported to France.[53]

Charcoal-makers continued to work in the Spanish woods until the 1940s.

The navies of France and Spain also extracted Pyrenean timber for masting ships during the seventeenth and eighteenth centuries. Fir trees were especially valued for masts and spars, and by then tall, straight trees grew only where their remoteness had protected them. The Pyrenean forests held firs which could be fashioned into masts 100 feet tall and 6 feet in circumference at the base: dimensions necessary to fit out the large warships of the time, but which were difficult to obtain elsewhere in France or Spain. In France the forests' strategic value was one reason for the promulgation of France's first *Ordonnance des Eaux et Forêts* in 1669. The law became the basis for a French forestry service, although not until the nineteenth century did government foresters exercise effective jurisdiction in the Pyrenees.[54] But naval engineers prevailed where foresters did not. The French Pyrenean forests of the Aspe valley and the Irati forest (Soule and Cize) provided masts for the naval shipyards of Bayonne in the late seventeenth century.[55]

The masting operations in France were conducted on a vast scale despite great difficulties of transport. In the last half of the eighteenth century, when the French navy's logging was most extensive, naval engineers built roads, cables, slipways, and sluices, often over difficult terrain. An extensive network of roads served the Issaux forest in Aspe, for example. Above Etsaut, a logging road was chiselled along the face of a sheer rock wall for 1,000 metres. The massive trunks could be taken down to Athas, whence they were floated to Bayonne in groups of three. Around 1770 the Navy launched about 900 masts a year at Athas. Ten years later most of the tall firs in the Aspe valley had been cut.[56] By 1800 the search for masts had nearly ended in the French Western Pyrenees.[57] Except for a few remote stands, the great trees were gone.

Almost nothing has been written about the exploitation of Spanish Pyrenean forests for masts. The economist D. Gerónimo de Uztáriz included an account of logging masts in the Roncal valley in an obscure treatise published in 1742. The logs were made into rafts at Isaba, where they were launched to float down the Esca and the Aragon rivers to the Ebro, which carried them to the Mediterranean.[58] Logging for masts continued longer in the Navarrese Pyrenees than in the French Western Pyrenees. The 1802 *Diccionario* tells that masts were cut in Aezcoa (in the Irati forest) as well as in the valley of Roncal. The pine forests of Salazar yielded turpentine, but apparently no masts.[59] In 1849 Madoz briefly mentioned naval logging operations, but gave few details.[60]

We cannot be sure whether mast-cutting in the Navarrese Pyrenees equalled the French navy's efforts, but the Navarrese forests do not show the effects of such intensive exploitation. More relics left by the logging operations themselves (roads, especially) can be found in French forests than Navarrese.

Commercial lumbering by the municipios themselves (not necessarily for masts), however, was a mainstay of the economy of the three easternmost Navarrese valleys (Aezcoa, Salazar, and Roncal) during the nineteenth and twentieth centuries. The great rafts of logs (almadías) floating downriver, piloted by four men using long sweeps, became the picturesque hallmark of these operations.[61]

After the mid-nineteenth century, most Pyrenean forests benefited from the decreasing demand for fuel and masts. At the same time they suffered from the extension of grazing activities in some areas. On the French side deforestation for charcoal diminished during the nineteenth century. Logging for masts had ceased by around 1800. After about 1850 little cutting was done in the region's forests. By 1902, after having been cut to exhaustion 64 years before, the Hayra forest had grown up again.[62] The Irati forest was cut very little between 1870 and 1927.[63] The forests of the Aspe valley also rested.[64] In a modern context these forests were difficult of access and expensive to log for commercial purposes. But they also benefited from official protection. Based on the law of 1827, the French forestry service acquired supervisory powers over large forests in the area after the 1830s, even though the valley syndicates retained title to the forests.

However, the forest service's influence was limited by the French syndicates' traditional preoccupation with livestock. Pasture was esteemed more highly than woods. For example, reafforestation in the syndical forests of the French Western Pyrenees was almost non-existent. Between 1949 and 1964 only 7,650 hectares were reafforested in the entire department of Basses-Pyrénées.[65] These were mostly in the lowlands. The forests increased mainly by natural regeneration and growth, wherever they were not grazed. The syndicates have logged them since after World War I, according to plans designed to give constant yields over the years, but compared with the Navarrese valleys (which have a longer history of commercial logging and forest conservation) the French syndicates seem to have been indifferent to the value of their forests' resources until recently.[66]

The growth of livestock husbandry kept the French forests from recovering more completely after the nineteenth century. The *Direction des eaux et forêts* could not prevent the syndicates from allowing grazing in and around their forests, nor could it control the firing of the heaths every Spring. In fact the forests which recovered best during the twentieth century were those in the east, where grazing grew least, or even declined (compare Figures 19 and 20). The relative importance of pasture also accounts for much of the cross-boundary contrasts these maps show. During the nineteenth century livestock densities grew more on the French side than the Spanish.

The state-owned forests of Navarre also were not cut during the nineteenth century. Surveys made in 1903 and 1904 showed that nearly all the trees in them were between 90 and 115 years old.[67] How they were protected is unclear, since documents in the archives of the *Patrimonio*

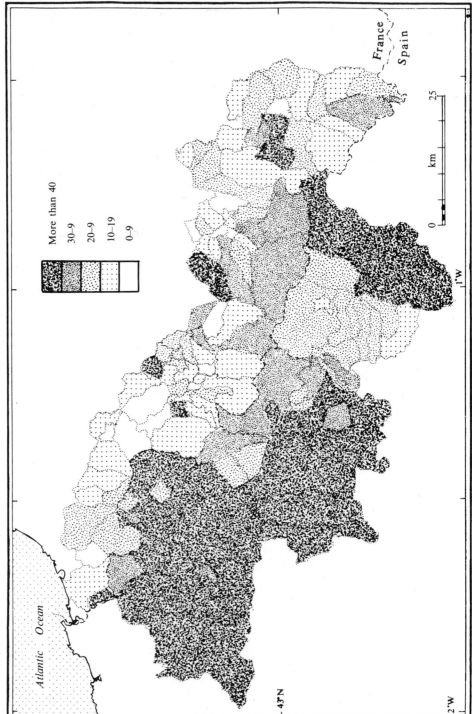

Fig. 19 Percentage of land in forest (1890s, 1914)

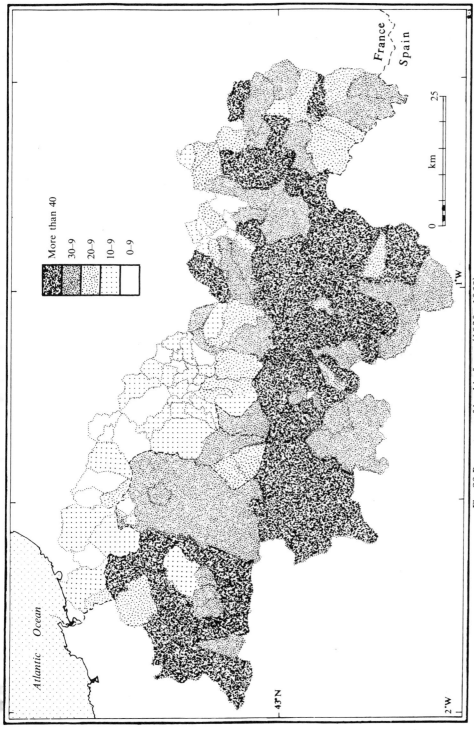

Fig. 20 Percentage of land in forest (1930s, 1962)
Source: 1962 Spanish agriculture census; latest French cadasters.

forestal del estado at Pamplona indicate that the foresters' effective control of these reserves dates from about 1870, but evidently there was little need to use them either for timber or pasture. Since about 1920 these forests have been logged according to plans designed to ensure a sustained yield of wood. The state has built service roads in most of them. But these national forests, located near the boundary in the central part of the study area, occupy relatively little land.

Elsewhere, in the eastern valleys, the importance of commercial lumbering to the local economy kept the forests in better condition and they occupied relatively more land (compared to pasture) than they did on the other side of the boundary.[68] This is not surprising when viewed in the context of Spain's forest resources as a whole. They are much less abundant than those of France. The Spanish Pyrenean forests are relatively more important to Spain than the French Pyrenean forests are to France. Indeed many of the cuts authorized in the French Pyrenean forests are sold to Spanish firms.

In north-western Navarre the large proportion of forested land in the 1890s does not appear to agree with the persistence of forges there. The problem may arise from the difficulty of knowing what the cadaster's surveyors meant by 'forest'. Pasture under sparse plantations of pollards may well have counted as forested land. On the other hand, reafforestation after the 1860s may have replaced some woods; a document from Echalar (dated 1861) indicates that the village had a nursery and that its inhabitants were required to work two days each year reforesting.[69] Certainly the Bidasoa valley has been the object of several reafforestation programmes. In a recent campaign, 7,280 hectares of trees were planted there between 1955 and 1961. Indeed, farmers in north-western Navarre no longer dislike trees. By the 1960s the visible growth of the earlier plantations encouraged many private owners to convert heath to woods, even at their own expense.[70]

Despite all the reafforestation in the Bidasoa valley, however, there was a net decrease in forested land (and an increase in pasture) between the 1890s and 1962. This reflects both the charcoal burning of the early twentieth century as well as the increasing importance of livestock husbandry since then. Field observations also suggest there was an increase in the quality and density of the stands while their area decreased. Thus plantations of conifers replaced the aged trees and pollards, and the formerly blurred distinction between grazing land and forest became much sharper.

RURAL ECONOMY

The major change in agricultural economy of the Western Pyrenees during the last century was the gradual replacement of subsistence polyculture with commercialized livestock husbandry. This happened earlier in the French than in the Spanish borderland. In the traditional system, although livestock were the hallmark of the valleys' economy, they were by no means the population's only sustenance. Foodstuffs grown in gardens and fields, barnyard chickens, ducks, and rabbits, a few forage crops, the forest and pasture, were the components of subsistence. Few families owned more than 20 to 40 sheep, a pair of cows, perhaps a mule, ass, or horse, and one or two pigs. The cattle gave milk and meat, but were especially useful as draft animals.[71] Sheep yielded meat, milk, and wool for the family. Relatively few of these livestock products entered commerce. Most were consumed locally. Occasionally the surplus of the least perishable might be sold away from the farm: cheese, wool, and hides.

Although the definitive shift to commercial livestock production took place during the twentieth century, it began in the nineteenth. In both parts of the borderland the numbers of sheep and cattle grew during the 1800s.[72] This is noteworthy, because at the same time the numbers of people living in the region decreased. Not only did people emigrate, but a few left farming for other occupations. As the number of farms and farmers declined, farm sizes grew. Abandoned arable became meadow or pasture. The average size of farmers' flocks and herds also increased.

The data are incomplete, but it is fairly clear that the numbers of cattle and sheep increased much more on the French side of the border than in Navarre.[73] Since both the population decline and the livestock increase were greater in the French Western Pyrenees than on the other side of the boundary, it follows that the average size of farmers' flocks and herds grew much faster there too. Larger holdings of sheep and cattle in the French Western Pyrenees around the end of the nineteenth century suggest an earlier specialization or a greater degree of commercialization there than in the Navarrese Pyrenees, or at least greater prosperity.[74] The contrast persisted. In 1956/1962 the numbers of cattle per farm were greater in the French communes than in the Spanish municipios (see Table 2 and Figure 21).[75]

Table 2

	Total farms	Total sheep	Sheep per farm	Total cattle	Cattle per farm
France 1956	5,386	150,610	27·96	34,005	6·31
Spain 1962	7,724	219,965	28·44	24,669	3·19
Total	13,110	370,575	28·27	68,674	4·48

The mean number of sheep per farm is similar in the two countries. But this is misleading because it reflects the predominance of large bands of sheep in the economy of the Roncal valley. The Roncalese own not only the vast upland summer pastures on their own territory but also large portions of the Bardenas Reales—the winter grazings south of the Pyrenees.[76] Thus

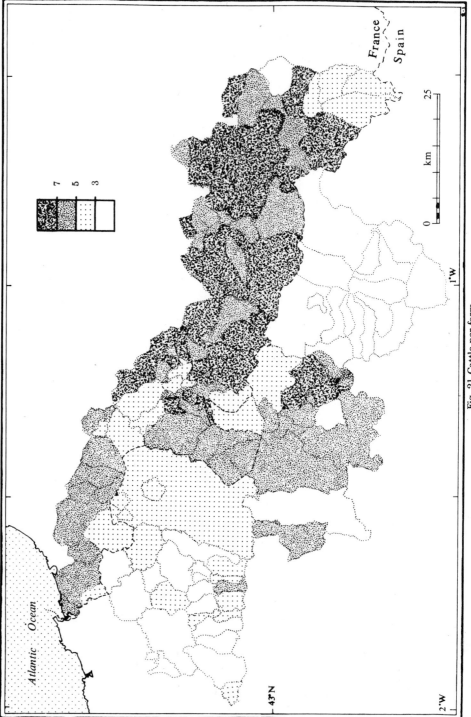

Fig. 21 Cattle per farm

Source: 1956 French agriculture survey 1958 Spanish agriculture survey

Roncal is one of the few Pyrenean valleys where long-distance winter transhumance continues to be feasible. Roncal's sheep raise the Spanish mean considerably. The distribution of municipal means about the grand mean, however, shows that most of the Navarrese farm flocks are smaller. In France 37 communes average more than 28 sheep per farm and 44 communes have smaller averages, whereas only 18 Spanish municipios have averages larger than 28 but 41 have smaller averages.[77]

Changes in land use and in agricultural practices accompanied the growing emphasis on livestock husbandry. Pyrenean farmers extended their meadows during the nineteenth and twentieth centuries.[78] In the 1830s, meadows accounted for 8·6 per cent and arable for 7·4 per cent of the French communes' area. The arable/meadow ratio was 0·87. By 1914 meadow had grown to 11 per cent and arable had decreased to 5·8 per cent; the same ratio was 0·53. In the latest French cadasters (1930s–1960s) meadow occupied 12·7 per cent of the land, and arable but 4·5 per cent, and the arable/meadow ratio was 0·36. Unfortunately we cannot compare the nineteenth-century evolution in France with that of the Navarrese Pyrenees, for lack of early statistics. In the cadasters of the 1890s in Navarre, however, arable (7·7 per cent) still exceeded meadow (2·6 per cent) in importance. The arable/meadow ratio was 3·03. By 1962 Navarre resembled France (1914–30) with an arable/meadow ratio of 0·47. An almost total absence of meadows in Roncal and Salazar exaggerates the disparity, but Figure 22 shows that in general the predominance of meadow came much earlier in France.

Besides converting the arable to meadow and pasture, farmers planted fewer foodstuffs and more forage crops on the arable that was left. In the rotation which had become common as maize spread during the seventeenth and eighteenth centuries, wheat and maize alternated with one another, and sometimes with a third year of fallow. Beans, sown between the rows of maize as a catch crop, and (where farmers were more progressive) turnips sown in autumn and pulled in spring, were early additions to the traditional rotation in both France and Spain. During the nineteenth and twentieth centuries farmers began intercalating other plants, especially mangels and clover, and sometimes vetch, fenugreek, or rye, and making meadows of sown clover and alfalfa. The innovations seem to have begun in the French part of the borderland, though rigorous proof of this is lacking.[79] Indeed, innovation may have been more difficult in the Navarrese Pyrenees. Rights of common such as common of pasture and the right to assart persisted there long after they had disappeared from the French valleys.

Later, wheat itself slowly gave ground to continuous crops of maize with roots and legumes. Wheat yielded less reliably than maize, but it could not be abandoned completely until it was regularly supplied from outside, for every village needed at least some wheat to make bread. It would be interesting to know more about the chronology and distribution of wheat's

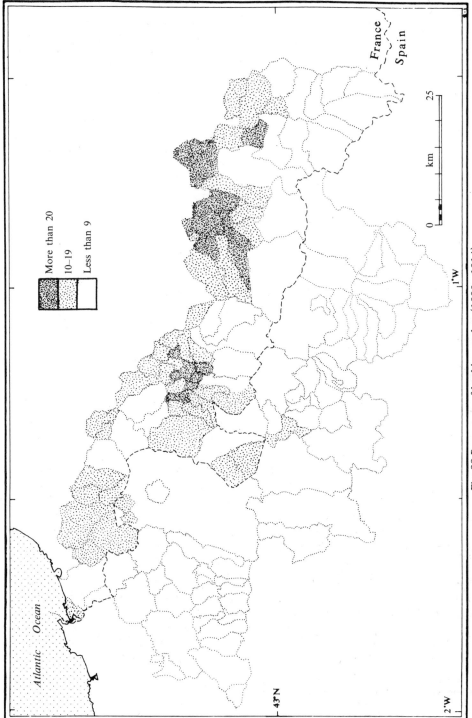

Fig. 22 Percentage of land in meadow (1890s, 1914)

demise, but the data are lacking. Today a little wheat is still found in most villages, but it is common only in the eastern Navarrese valleys, where greater aridity favours it.

Commercial dairying and cheese manufacture became the major outlets for the new husbandmen of the Western Pyrenees. Again the French sector showed an earlier dependence on such markets. It is true that in the late nineteenth century in the Navarrese Pyrenees a gradual increase in fodder crops and stabling allowed farmers to keep more cattle than they had been able to do with pasture alone, but most of these cattle still served the traditional needs for draft animals and beef for local consumption. In autumn Navarrese farmers sold whatever cattle they could not feed through the winter to drovers from city markets to the south (or smuggled them to French markets), but there was little specialized production of beef for sale. Only in the westernmost municipios was there some dairying and beef production for Guipuzcoan towns.

The widespread commercialization of cattle husbandry in the Navarrese Pyrenees only began after World War II with the production of meat and especially milk for Pamplona and San Sebastian. Until the 1960s, however, the farmer himself had to arrange to send these products to market. In 1958 and 1967 two large dairies in Pamplona began buying Pyrenean milk and their daily collections by trucks passing through each village made milk production more remunerative in north-western Navarre. During the last ten years the more prosperous dairy farmers there have been replacing the traditional Pyrenean Blond cows with milch breeds such as Brown Swiss.

Sheep are kept in every village in the Navarrese Pyrenees but they have not been the object of intensive commercial development. Most farmers manage their flocks in the traditional ways. In the west, the ewe's milk is made into cheese at the farm or in the summer *bordas*, and the wheels (weighing two or three kilogrammes) are either kept for family use or sold in local markets. Similarly the wool and meat are both used at home and sold locally. No modern marketing facilities or uniform standards of quality exist for these products; sales of cheese at least are generally casual or sporadic.[80] In Roncal, in the east, most of the sheep are managed differently, though still in traditional ways. Rather than small farm flocks, large transhumant bands of sheep predominate. They are kept primarily for mutton and wool.

In Basses-Pyrénées, on the other hand, raising calves or feeding beef cattle for urban markets became common in some districts even in the first decades of the twentieth century. Rising standards of living enlarged the demand for meat, and this happened earlier in France than in Spain. Although milking breeds were still rare (the Pyrenean Blond predominated), farmers on the northern fringes of the study area also produced milk for towns such as Bayonne and Pau even in the last decades of the nineteenth century. The eastern French valleys sold a cheese made from a mixture of sheep's and cows' milk. Because of the importance of sheep husbandry, cattle are relatively less important in the agricultural economy of the French Western Pyrenees, but French farmers produced for urban dairies earlier than did their Navarrese neighbours. By 1952 trucks collected milk in most communes.[81] French farmers began to replace their Pyrenean Blond cattle with dairy types, and by 1962 very few Pyrenean Blond cattle remained in the dairying districts. Today cows' milk production is most important in the eastern valleys, where sheep husbandry declined along with the loss of lowland winter pastures, and in communes close to urban centres (on the northern edge of the area and near the Atlantic coast).

Even though over-all sheep densities are similar on both sides of the boundary, sheep husbandry provides the greatest contrast between the two sectors' agricultural economy. In Baïgorry, Cize, and Soule, keeping sheep became the most remunerative agricultural activity after 1910, because the ewes' milk could be sold to make Roquefort cheese. Around the turn of the century the rising demand for the famous cheese began to exceed the capabilities of the flocks in the Causses, the district surrounding the village of Roquefort-sur-Soulzon (in the department of Aveyron, in the southern Massif Central).[82] In the 1890s Corsican milk was first used for Roquefort. Soon after, Roquefort cheese factories were built in the French Western Pyrenees. Milk for Roquefort brought very high prices, and suddenly sheep raising became quite profitable in the region. In fact sales to Roquefort are the largest source of income for many French Basque and Béarnais farmers. Producing milk for Roquefort has also altered the traditional patterns of flock management, for instance by encouraging the very early sale of milk lambs (at around three weeks) and by postponing the dates of spring transhumance to keep the ewes close to the factories for longer periods. Trucks collect the milk at each farm. Before the 1940s shepherds could not sell the milk produced by ewes on summer pastures because the cheese factories were too far away, so they continued to make the traditional cheeses in the *bordas*. But after 1946 jeeps began collecting milk for Roquefort even in the mountains. The milk that ewes give while grazing alpine pastures is richer in fat and makes more cheese.

Sheep farmers in Navarre have no such commercial outlet. They raise sheep as much for lamb, mutton, and wool, as for milk, and their income from sheep is less. In 1968, for example, a farmer in Baztán with 120 sheep could make about 250 pesetas ($3·57) per sheep per year by selling about 150 of his home-made cheeses in the Elizondo market. His counterpart in Baïgorry might own 220 sheep, selling an average of 7,000 litres of milk per year to Roquefort (at 1·30 f. per litre) for an annual income per sheep of 41·36,f. ($8·27).[83] Such differences in prosperity are characteristic. Farmers on the French side of the boundary have larger flocks and herds, and sell more of their production.

It is not only livestock husbandry, but the entire range of agricultural activity which has been touched by the increasing dependence upon markets.

This is especially visible on the French side of the boundary. Since World War II French farmers have simply found themselves handling more money. They sell more in markets than they did before and they depend more on purchased seeds, feed, fertilizers, pesticides, tools, and services.

Up to 1949, for example, the varieties of maize grown throughout the borderland were of the free-pollination type. Carefully selected in field and barn by the farmers themselves over the last three centuries, these local strains were well adapted to the local climates, and resistant to local diseases. In 1949, much higher-yielding American hybrid varieties of maize were introduced in Basses-Pyrénées. Farmers adopted them rapidly, and by 1964 only a few farmers in the French part of the borderland still grew the old types.[84] Yet the new seed had to be purchased each year, and it entailed chemical disinfection of the soil and chemical weed-suppression instead of cultivation by hand. At the same time growing maize for sale rather than for consumption on the farm gained ground in the French part of the borderland. Both hybrids and commercial crops are much rarer amongst Navarrese farmers.[85]

Not all the money entering the rural economy came from farming. On both sides of the boundary smuggling provided substantial cash incomes to many families until the early 1960s, when diminishing price differences decreased its appeal. Remittances from relatives abroad also injected cash into the Basque economy. It is unfortunately not possible to ascertain the exact importance of these two sources of income, but farmers cite them often enough to make it obvious they were substantial. Additionally, French families benefit (much more than Spanish families) from the country's programme of social welfare. Many French farm families frankly admit that they would be hard pressed to make ends meet without such transfer payments as social security pensions and family allowances for children.

Most French farmers in the borderland trace the tangible beginnings of their growing prosperity to the years just after World War II. The examples they cite generally represent investments in equipment which the increased 'cash flow' of their operations allowed them to make. For many of them the great change was the mechanization of their operations which came after 1946 with the purchase of a used U.S. Army jeep from the French government. The surplus jeeps were not very expensive and apparently many farmers had been able to save some of the money they earned—by smuggling in many instances—during the years of German occupation. The jeeps took produce to market and helped to accelerate the transition to commercialized agriculture in a region where most farms were dispersed.[86]

The next machine most farmers purchased was a motor scythe or a motor tiller (usually the former). By 1969 68 per cent of the farms in the French part of the borderland owned one. The 1966 agricultural questionnaire listed only 31 such machines in the Navarrese Pyrenees—clearly an understatement—but nevertheless in 1968 it was about as rare to see a farmer mowing with a motor scythe in Navarre as it was to see a French farmer scything his meadow by hand.[87]

Tractors are much less conspicuous, but this is because steep slopes and small plots are unsuited to them. However, the data on tractors' diffusion exemplifies the lag of the Spanish borderland behind the French. In 1946 there was only one tractor in the French part of the borderland. The number grew to 159 tractors in 1956 and 631 in 1968. In 1966 there were 158 tractors in the Navarrese Pyrenees.[88] Similarly, cars are much more common on the French side of the boundary than in the Navarrese Pyrenees. In 1968 most French farmers in the area owned a car, whereas one might say the same for motor cycles on the Spanish side of the bouundary. Other forms of mechanization such as milking machines (for cows), four-wheel-drive trucks, electric fences, motor rakes, hay-balers, and manure pumps and spreaders, are much more common in France than Spain. Farm families on the French side enjoy more domestic appliances also.

Although the majority of families in the borderland are farm families, there are fewer persons engaged in agriculture in the French Western Pyrenees than in the Navarrese Pyrenees. Since municipal statistics on occupation are published only in France, it is not possible to make direct comparison, but an indirect measure of the same tendency is the mean number of persons per farm. The number of persons per farm in the Spanish sector in 1960/1962 was 5·57. In France in 1954/1956 it was 9·73. This does not mean that French families are larger—quite the contrary—it means that there are more non-farming families (i.e. fewer farms) in France than in Spain. The borderland's over-all average was 7·28 persons per farm. Only two Spanish municipios exceeded this figure, but 43 municipios (73 per cent)—and only 12 communes (15 per cent)—had fewer than six persons per farm.

Employment in industry, commerce, and services supports a larger percentage of the population in the French part of the borderland. But if Hendaye (France) is excepted, about the same number of persons are wage-earners in industry in the Navarrese Pyrenees as in the French Western Pyrenees. However, the number of industrial workers employed in the French Western Pyrenees is not the same as the number of industrial workers living in the borderland. In fact it is about half; that is, about as many workers as are employed in the area commute to industrial jobs outside the area.[89] There is much less commuting to work in the Navarrese Pyrenees. Rural industry in Navarre is encouraged by the *Diputación foral*, which has subsidized industrial parks in rural locations. Thus two *poligonos industriales* have been established in the study area: in Vera de Bidasoa and in Santesteban.[90] Vera de Bidasoa has a distillery and several metal fabricating plants employing a total of about 250 workers. An abrasives plant and a garment manufacturer employ about the same number in Santesteban. Three other establishments in the Navarrese Pyrenees are quite large: two paper mills in Leiza employ 600 persons, and Magnesitas de Navarra, S.A. (quarrying) employs a like number in Eugui and Zubiri. The factories in Eugui, Zubiri, Leiza, Santesteban, and Vera de Bidasoa thus employ two-thirds of the industrial workers of the Navarrese Pyrenees. No parallels to these large industrial plants exist in the French part of the borderland.[91] Most other industries—on both sides of the boundary—employ smaller numbers of workers in quarrying, food processing, electricity generating, and wood processing.

More people are employed in commerce and services in the French villages than in the Navarrese Pyrenees. The biggest difference is the far greater importance of tourism in France, which has its origins in the spas of the seventeenth and eighteenth centruies. Not only are Frenchmen better able to afford summer vacations, but the French Pyrenean borderland has become an extension of the internationally-popular *Côte basque* of Biarritz and St. Jean de Luz.

The Navarrese Pyrenees are much less frequented by tourists. In 1967 there were as many hotels in St. Jean Pied-de-Port, or in the valley of Baïgorry, as there were in the entire Navarrese Pyrenees.[92]

The population of the French villages swells in summer as thousands of urban French families come on vacation, perhaps to rent a farmhouse for their month of *congés payés*. In the Aspe valley (France), where the proportion is highest, one-quarter of the houses were owned by outsiders as vacation homes in 1964. Ten per cent of the valley of Cize's houses were summer houses.[93] These proportions have increased in the last decade, as affluent, urban-dwelling Frenchmen have purchased and renovated the farmhouses left vacant by a century of emigration. French farmers also augment their income by renting rooms or spare houses to summer visitors. The practice is becoming increasingly common and the local *Syndicats d'Initiatives* (chambers of commerce) keep lists of rooms available to tourists. In the Irati forest, the pastoral syndicates of Soule and Cize have allowed the construction of chalets for summer visitors, and the rentals are becoming important components of the syndicates' revenues. The French Western Pyrenees also have a winter sports resort above Arette on the road to the Col de la Pierre St. Martin.[94]

There is another economic activity of considerable importance on both sides of the boundary which illustrates the borderland's responsiveness to changing national circumstances. It is the movement of contraband.

Contraband in the Western Pyrenees is a well-organized business, backed by a few wealthy men who never touch the merchandise, and carried by numerous paid runners who never meet the wealthy men. Contraband is very sensitive to cross-boundary differences. For example, during World War II, while France was occupied by German troops and many necessities and most luxuries were in short supply, smuggling fuelled the French black market. From Spain the Basques smuggled medicines (especially penicillin), alcohol, buttons, lace, thread, sugar, coffee, olive oil, lemons, oranges, and even tomatoes. But their knapsacks returning to Spain contained mostly money: specie, jewels, and gold. After the war the contraband quickly reverted to pre-war patterns, despite the fact that the boundary remained officially closed (it was closed from 1936 to 1948). From France to Spain went spare parts for cars and other machinery, ball bearings, copper, precision instruments, and small manufactured articles such as needles and buttons. From Spain to France the smugglers took alcohol, sheep, mules, cattle and horses.

There was a decline in smuggling during the 1960s. Price differences decreased and the value of labour on both sides increased, so that the profits smugglers might make began to pale in comparison with the risks they ran. The farmhouses on small holdings nestled against the boundary line were abandoned; their income from farming never had been their *raison d'être*. Today a few sheep, and pure alcohol (taxed in France but not in Spain) are the only items still smuggled into France, while gold (not freely available in Spain) moves in the other direction.[95]

Besides transporting merchandise, Basques can also arrange to take people across the boundary: in World War II some members of the French Resistance fled from the Gestapo by this route;[96] and in the 1960s Portuguese workers entered France clandestinely.

Finally there is household smuggling, or *pacotille*: the weekly bag of groceries carried from a Spanish store (there is almost no movement in the other direction). This is very common, and French customs men are fairly tolerant towards it. To serve their French clientele, Spaniards have built many stores (called *ventas*) right beside the boundary. Often the *ventas* are far from any settlement, but served at the back by a dirt track from the nearest Spanish village and at the front by a paved road built by the nearest French commune. The paved road ends in a small parking area exactly at the boundary, a few metres from the Spanish store's entrance. Since it is not officially a vehicular crossing-point, there is no French customs control. The *ventas* sell meat (especially sausages and hams), fresh vegetables and fruits, wines and spirits, cigarettes, and canned fruit to French housewives. They also serve as *entrepôts* for huge consignments of pure alcohol from Spanish distilleries, but the alcohol moves only at night.

Most of the cross-boundary contrasts described in this study have related in some way to differences in the standard of living. Yet an important cultural contrast has also developed.

It is true that the borderland appears to be culturally homogeneous, at least in the west, because Basques live on both sides. There are, of course, numerous cultural and linguistic subdivisions in the Basque country. Some straddle the political boundary, such as the affinity between the dialects of Baïgorry and Baztán. But the Basques' 'culture' today depends almost entirely upon their linguistic identity.

In fact most Basques in the borderland, like their neighbours the Béarnese and the inhabitants of the valleys of Roncal, Salazar, and Aézcoa, are quite conscious of their 'French-ness' or 'Spanish-ness'.[97] They learn to speak French or Spanish in school, and they trade primarily with their fellow countrymen, and in the national language. The French participate in their country's political affairs. Like the Spaniards, they are governed by their country's laws. They pay its taxes and depend upon its civil servants and its public services. On either side people tend to buy their own country's newspapers and magazines and listen to its radio and televison stations. It is more expensive to telephone or send a letter a short distance across the boundary than within one's own country. The boundary hinders travel. The French village of Banca, for example, is equally distant from Pamplona and Bayonne, but it is much easier to travel thence to Bayonne. Not only customs formalities but discontinuities in public transportation services make the trip to Pamplona much more complex. Besides, the people of Banca have more business in Bayonne. Many inhabitants of the borderland have never crossed the international boundary. Thus as the landscape of the borderland has come to reflect its administrative division, so has the inhabitants' sense of national identity.

---

[1] Elisée Reclus similarly perceived the forces of 'modernization' at work in the region. He saw roads, railways, and schools (and emigration) eroding Basque culture even in the 1860s. 'Les Basques: un peuple qui s'en va', *Revue des Deux-Mondes*, 15 mars 1867. One might also relate these developments to Von Thünen's ideas about the location of economic activity. The local markets represented by the valleys (in which there is a declining intensity of land use with increasing distance from the villages) give way to the metropolitan markets (in which the intensity of land use—on a much larger scale—declines with distance from the large cities of France and Spain, or even Europe). This has been done for Europe as a whole by several authors. See: Michael Chisholm, *Rural settlement and land use* (London: Hutchinson, 1962), pp. 106–9; Olof Jonasson, 'The agricultural regions of Europe', *Economic Geography*, I (1925), 277–314; and the maps on pp. 7, 21, 22 of Samuel Van Valkenburg and Ellsworth Huntingdon, *Europe* (New York: Wiley, 1935).

[2] In part this may be because the very data which make it possible to measure some differences first become available during the nineteenth century. Archival work which threw more light on regional peculiarities before the nineteenth century, would doubtless prove that the map of traditional life or economy in the Western Pyrenees was far more variegated than has been shown here. But the roots of the economic disparity which today marks the borderland lie largely in the last two hundred years.

[3] Chevalier, *Les Pyrénées ariégeoises*, pp. 664–8. The potato appears in the Navarrese Pyrenees around 1800; Floristán Samanes & Torres Luna, *Pirineos*, vol. XXVI, no. 95, p. 20.

[4] Dralet, *Description des Pyrénées*, I. 206–9.

[5] Michel Chevalier, 'Note sur les usurpations de terre en Couserans au milieu du XIXe siècle', *Annales du Midi*, LXI (1949), 325–9.

[6] The figures for 1802 come from the *Diccionario* of the Real Academia; those for 1857 come from the census.

[7] The data are from the 'Napoleonic' cadasters of the 1830s. See the appendix for a discussion of the sources. No comparable source exists in Navarre before the 1890s.

[8] From contemporary writers, such as the Real Academia or Madoz for Navarre, and for Basses-Pyrénées Dralet, and Alexandre Dumège, *Statistique géénérale des départements pyrénées* ... (2 vols.; Paris: Treuttel et Wurtz, 1828–9), *passim*.

[9] Viers, *Les Pyrénées*, pp. 78–84. Michel Chevalier's chapter on depopulation gives an excellent description of the situation in Ariège: *Les Pyrénées ariégeoises*, pp. 663–753. See also: David

Lowenthal and Lambros Comitas, 'Emigration and depopulation: some neglected aspects of population and geography', *Geographical Review*, LII (1962), 195–210; and Pierre George, 'Structure agraire et problèmes démographiques dans la vallée d'Aspe (Basses-Pyrénées)', *Travaux et documents de l'Institut national d'etudes démographiques: cahier no. 8: 'Dépeuplement rural et peuplement rationnel'* (Paris: 1949), pp. 91–100.

[10] An interesting analysis of Roncal's adjustment to the new conditions in terms of energy input and output is presented in J. E. Puigdefábregas and E. Balcells R., 'Relaciones entre la organización social y la explotación del territorio en el Valle de Roncal (Navarra oriental)', *Pirineos*, vol. XXVI, no. 98 (1970), pp. 53–89.

[11] Of course the decline, which outsiders might view as salutory, is painful to the inhabitants themselves. They ask, why should decline be so pervasive in the mountains when everywhere else knows growth? They despair over what seems most visible: the loss of people. They see villages withering, aged farmers without heirs, and fields reverting to pasture.

[12] See *Enqête montagne*, I. 40, 41. Viers summarizes Pyrenean depopulation in *Les Pyrénées*, pp. 77–84.

[13] I lack data on some communes for some of the censuses before 1876. Of those communes for which I do have figures, 10 attained population maxima in 1831, 10 in 1836, 12 in 1841, 13 in 1846, 17 in 1851, 8 in 1856, and 1 in 1861. M. Gilbert Dalla-Rossa of Pau kindly lent me this pre-1876 census material. He obtained it from M. Serge Lerat.

[14] The rise in 1911 is due to the presence of workers building the railway in the Aspe valley.

[15] But the carnage of two world wars, especially the first, postponed significant gains in the department until the late 1940s.

[16] Centre d'Expansion Bordeaux–Sud-Ouest, 'Inventaire démographique du Sud-Ouest', *Revue juridique et économique du Sud-Ouest*. Série économique, V (1956), 213–68; France, Institut national de la statistique et des études économiques, Direction régionale de Bordeaux, *Population par commune de 1876 à 1954; Département des Basses-Pyrénées* (Mimeographed; Bordeaux: I.N.S.E.E., n.d.), pp. 6–8; Arsène Dumont, 'Natalité des Basques de Baïgorry', *21e session de l'Association française pour l'avancement des sciences*, Pau, 1892, II. 597–612.

[17] Several peculiarities of this graph need explanation. The broken line for the French Western Pyrenees before 1876 indicates extrapolation from incomplete data. The hump in 1911 was due to the presence of construction workers building the railway under the Somport pass in the Aspe valley. Similarly the slight hump in the line for the Spanish Western Pyrenees in 1940 reflects wartime garrisons near the boundary. The discontinuities in the French curve show France without Nice and Savoie before 1861, and without Alsace and Lorraine in 1872–96. The French line is discontinuous after 1962 because the definition of what constituted an 'inhabitant' was changed. After 1900 the Spanish population includes the Balearic Islands and the Canary Islands.

[18] This reflects national trends. In the same period the population of Spain doubled, but that of France increased by only 14 per cent.

[19] Evidence and some support for this interpretation may be found in the censuses, and in: Spain, Instituto nacional de estadística, *Reseña estadística de la Provincia de Navarra* (Madrid: I.N.E., 1950), p. 165; Viers, *Les Pyrénées*, p. 82; Carr, *Spain*, pp. 413–14; Lefebvre, *Les Pyrénées atlantiques*, p. 696; Jaime Vicens Vives, *An economic history of Spain* (Princeton, New Jersey: Princeton University Press, 1969), pp. 617–23; José Ros Jimeno, 'El decrecimiento de la natalidad y sus causas', *Revista Internacional de Sociología*, VI (1944), 79–123; Angel Abascal Garayoa, 'Los origenes de la población actual de Pamplona', *Revista Geográfica*, II (1955), 117–18; Jorge Nadal, *La población española (siglos XVI a XX)* (Barcelona: Ariel, 1966); and Margarita Jimenez-Castillo, *La población de Navarra; estudio geográfico* (Saragossa: Consejo Superior de Investigaciones Científicas, 1958).

[20] Unfortunately it was not possible to collect the French 1856 census totals for all communes. This would have been approximately contemporaneous with the first Spanish census (1857).

[21] Because of the different dates, growth rates are expressed as per centum per annum, obtained from the formula (as for compound interest): $P = p(1 + i)^n$, where P is the population at the end of a period of n years, p is the initial population, and i is the annual rate of growth expressed as a decimal fraction.

[22] Burguete and tiny Roncesvalles (dominated by the fluctuating population of its monastery) grew.

[23] Two French communes (St. Martin d'Arrossa; and Ossès, from which it was created after 1920) and four Spanish municipios (which had large garrisons in 1940) were not included in these computations.

[24] The last clauses are paraphrased in translation. The original is cited by Lefebvre, *Les Pyrénées atlantiques*, 286 n.

25 Lefebvre, *Les Pyrénées atlantiques*, 693–4. The only article which describes patterns of seasonal migration in the Pyrenees contains little information on the inhabitants of the Western Pyrenees: Lucien Goron, 'Les migrations saisonnières dans les départements pyrénéens au début du XIXe siècle', *RGPSO* IV (1933), 230–72.

26 Georges Viers, *Mauléon-Licharre; la population et l'industrie; étude de géographie sociale urbaine* (Bordeaux: Bière, 1961).

27 Pierre Laborde, 'Les travailleurs frontaliers sur la Côte basque française', *RGPSO* XL (1969), 243–52. Another study describes boundary crossing by workers in the Eastern Pyrenees: Emile Fornier, 'Les passages frontaliers en Cerdagne et Haute-Ariège', *RGPSO* XL (1969), 235–38.

28 *Enquête montagne*, I. 53–5.

29 Spain was a relatively unimportant destination for emigrants from Basses-Pyrénées. Christiane Pinède, 'L'émigration dans le Sud-Ouest vers le milieu du XIXe siècle', *Annales du Midi*, LXIX (1957), 237–51.

30 Cf. for example the attention devoted to the subject at the twenty-first congress of the Association pour l'avancement des sciences (1892): *Mémoire*, 21ème session, Association française pour l'avancement des sciences (Pau, 1892), I. 357–65; II, 1092–1104; with articles by Louis Etcheverry and Adrien Planté. Also: Louis Etcheverry, 'L'émigration des Basques en Amérique', *La Réforme sociale*, 2ème série, I (1896), 491–515.

31 Pierre Deffontaines, 'Participation des Pyrénées au peuplement des pays de la Plata', *Actas*, I CIEP, V. 269–77. Christiane Pinède, 'Une tentative d'émigration pyrénéenne organisée en Republique Argentine', *RGPSO* XXVIII (1957), 245–74.

32 Adrien Gachitéguy, *Les Basques dans l'ouest américain* (Bordeaux: Éditions Ezkila, 1955); Sol Silen, *La historia de los vascongados en el oeste de los Estados Unidos* (New York: Las Novedades, 1917).

33 Deffontaines, 'Participation des Pyrénées', p. 272; Urabayen, *Geografía de Navarra*, map 28; Albert Girard, 'L'émigration espagnole', *Annales de Géographie*, XXI (1912), 418–25; Daniel Gómez-Ibáñez, 'The rise and decline of transhumance in the United States' (M.A. thesis, University of Wisconsin, 1967).

34 But the resultant tendency towards a greater percentage of owner-occupied caseríos was probably offset by rural-to-urban migration which at the same time put caseríos of urban emigrés onto the rental market. See Douglass, 'Opportunity, choice-making, and rural depopulation in two Spanish Basque villages'; and José Luis Martín Galindo, 'El caserío vasco como tipo de explotación agraria', *Estudios Geográficos*, XXIX (1968), 205–44.

35 For a personal account, see the novel by Robert Laxalt, *Sweet promised land* (New York: Harper, 1957).

36 Pyrenean deforestation is treated in Lefebvre, *Les Pyrénées atlantiques* pp. 230–5; Chevalier, *Les Pyrénées ariégeoises*, pp. 495–539; Cavaillès, *La Vie pastorale*, pp. 41–7; and Axel Loze, *Déforestation et reboisement dans la région pyrénéenne* (Doctoral thesis, Faculté de Droit, Université de Paris) (Paris: Lib. Recueil Sirey, 1910). Loze cites (p. 32) a report by de Froidour, who was Grand Maître des Eaux et Forêts in the Languedoc region in 1666–73: 'There is not a single forest which has not been burned several times either through the malice of the inhabitants or to convert the woods to meadow or arable.' (*Procès-verbal*, 8 mai 1670).

37 There are several articles on the chestnut and the chestnut blight in the region. Because of the nuts' importance, foresters introduced Japanese species of chestnut to replace the dying trees. See, for example, Henri Gaussen, 'Les châtaigners japonais au Pays basque et dans le Sud-Ouest pyrénéen', *Travaux du Laboratoire forestier de Toulouse*, t. I, vol. IV, art. XIII (1946).

38 Cavaillès (*La Vie pastorale*, pp. 41–2) points out that the medieval forests were protected by most communities. Cutting was subject to permission of the magistrats. The *For général de Béarn* (arts. 79, 81) required replanting after cutting. Yet the general increase of population ensured that deforestation predominated. See also: P. Tucoo-Chala, 'Forêts et landes en Béarn au XIVe siècle', *Actas*, II CIEP, VI. 161–73.

39 Manuscript reports on individual forests, and interviews (1968) with foresters: Office national des forêts (Bayonne); Patrimonio Forestal del Estado (Pamplona); Diputación foral de Navarra, Dirección de Montes (Pamplona).

40 See e.g.: Monique Guitard, 'Les forêts d'Aspe et d'Ossau' (unpublished Diplôme d'études supérieurs de géographie, Université de Bordeaux, Faculté des Lettres, 1954), 71–90.

41 Idoate, *Principe de Viana*, nos. 78–9, pp. 125–9. Many must have been very small operations.

42 Muthuon, 'Rapport sur les forges du pays conquis en Espagne, dans les Pyrénées occidentales',

Journal des Mines, no. XI, Thermidor, an. III [1795], pp. 1–18. In a table on p. 16 he lists seven forges in the Bidasoa valley.

43'Informe de Don Lucas de Olazábal, Ingeniero de Montes; 26 de enero 1860; Pamplona' MS. of 8 folios in the archives of Patrimonio forestal del estado, Pamplona office.

44d'Étigny, correspondence 2 septembre 1752 (Gers archives, C–3–94 ff.) cited by Loze, *Déforestation*, pp. 37–8.

45Dralet, *Déscription des Pyrénées*, II. 139–42.

46Dumège, II. 571.

47France. Ministère de l'Agriculture. Direction générale des eaux et forêts, Inspection de Bayonne, 'Rapport de M. Georges Duplan . . . sur la Forêt Syndicale de la Vallée de Baïgorry', typescript (n.d. but *c.* 1966) kept at Bayonne office of the Office national des forêts. Studies of French forests are numerous, and all tell essentially the same story, e.g.: Georges Viers, 'La forêt d'Irati', *RGPSO* XXVI (1955) 5–27; or Henri Gaussen, 'Les forêts de la vallée d'Aspe', *RGPSO* III (1932), 5–17.

48Eugène Trutat, *Les Pyrénées* . . . (Paris: J.-B. Baillère, 1894), p. 188; Lefebvre, *Les Pyrénées atlantiques*, p. 329.

49Madoz, *Diccionario*, XII. 86–7.

50Caro-Baroja, *Vera de Bidasoa*, p. 109; id., *Los vascos*, pp. 229–39.

51Lefebvre, *Les Pyrénées atlantiques*, p. 329.

52M. Espesset, 'L'exploitation des forêts des Basses-Pyrénées', *Annales de la Fédération pyrénéenne d'économie montagnarde*, XI (1944–5), 162. During the German occupation of France in the 1940s there was a brief revival of charcoal-making in the French forests.

53Lefebvre, *Les Pyrénées atlantiques*, pp. 300–4.

54After the enactment of the *Code Forestier* of 1827. The law of 1669 and its application to the Pyrenees are discussed in Loze, *Déforestation*, pp. 64–7.

55See Dralet, *Description des Pyrénées*, II. 22–8. Beginning in 1629 the Irati forest yielded 7,000 fir trees for masts.

56France. Direction génerale des eaux et forêts, Inspection d'Oloron, 'Notice descriptive des Services, 1948'. See also, Maurice Moreau, 'Les forêts béarnaises au XVIIIᵉ siècle', *Pyrénées*, no. 7 (juillet–sept., 1951), pp. 9–13.

57In 1813 Dralet reported that only Gabas, in the Ossau valley (east of the study area) was furnishing masts. *Description des Pyrénées*, II. 32.

58Gerónimo de Uztáriz, *Theorica y práctica de commercio y de marina en differentes discursos* (2nd ed.; Madrid: Sanz, 1742), chap. LXIII, cited by Jean Sermet, 'L'extraction des bois pour la mature dans les Pyrénées françaises et espagnoles', *RGPSO* XXV (1954), 84–91. Uztáriz mentions two other Pyrenean forests similarly logged: in the Cinca valley and in the valley of Hecho. Rafting the logs downstream is described in the regional novel, *Oro del Ezka* by Mariano Estornes Lasa (San Sebastian: Auñamendi, 1958).

59Real Academia . . . *Diccionario*, I. 379; II. 277–8; II. 172; I. 391. Dralet (1813) mentions masting the Spanish navy with Pyrenean timber, but the examples are from the Central and Eastern Pyrenees. *Description des Pyrénées*, II. 33–4.

60Madoz, *Diccionario*, XIII. 55–72.

61Pío Baroja y Nessi includes a photograph of an *almadía* descending the Esca river in *El país vasco* (3rd. ed.; Barcelona: Ediciones Destino, 1966), p. 296.

62France. Ministère de l'Agriculture, Direction générale des eaux et forêts . . ., 'Rapport de M. Georges Duplan . . .'.

63Viers, 'La forêt d'Irati', pp. 17–20.

64France. Ministère de l'Agriculture, Direction générale des eaux et forêts . . . 'Notice descriptive des services, 1948'.

65Association départementale d'économie rurale des Basses-Pyrénées, *L'Agriculture départementale; son évolution de 1954 à 1964* (mimeographed; Pau: A.D.E.R., n.d.), p. 63. On the very limited extent of reafforestation projects in the mountains, see C. Sulzlée, 'Le problème du reboisement au Pays basque', *Annales de la Fédération pyrénéenne d'économie montagnarde*, XI (1944–5), 172–6. Since 1960 the Hayra forest has been reafforested—but only at a rate of three or four hectares per year. (Interview with syndical warden, 15 April 1968).

66See Michel Chadefaud & Gilbert Dalla Rosa, 'L'aménagement d'une moyenne montagne forestière: Iraty', *RGPSO* XLIV (1973), 5–27.

67Spain. Patrimonio forestal del estado, 'Proyecto de ordenación de los montes "Aezcoa" y "La Cuestión" ' (Madrid: P.F.E., 1904; typescript kept in Pamplona office of P.F.E.); and 'Proyecto de ordenación de los montes "Erreguerena", "Vertiente meridional de Quinto Real", y "Legua Acotada",' (Madrid: P.F.E., 1903; typescript kept in Pamplona office of P.F.E.).

68 I do not know why the forests of Salazar, where lumbering is very important, were so diminished in the cadaster of the 1890s.

69 Cited by Douglass, (Ph.D. dissertation), p. 125. I was unable to consult an apparently valuable book by Lucas de Olazábal which recounts the history of Navarrese forests: *Ordenación y valoración de montes* (Madrid: 1883).

70 See H. de Coincy et Georges Roux, 'Les reboisements en Pays basque espagnol', *Revue des eaux et forêts*, LXV (1927), 167–77. The information on modern programmes comes from typewritten accounts on file in the Pamplona office of the Dirección de Montes of the Diputación foral de Navarra. The most popular species are *Pinus insignis* and *Larix japonica*.

71 The herd book's standard of conformation for the local variety of cattle (Pyrenean Blond) still emphasizes its working qualities above meat or milk. Georges Guyonnet, 'Race bovine blonde des Pyrénées', in France, Ministère de l'agriculture, *Statistique agricole de la France, annexe à l'enquête de 1929; Monographie agricole du département des Basses-Pyrénées* (Pau: Imp. 'L'Indépendant', 1937, pp. 310–29.)

72 Pigs, horses, asses, mules, and a few goats also contributed to the area's livestock economy, but they will not be considered here. They are relatively much less important than cattle and sheep. Most of the references cited on the following pages also contain information on the minor varieties.

73 Archival material for 1817 (Navarre) and 1812 (France), and 1891 (Navarre) and 1892 (France), quoted by Torres Luna, *La Navarra húmeda*, pp. 80, 81; Dumège, *Statistique*, II. 562; *Monographie agricole* (1929), p. 328; Lefebvre, *Les Pyrénées atlantiques*, pp. 428, 444–5, plates XV–C, XX–A. The difficulty in interpreting these trends arises from the authors' presentation of aggregated percentages rather than the original figures. I lack information for the eastern Navarrese villages.

74 This assumes that average livestock holdings at the beginning of the nineteenth century were of similar size on either side of the boundary. Although unproven, it seems the only reasonable assumption in view of twentieth century performance: cattle, for example, increased more in Navarre than in France from 1901 to 1960, yet in 1956/1962 the cattle/farm ratio was still higher in France. For the twentieth-century material on which the pages which follow are based, see Torres Luna, *La Navarra húmeda*, Appendixes VII, VIII; Lefebvre, *Les Pyrénées atlantiques*, pp. 428–31; Serge Lerat, 'L'économie des Pyrénées basques et béarnaises', *RGPSO* XXXIX (1968), 435–57; Association départementale d'économie rurale, *L'Agriculture ... 1954 à 1964*; France, Institut national de la statistique et des études économiques, 'Enquête agricole de printemps 1946 (Basses-Pyrénées)' (computer print-out kept at Bordeaux office of I.N.S.E.E.); id., 'Enquête agricole–année 1951 (Basses-Pyrénées)' MS. totals kept at Bordeaux office of I.N.S.E.E.; id., 'Recensement agricole, 1956, "Inventaire communal" (Basses-Pryénées)' (computer print-out kept at Bordeaux office of I.N.S.E.E.); plus other sources cited in this section.

75 The numbers of farms, sheep, and cattle are from the 1962 census of agriculture (Spain) and the 1956 agricultural census (France). Spain, Instituto nacional de estadística, *Primer censo agrario de España, año 1962*, serie B, vol. 31: 'Navarra' (Madrid: I.N.E., 1964), part 3, table 1 (farms); and unpublished manuscript lists from the same census kept in the Ministry of agriculture in Madrid (sheep and cattle); France, Institut national de la statistique et des études économiques, Recensement agricole, 1956, 'Inventaire communal' (Basses-Pyrénées) (unpublished; computer print-out kept in the Bordeaux office of I.N.S.E.E.).

76 Alfredo Floristán Samanes, 'Juntas y mestas ganaderas en las Bardenas de Navarra', *Actas*, I CIEP, V. 111–30.

77 The standard deviation of French communes' means is 17, but it is 35 in Spain.

78 'Meadows' are cultivated or tended grasslands where hay can be cut for stall feeding. They are not pastures, except that they may be grazed after the summer's last mowing. This corresponds to the definition adopted by the 1962 Spanish agricultural census. How closely the cadasters adhered to this definition is questionable, however, so comparisons must be made with caution. The 1890s cadaster in Navarre apparently used the strictest definition ('prados artificiales'). The French cadaster's definitions are somewhat ambiguous, but probably are comparable to those of the Spanish census.

79 See Lefebvre, *Les Pyrénées atlantiques*, pp. 527–9. My own field observations and conversations with French and Spanish agronomists support this. Torres Luna also discusses crop changes on pp. 67–71 of *La Navarra húmeda*. See also: Alfredo Floristán Samanes, 'Las transformaciones modernas de la agricultura navarra', in *Aportación española al XXI Congreso geográfico internacional* (Madrid: Consejo superior de investigaciones científicas, 1969), pp. 100–3.

[80]In 1968, however, *Roquefort Española* began to set up a small cheese factory in Baztán to use the local ewes' milk. If successful, it will drain all of the production of north-western Navarre by 1973 and will doubtless do much to stimulate sheep husbandry in the region.

[81]Although the average yield was only about 7·5 litres per day per farm. Georges Viers *et al.*, 'La XLIe excursion géographique interuniversitaire (8—13 mai 1959)', *Annales de Géographie*, LXVIII (1959), 519.

[82]By French law (and international treaty after 1926) only cheese made from pure ewe's milk which has been aged in the caves under the village of Roquefort-sur-Soulzon can be called 'Roquefort'. True Gorgonzola (from Italy) resembles it; so does Bleu, which contains cow's milk, but Roquefort has a more subtle flavour. The factories in Basses-Pyrénées (and Corsica) only begin the process of making Roquefort. The milk is curdled, sprinkled with *Penicillium Roquefortii*, made into 'breads' (wheels about 25 centimetres across), drained, salted, and dried. Then the cheeses are taken by truck to Roquefort for the ageing which produces their distinctive flavour. An alliance of Roquefort producers maintains uniform standards of quality. Roquefort commands high prices and large quantities are exported all over the world. Information on the Roquefort industry of the French Western Pyrenees came from interviews with local farmers and with M. Coste, regional director of the Société Anonyme des Caves et des producteurs réunis de Roquefort (St. Jean Pied-de-Port). See also: Gisèle Espinasse, 'Le rayonnement d'une industrie agricole locale: le Roquefort', *RGPSO* II (1931), 377—430.

[83]Based on interviews with farmers, 1968. The Spanish farmer's total gross income from milk was 30,000 pesetas ($430), less the labour of making the cheese. The French farmer earned 9,100 f. ($1,820).

[84]The most common varieties were Iowa 4417 and Funk's 72, 34, and 17. They increased yields by about one-third over the traditional varieties. *Enquête montagne*, p. 63; *Monographie agricole (1953)*, p. 37.

[85]Robert Lassalle, 'Les maïs hybrides dans les Basses-Pyrénées', *RGPSO* XXV (1954), 78—80; Serge Lerat, 'L'introduction du maïs hybride dans les pays de l'Adour', *RGPSO* XXXII (1961), 97—117.

[86]Interviews with 'Pedro', the first person in the area to buy a jeep and the first to collect ewes' milk in the summer grazings; and with other French farmers, in 1968.

[87]In 1967 a sample of 1,139 farms in the French part of the borderland owned 775 'motoculteurs et assimilés'—a ratio of 68 per cent. (France, Ministère de l'agriculture, Service centrale des enquêtes et des études statistiques, 'Basses-Pyrénées: enquête communautaire sur la structure des exploitations agricole (sept. 1967—jan. 1968)', unpublished data kept in the Direction départementale de l'agriculture, Pau.) The 1964 *Enquête montagne* (Annexe, p. 72), which was based on a more comprehensive census, also showed that 67 per cent of farms owned a motor scythe.

[88]The data on tractors are quite accurate and comparable, except that the 1968 figures for France should probably be increased by about 10 per cent since they are based on petrol tax exemption permits issued for each tractor—and not all farmers apply for these. The other figures are based on motor vehicle registrations. For Spain: the manuscript 'hojas declaratorias' of the 1966 agriculture questionnaires. France: Institut national des statistiques et des études économiques, 'Enquête agricole de printemps 1946', and 'Recensement agricole, 1956', unpublished data for Basses-Pyrénées kept in the Bordeaux offices of I.N.S.E.E.; and Direction départementale de l'agriculture des Basses-Pyrénées, Pau: typescript lists of 'bons de carburants'.

[89]See *Enquête montagne*, p. 98. Note that the total population of the French communes is slightly more than that of the Spanish municipios. Industrial employment in the borderland totals about 2,500 workers in each country. See: Diputación foral de Navarra, Dirección de industria. *Catálogo de la industria de Navarra* (Pamplona: Diputación foral, 1968); id., *Programa de promoción industrial de Navarra (texto refundido) año 1966* (Pamplona: Diputación foral, 1966); and typescript of 1966 census of industry kept in the Dirección de industria (Pamplona) and MS. municipal questionnaires (30 November 1967) on file in the same offices. France. Institut national de la statistique et des études économiques, *Recensement général de la population de 1962: Basses-Pyrénées; resultats du dépouillement exhaustif; population par région agricole*; and mimeographed lists of industrial and commercial establishments from the Chambres de commerce et de l'industrie of Pau and of Bayonne (1968).

[90]Manuel Ferrer, 'La industria navarra,' *Actas*, V CIEP, III. 121—36.

[91]In December 1972 the *Commission Internationale des Pyrénées* discussed the industrial pollution of the Bidasoa River after French fishermen complained of contamination by effluents from the new factories in Vera de Bidasoa and Santesteban. (Jean Sermet, personal communication, 12 June 1973.)

[92]The Syndicat d'Initiatives of St. Jean Pied-de-Port listed 20 hotels and 'pensions' in the three

contiguous villages of St. Jean-Pied-de-Port, Ispoure, and Uhart-Cize. The Syndicat d'Initiatives of St. Étienne de Baïgorry listed 17 hotels and 'pensions' in St. Étienne de Baïgorry, Banca, Aldudes, Urepel, and Ossès. In Navarre, the provincial office of Spain's Ministerio de información y turismo listed 16 hotels and 'pensions' in the entire Pyrenean borderland. In addition there are about the same number of small guest houses (*fondas*) in the Navarrese Pyrenees. Very few of the Navarrese hotels match the degree of luxury offered by the average French Pyrenean hotel.

93*Enquête montagne.* II. 91.

94On tourism and recent developments in the economy of the French Western Pyrenees, see: Michel Chadefaud, 'Une formule originale de tourisme social: les gîtes ruraux', *RGPSO* XXXIX (1968), 273–97; Georges Cazes, 'Nouveaux aspects du tourisme d'hiver dans les Pyrénées', *RGPSO* XXXVIII (1967), 69–78; Michel Chadefaud & Gilbert Dalla Rosa, *RGPSO* XLIV (1973), 5–27; and Gilbert Dalla Rosa, *Documents pour un livre blanc des Pyrénées—Pyrénées atlantiques, 1972* (2 vols., text & atlas; Pau: Direction départementale de l'agriculture, 1972), which amplifies the *Enquête montagne* and brings it up to date.

95The gold is not freely available in France, either. It comes from Switzerland, and it is hoarded by those Spaniards who can afford to indulge their mistrust of the peseta.

96See: Remy, *La Ligne de démarcation; histoires du Pays basque, de Béarn et de Bigorre* (Paris: Librarie Académique Perrin, 1973).

97Although Basque nationalism in Spain is sometimes conspicuous, very few Navarrese participate in the movement, and in France it is the concern of only a handful of people.

CHAPTER VIII

Conclusion

The first chapters of this study, describing the period from the eleventh to the seventeenth centuries, emphasized the role of the valley communities in the Western Pyrenees. The last chapters, which covered the period since the Treaty of the Pyrenees in 1659, described the growing importance of administrative division in the mountains as national forms of territorial organization were added to the older arrangement based on valleys. These have been the major themes of this regional study, and they are both found in the modern landscape.

The old valley communities had several interrelated attributes. First, the complementary nature of their upland and lowland resources suited them for a pastoral economy in which the valley was the fundamental unit and in which all parts of the valley were integrated. The seasonal rhythm of transhumant herds linked the meadows and fields around the villages below with the alpine pastures above. So important was this livestock husbandry based on transhumance that most other forms of rural economy were subordinated to it.

Another attribute of the valleys was their social cohesiveness; whence the term 'valley community'. Transhumance involved all the inhabitants in a common enterprise. Villagers upstream and villagers downstream depended upon one another's co-operation. From these bonds, and from the need to manage the vast common pastures, Pyrenean countrymen developed systems of local government in which all households participated and which embraced whole valleys, not just villages, reinforcing the valleys' status as the most important units of economy and society.

At first the valleys' institutions were relatively isolated from those of the world outside the mountains. In fact, if not always in law, the valley communities enjoyed a large degree of autonomy. They treated with their neighbours in the manner of sovereign states. The *traités de lies et passeries* which the valleys signed not only resolved their disputes over grazings, but also wove the Pyrenees into what Cavaillès called a 'confederation' of valley communities.

The present landscape of the mountains still reflects its former organization. Grazing and transhumance remain the mainstay of the valleys' rural economy and thus they still function as local economic units. Further, the modern landscape still bears the imprint of centuries of livestock husbandry. The heaths' fire-climax vegetation, the bracken mown in autumn, the extensive upland grazings dotted with herders' cabins, the system of land tenure combining private property and commons, and even the dispersed pattern of settlement itself; all reflect the valleys' pastoral vocation.

The valleys also encompass much of the mountains' social life. People still think of themselves as inhabitants of a valley rather than a village or a larger district. If one examines the valleys in detail, cultural differences between them can still be discerned in such matters as the varieties of dialect or forms of speech, in folklore and games, in the vernacular architecture, in the traditional varieties of seed (if they still be sown), and in some of the tools and artefacts still made and used by farmers and shepherds.

The valleys' governmental functions, however, gave way before the rise of the modern nation-states during the seventeenth century and after. Over the loose confederation of Pyrenean communities the Treaty of 1659 imposed the modern administrative boundary of France and Spain. Yet the 'new' boundary was remarkable in the degree to which it followed the valleys' ancient usages. With very few exceptions the boundary commissioners of the nineteenth century respected local boundary lines, and what is more they even formalized the peculiarities of status by which the valleys shared the summer pastures on the crests. And despite the valleys' apparent loss of 'autonomy' they continued to regulate their own pastoral affairs, even to the extent of signing grazing agreements across the international boundary.

Nevertheless, political division gradually became an important component of the Pyrenean landscape. What made it so was the great economic transformation of Europe during the last two centuries. The Pyrenees experienced this not only through shifts in the nature of their economic activity but also through rural depopulation and a decreasing intensity of land use. The valleys evolved in broadly similar ways on both sides of the modern political boundary, but the timing and rates of the change were not the same, especially after 1800. Thus, important differences grew up between the French and Spanish parts of the borderland. The two sides of the boundary differed because in general change came sooner to the French side. French farmers enjoyed the opportunities—and experienced the traumas—of an enlarged market before their neighbours did, and so the boundary became a major discontinuity in the social and economic landscape of the borderland.

In part this was because the French built the infra-structures of change earlier and so tied the Pyrenees to their national economy sooner. But we should be wary of assigning too much weight to the development of the regional infra-structure as a cause of cross-boundary differentiation. The very fact that it was built earlier in France points to a more fundamental reason for the greater and more precocious prosperity of the French borderland, and for its earlier depopulation: simply that the French economy as a whole was at most times more vigorous and powerful than that of Spain. It also had a broader base. France's bourgeoisie or middle class was always more numerous than Spain's. Therefore, even had both sides of the borderland been integrated with their national economies at the same time, the French Western Pyrenees would have changed more, and prospered more. Both sides reflected national circumstances.

Indeed, when the borderland's contrasts are viewed in the contexts of France and Spain as a whole, the disparities of the two countries appear even more striking. In Spain, the north is a relatively wealthy region. South-western France, on the other hand, is one of France's less prosperous areas.

Quite apart from their relative strengths, the specific opportunities offered by each national market also influenced economic developments in the borderland. Thus lumbering is profitable in Roncal and Salazar, and the production of ewes' milk for Roquefort cheese is important in Baïgorry, Cize, and Soule.

The special status of the Spanish province of Navarre is another element in the Western Pyrenean landscape. Because the province retained some of the privileges of its medieval charters, it may have prospered more than others. The better development of Navarrese roads, for example, contrasts with the rest of the Spanish Pyrenees. The *Diputación foral*'s encouragement of rural industrial parks has given the Navarrese Pyrenees factories which are much larger than any in the French Western Pyrenees.

Although not specifically analysed in this study, there is a contrast in the Western Pyrenees between the eastern valleys and those closer to the Atlantic Ocean. The most striking differences are physical: the western valleys are much less rugged and mountainous than those closer to the Central Pyrenees. There are cultural contrasts: for example, the vernacular architecture of the west, with its whitewashed and red-roofed houses, differs from the fieldstone walls and slate roofs of the eastern valleys. Settlement is also more dispersed in the west; more nucleated in the east. The whitewashed and red-roofed houses of the west are often termed 'Basque' but in fact there is little evidence linking the Basque language with a style of architecture besides their coexistence today in the same valleys. Now heard only in the western part of the study area, Basque speech was once more widespread. The rural economy of the eastern valleys also differs somewhat from that in the rest of the study area. Roncal and Salazar, for example, pursue a different type of sheep husbandry than the valleys to the west, and lumbering is also more important there. Similarly, Roquefort cheese production is limited to the central part of the French borderland. The Aspe valley to the east makes cheese from cows' milk, and the agriculture of the French coastal region is more oriented towards local urban markets.

Examined closely, these east—west differences are primarily differences between valleys, and thus lead back to the observation that the modern landscape is a composite of the valley communities and the nation-states. For example, shepherds still utilize the valleys' complementary resources, but they now serve metropolitan markets. The old valley communities and the Pyrenean web of pastoral agreements which bound them together coexist with the links forged by modern commerce and government. Vestiges of tradition and custom still animate valley life in the Western Pyrenees, but they do not hide the contrasts which have developed between the French and Spanish sectors.

Appendix

Minor civil divisions

The map of communes and municipios in the borderland (Fig. 23) is based on maps obtained from the Institut national de la statistique et des études économiques (France) and from Professor Casas Torres of Madrid (Spain) and from the 1:50,000 topographic surveys of both countries. Where fusions of minor civil divisions (e.g. Larrasoaña–Esteríbar) or divisions (e.g. Ossès–St. Martin d'Arrossa) have occurred, the map portrays the situation in 1968 and the earlier statistical data have been transformed accordingly.[1] The Montes de Bidasoa and other pastures common to several minor civil divisions were not separately delineated (thus the Montes de Bidasoa, for example, are shown on this map as part of the municipio of Sumbilla).

The areas of minor civil divisions (used to compute densities) presented no problems in France, where figures used by the cadaster agree with those used by the census or by other agencies. In Spain, however, no two sets of numbers on municipal areas agreed: those consulted were the areas according to the cadaster, the 1960 census *Nomenclator*, the 1962 agriculture census, and the *Jefatura Agronomica*. In general the procedure adopted (since there seemed to be no consistent bias to any of the sources) was to compute densities for population using the census's figures, densities for categories of land use using the cadaster's figures, etc. Where discrepancies were large the area was measured on the 1:50,000 maps with a planimeter.

Dispersed population

Because the French and Spanish census definitions of dispersed population are different, international comparison must be made with caution. The problem is that the French census defines as agglomerated, the population of the town or village in which the *mairie* (town hall) is located, and as dispersed, not only people living in dispersed farms but also inhabitants of other villages in the commune—villages which do not have a *mairie*. In Spain, the agglomerated population includes all persons living in nucleated villages and towns, whether or not they are the seats of their minor civil division's administration. The problem is not acute, however, because the French communes are generally much smaller than the Spanish municipios. Most French communes in fact have only one village (the site of the *mairie*) and it is generally only the larger Spanish municipios which contain more than one nucleated settlement.

Forests

Some of the cross-boundary contrasts shown on Figures 19 and 20 may represent a difference in the two nations' definition of forested land. In France the first cadaster measured the actual forested area. The most recent cadasters may have exaggerated the forested area slightly because in some places they used the original parcel lines, whereas the edge of the forest had retreated somewhat, as a result of fires set in Spring on the surrounding heaths.[2]

In Spain, however, there are areas legally defined as forests, not all of which are covered with trees. The area of legal forests bears no consistent relationship with the cadastral area. But the exact definition of forest used by the 1890s cadaster is uncertain. The 1962 agricultural census defined forested land simply as 'land covered with trees ... from which forest products can be obtained', but we do not know how the definition was applied in each municipio.

Certainly the comparability of the French and Spanish data is only approximate. Nevertheless, observations in the field support the statistics: in general the Navarrese

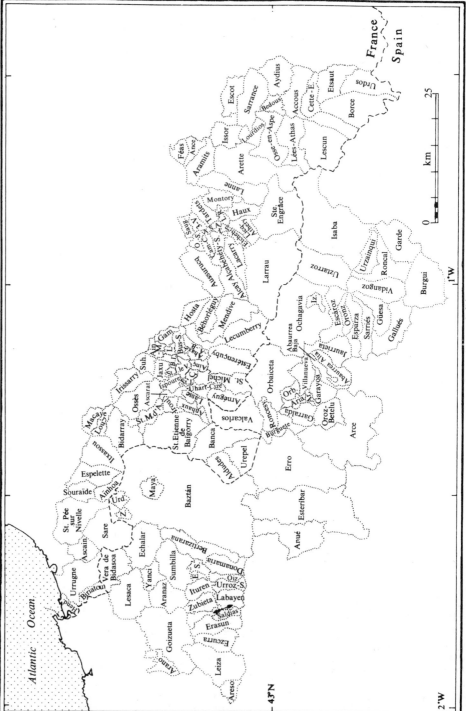

Fig. 23 Communes and Municipios

Pyrenees are more extensively forested than the French borderland. An analysis of aerial photographs would yield better information, but it was not possible to obtain photographs of the entire borderland.

Land use and agriculture

There are good quality data on land use in the borderland. The first comprehensive survey exists in the ledgers of the so-called 'Napoleonic' cadaster of French communes.[3] Those in the study area were first surveyed according to a uniform system between about 1821 and 1842. Most of the surveys date from the 1830s. The purposes of the cadastral survey were to establish individuals' title to real property and to determine taxable land values. Each parcel of land was surveyed, measured, and mapped, and its location, size, and use was recorded in the cadastral ledger with the owner's name. The cadastral maps, at large scales (e.g. 1:2,000), are very precise. The surveyors used a consistent scheme for classifying land use, and the surveys and their maps make valuable if somewhat cumbersome sources for historical—geographical studies. At the beginning of each commune's ledgers the total area in each category of land use is given, making a parcel-by-parcel search unnecessary. The ledgers and map folios are kept in the archives of the regional offices of the Administration des Contributions Directes et du Cadastre (in the sub-prefectures).

The cadastral offices kept a running account of changes in ownership and land use, but eventually it became necessary to carry out revisions or resurveys. In 1914 (in the Basses-Pyrénées) the cadaster was revised—not resurveyed—on the basis of a commune-by-commune inquiry. The revision, which was fairly accurate, was entered into a new ledger, and this also included a recapitulation of the amount of land in each category. There were revisions made again in 1951 and 1963, but they represent mainly adjustments to the valuation of land, not to the size or categorization of the parcels. The 1951 and 1963 revisions were 'armchair' inquiries, based on questionnaires mailed to each *mairie*. In most cases, if the commune's secretary bothered to reply at all, he usually stated simply that there had been no changes.

In the 1930s a programme of cadastral resurvey began. The first commune in the study area was resurveyed in 1932, the last in 1969. This resulted in a new series of data and maps comparable in quality to the original cadaster, but unfortunately spread over 37 years for the whole study area. Nevertheless, for each commune there are three dates for which accurate land-use information exists: the first around the 1830s, the second in 1914, and the third between 1932 and 1969.[4]

In Navarre the cadastral service assessed the taxable valuation of livestock, arable, forests, and land of various categories from about 1817. The statistics were not gathered in the field, but based on declarations by the municipal secretaries. The declarations (and the ledgers recapitulating them) became annual questionnaires after the late 1880s. The Archivo General de Navarra preserves the 1817 survey and others made in the 1830s, and the annual declarations after the 1880s are found in ledgers kept in the offices of the Servicio Catastral in Pamplona. But the fiscal purpose of the surveys makes them suspect. And because the manner in which the earlier statistics were gathered is uncertain, we cannot verify their accuracy either. They have not been used in this study except as checks to other sources. There is thus no counterpart to the French cadaster of the 1830s.

In the 1890s, however, Navarre did complete an accurate cadastral survey of the Pyrenean municipios.[5] It was approximately comparable to the French cadaster in method, quality, and definitions. The ledgers, which also contain recapitulations of the total area in each category of land use, may be found in the Archivo General de Navarra. The Navarrese cadaster employs the traditional measure of Navarre, the *robada*, rather than the metric units of France, and so must be converted.[6]

In some parts of Navarre the cadaster is periodically resurveyed (now photo-grammetrically), but the Pyrenean region, relatively unimportant as a source of revenue, has never been revised. The secretaries' annual declarations are the only source of data for cadastral information after the 1890s, but they are not of comparable accuracy.

There are other sources of information on modern land use. One, a 1951 publication of the Spanish Instituto nacional de estadística, proved unsuitable both because its categories were not comparable with the French ones and because the way in which the data had been gathered—and so their quality—could not be discovered.[7] The second possible source is the results of the annual questionnaire sent to each municipio by the Spanish Ministry of Agriculture every May.[8] This source is unreliable. The questionnaires are filled out by a representative of the Hermandad Sindical de Labradores y Ganaderos in each municipio, not on the basis of any formal survey, but according to the best knowledge of the individual. Examination of the manuscript questionnaires, rather than the ledgers aggregating them, reveals a predominance of dozens and tens in the figures for various categories. At the end of each questionnaire, the Jefatura Provincial de Agricultura has typed in the total area of the municipio in hectares and ares (1 are = 100 m^2). Often the respondent, seeing that his figures are supposed to yield a certain sum at the bottom of the page, writes in an uncharacteristically precise figure in the last category (e.g. 103·47 rather than 100), so that when it is added to the dozens and tens above, the total agrees with that which already appears at the bottom of the column—to the last 100 square metres. Inquiry amongst municipal secretaries and mayors in the study area revealed that the questionnaires are not taken very seriously. In one municipio the mayor said that the information to answer the questionnaires was taken from the cadaster. When asked how this was possible since the cadaster dated from the 1890s, he replied that it was of little moment, since nothing ever changed. Some municipios do not bother to return the questionnaires. When this happens, the provincial office uses one from a previous year when making up the sums for the whole province. Only the provincial totals are published.

Table 3

English	France: three cadasters	Navarre: 1890s cadaster	Spain 1962 census
Forest	Bois, Châtaigneraies	Arbolado	Forestal
Grazing	Landes	Pastos sotos	Pastos
Meadows	Prés	Prados artificiales	Prados permanentes
Arable	Labourables, Jardins, Vergers	Huertos, Labor (de secano, de regadio)	Agricola
Vines	Vignes	Viña	none in area

The third possible source for information on land use is the 1962 census of agriculture. This is the one which was chosen. The figures for land-use categories are based on actual field inspection and interviews. They are not as accurate as a cadastral survey might be, but they appear to be the best available.

Table 3 summarizes the categories used for land-use analyses in the Western Pyrenean borderland.

Figures on crops and livestock from the 1962 agricultural census are probably not so accurate as those relating to land use. The 1962 agricultural census was Spain's first, and suspicious farmers, fearing taxation, tended to under-report. Nevertheless they have been used here in preference to the same information from the Servicio Catastral, because they followed definitions more comparable with those used in French agricultural statistics.

Of the five French agricultural censuses (1946, 1951, 1953, 1956, 1967) used here, the first three are of doubtful accuracy since they were based on questionnaires sent to the secretaries of each commune. The 1956 survey is quite accurate, having been based on enumerations made at each farm. The 1967 census included only a sample of communes.

1 In 1969 Maya del Baztán became part of Baztán.

2 Between 1904 and 1963, for example, the edge of the Hayra forest (in the valley of Baïgorry) retreated a few metres almost everywhere along its margins. On the other hand some clearings within Hayra (usually pastures surrounding *bordas* which had been abandoned) had filled in. (From a comparison of the 1963 topographic sheet XIII–46/5–6, 1:25,000 (France, Institut géographique national), with 'Forêt syndicale de la vallée de Baïgorry. Plan de division à joindre au plan d'aménagement', 1:10,000, 1904 (MS. map kept at Office national des forêts, Bayonne).)

3 For some communes there are cadastral surveys from the 1790s, but the records which have survived are not complete.

4 I am indebted to M. Gauthier, Chef de circonscription du Cadastre at Bayonne, for discussions on the nature and quality of the cadastral surveys and revisions.

5 It did not include maps, however. This cadaster is technically an *amillaramiento*, or assessment, rather than a *catastro*.

6 One *robada* = 16 *almutadas* = 898 m2. The *robo*, a measure of grain (28·13 litres) was the amount needed to sow one *robada*.

7 Spain. Instituto nacional de estadística, *Estadística de propietarios de fincas rusticas de España, Cuaderno 2: Provincias vascongadas y Navarra* (Madrid: I.N.E., 1951).

8 Spain. Ministerio de Agricultura, Sección de Estadística Agricola. 'Hoja declaratoria de distribución de superficies en 1° de Mayo' (MS. municipal questionnaires on file in the Pamplona office of the Jefatura Provincial de Agricultura. Besides figures for various categories of land use the questionnaire includes crop acreages. There is also a similar questionnaire (1 September) covering hectares in late-sown crops, and agricultural machinery.

Selected Bibliography

(N.B. See the list of abbreviations on p. xiv)

Abascal Garayoa, Angel. 'Los origenes de la población actual de Pamplona.' *Revista Geográfica*, II (1955), 99—188.

Alimen, H., Florschutz, F., and Menéndez Amor, J. 'Étude palynologique sur le Quaternaire des environs de Lourdes.' *Actes*, IV CIEP, I. 7—26.

Alzola y Minondo, Pablo de. *Las obras publicas en España; estudio historico.* 'Biblioteca de la Revista de Obras Publicas.' Bilbao: Casa de la Misericordia, 1899.

Ancel, Jacques. *Géographie des Frontières.* 4th ed. Paris: Gallimard, 1938.

Antolín Monge, Francisco. *El Valle de Baztán.* Unpublished Ph.D. dissertation; Universidad de Madrid, 1966.

Arensberg, Conrad. *The Irish Countryman.* Cambridge, Mass.: Harvard University Press, 1938.

Arin y Dorronsoro, Felipe de. *Problemas agrarios; estudio juridico-social de las corralizas, servidumbres, montes y communidades de Navarra.* Segovia: 'Heraldo Segoviano' [Imprenta de Carlos Martin], 1930.

Arqué, Paul. *Géographie des Pyrénées françaises.* Paris: Presses Universitaires de France, 1943.

Association départementale d'économie rurale des Basses-Pyrénées. *L'Agriculture départementale; son évolution de 1954 à 1964.* (mimeographed.) Pau: A.D.E.R., n.d.

Babonneau, L. *L'énergie électrique dans la région pyrénéenne.* Toulouse: Privat, 1942.

Balié, Pierre. 'Les forêts de Chênes têtards du pays basque.' *Revue des Eaux et Forêts*, LXXI (1933), 741—53, 825—33, 905—15.

Barandiarán, José Miguel de. 'Bosquejo etnográfico de Sara, II.' *Anuario de Eusko-Folklore*, XVIII (1961), 107—80.

   El hombre prehistórico en el país vasco. 'Biblioteca de cultura vasca', No. 42. Buenos Aires: Editorial Vasca Ekin, 1953.

   'Vida pastoril vasca. Albergues veraniegos, trashumancia intrapirenaica.' *Anales del Museo del Pueblo Español*, I (1935), 88—97.

Baroja y Nessi, Pío. *El país vasco.* 3rd ed. Barcelona: Ediciones Destino, 1966.

Barrère, Pierre; Jean Sermet; Yves Doumergue. 'Les aménagements hydro-électriques dans les Pyrénées.' *RGPSO* XXX (1959), 88—99.

Berthaut, Henri Marie Auguste. *La carte de France 1750—1898; étude historique.* 2 vols. Paris: Imprimerie du service géographique de l'armée, 1898—99.

Billaut, Micheline; *et al.* 'Problèmes climatiques sur la bordure nord du monde méditerranéen.' *Annales de Géographie*, LXV (1956), 15—39.

Birot, Pierre. *Étude comparée de la vie rurale pyrénéenne dans le pays de Pallars (Espagne) et de Couserans (France).* Paris: J.-B. Baillière et fils, 1937.

Bloch, Marc. *French rural history; an essay on its basic characteristics.* Berkeley: University of California Press, 1970.

   'La lutte pour l'individualisme agraire dans la France du XVIIIe siècle.' *Annales d'Histoire économique et sociale*, II (1930), 329—83, 511—56.

Bombédiac, Christian, 'Les quarante français du Pays Quint.' *Sud-Ouest* (16 July 1967), p. 11.

Bordes, Maurice, 'Les anciennes céréales et les origines de la culture du maïs en Gascogne.' *Séances de l'Association Marc Bloch de Toulouse.* 1951—2 and 1953, pp. 6—9.

Bourde, André J. *Agronomie et agronomes en France au XVIIIe siècle.* 'Les Hommes et la terre', XIII. 3 vols. Paris: École pratique des hautes études VIe section, Centre de recherches historiques, 1967.

Brunet, Roger. 'L'équipement électrique des Pyrénées.' *RGPSO* XXXIII (1962), 123–28.

Burghardt, Andrew F. *Borderland: a historical and geographical study of Burgenland, Austria.* Madison: University of Wisconsin Press, 1962.

Butzer, Karl W. *Environment and archaeology: an introduction to Pleistocene geography.* Chicago: Aldine, 1964.

El camino de Santiago a través de Navarra. Pamplona: Diputación foral de Navarra, 1954.

Camena d'Almeïda, P. *Les Pyrénées; développement de la connaissance géographique de la chaine.* Paris: Colin, 1893.

Caput, Jean. 'Les anciennes coutumes agraires dans la vallée du Gave d'Oloron.' *Bulletin de la Société des sciences, lettres, et arts de Pau*, 3e série, XVII (1954), 62–70.

'La formation des paysages agraires béarnais, observations et problèmes.' *RGPSO* XXVII (1956), 219–42.

Caro Baroja, Julio. 'Dos notas descriptivas: La agricultura en Vera de Bidasoa y caza de palomas en Echalar.' *Eusko-Jakintza*, V (1951), 107–19.

Vasconiana, de historia y etnología. Madrid: Minotauro, 1957.

Los vascos. 2nd ed. Madrid: Minotauro, 1958.

La Vida rural en Vera de Bidasoa. 'Biblioteca de Tradiciones Populares.' Madrid: Consejo Superior de Investigaciones Científicas, Instituto Antonio de Nebrija, 1944.

Carporezen, Claudine. *Les biens d'équipement des Basses-Pyrénées.* Unpublished Mémoire, Diplôme d'études supérieurs de géographie; Université de Bordeaux, 1965.

Le tourisme hivernal dans les Pyrénées occidentales. Unpublished Mémoire, Diplôme d'études supérieurs de géographie; Université de Bordeaux, 1965.

Carr, Raymond. *Spain 1808–1939.* Oxford: Clarendon Press, 1966.

Carreras y Candí (ed.) *Geografía general del Pais Vasco–Navarro.* 6 vols. Barcelona: Alberto Martín, 1921.

'Carte géométrique de la France au 1/86.400, dite de l'Académie ou de Cassini.' Sheets 108, 139, 140.

Casas Torres, José Manuel. *Originalidad geográfica de Navarra.* Pamplona: Diputación foral de Navarra, 1956.

and Abascal, A. *Mercados geográficos y ferias de Navarra.* Saragossa: Estación de Estudios Pirenaicos & Institución Príncipe de Viana, 1948.

Caujolle, A. 'Gourette; Station pyrénéenne de sports d'hiver.' *RGPSO* XXXIX (1968), 457–60.

Cavaillès, Henri. 'Les chemins de la vallée d'Aure.' *Bulletin pyrénéen* no. 215 (1935), pp. 6–16.

'Une fédération pyrénéenne sous l'ancien régime—les traités de lies et de passeries.' *Revue historique*, CV (1910), 1–34, 241–76.

'La houille blanche dans les Pyrénées françaises.' *Annales de Géographie*, XXVIII (1919), 425–68.

La Route française: son histoire, sa fonction: étude de géographie humaine. Paris: A. Colin, 1946.

'La transhumance dans les Basses-Pyrénées.' *RGPSO* IV (1933), 490–8.

La Transhumance pyrénéenne et la circulation des troupeaux dans les plaines de Gascogne. Paris: A. Colin, 1931.

La Vie pastorale et agricole dans les Pyrénées, des Gaves, de l'Adour et des Nestes: étude de géographie humaine. Paris: A. Colin, 1931.

'Note sur les syndicats de communes dans les vallées pyrénéennes.' In: Congrès des Sociétés Savantes de 1908, *Bulletin de la Section des Sciences économiques et sociales*, an 1908, pp. 193–201.

Cazes, Georges. 'Nouveaux aspects du tourisme d'hiver dans les Pyrénées.' *RGPSO* XXXVIII (1967), 69—78.

   Le Tourisme à Luchon et dans le Luchonnais. Toulouse: Institut de Géographie de la Faculté des Lettres et Sciences Humaines, 1964.

Cénac-Moncaut, Justin Edouard Mathieu. *Histoire des peuples et des États Pyrénéens (France et Espagne) depuis l'époque celtibérienne jusqu'à nos jours*. 2nd ed. 5 vols. Paris: Amyot, 1860.

Centre d'Expansion Bordeaux Sud-Ouest. 'Inventaire démographique du Sud-Ouest.' *Revue juridique et economique du Sud-Ouest*. Série économique, V (1956), 213—68.

Chadefaud, Michel. 'Une formule originale de tourisme social: les gîtes ruraux.' *RGPSO* XXXIX (1968), 273—97.

   and Dalla Rosa, Gilbert. 'L'aménagement d'une moyenne montagne forestière: Iraty.' *RGPSO* XLIV (1973), 5—27.

   and Dalla-Rosa, Gilbert. 'Le parc national des Pyrénées occidentales.' *RGPSO* XXXIX (1968), 397—409.

Chambre de commerce et d'industrie de Pau. 'Rapport sur la situation économique et perspectives d'avenir (Janvier, 1968).'

Chambre départementale d'agriculture des Basses-Pyrénées. *Enquête montagne*. 2 vols. (mimeographed). Pau: Chambre départementale d'agriculture des Basses-Pyrénées, 1965.

Chevalier, Michel. 'Le Jura, montagne frontière.' *RGPSO* XXXI (1960), 425—35.

   'Note sur les usurpations de terre en Couserans au milieu du XIXe siècle.' *Annales du Midi*, LXI (1949), 325—9.

   La Vie humaine dans les Pyrénées ariégeoises. Paris: Genin, 1956.

Chisholm, Michael. *Rural settlement and land use*. London: Hutchinson, 1962.

Clark, Sir George. *The seventeenth century*. 2nd ed. New York: Oxford University Press, 1961.

Clark, J. G. D. 'Farmers and forests in Neolithic Europe.' *Antiquity*, XIX (1945), 57—71.

   Prehistoric Europe: the economic basis. London: Methuen, 1952.

Coincy, H. de. *Louis de Froidour en Pays basque*. Bayonne: Imprimerie du Courrier, 1929.

   and Roux, G. 'Les reboisements en Pays basque espagnol.' *Revue des Eaux et Forêts*, LXV (1927), 167—177.

Colas, L. *L'Habitation basque*. Paris: Massin, 1925.

Compañia Telefonica Nacional de España. *Guía telefonica: Pamplona y Provincia de Navarra, Julio 1968*.

Compte Freixanet, Alberto. 'El Alto Ampurdán.' *Pirineos*. XIX—XX (1963—4), 5—283.

Coppolani, Jean. 'Les capitales régionales des Pyrénées françaises.' *Pirineos*, X (1954), 493—513.

Cordero Torres, José María. *Fronteras hispanicas: geografía e historia, diplomacia y administración*. Madrid: Instituto de Estudios Politicos, 1960.

Crouzet, F. 'Les origines du sous-développement économique du Sud-Ouest.' *Annales du Midi*, LXXI (1959), 71—9.

Cuzacq, Pierre. 'Introduction du maïs dans les Basses-Pyrénées et les Landes.' *Bulletin de la Société des sciences et lettres de Bayonne* (1902), 193—206.

Cuzacq, René. 'Origine de la culture du maïs en Gascogne.' *Bulletin de la Société archéologique, historique, littéraire, et scientifique du Gers*, (1952), 79—97 and 246—60.

Dalla Rosa, Gilbert. *Documents pour un livre blanc des Pyrénées—Pyrénées atlantiques, 1972*. 2 vols., text and atlas. Pau: Direction départementale de l'agriculture des Pyrénées-atlantiques, 1972.

   'Les migrations des montagnards basco-béarnais en France.' *RGPSO* XLI (1970), 43—52.

Daranatz, J.-B. 'La chapelle de Saint Sauveur ou de Charlemagne, à Ibañeta.' *Bulletin du Musée Basque*, I—II (1935), 149—60.

Darby, H. Clifford. 'The clearing of the woodland in Europe.' in *Man's role in changing the face of the earth*. Edited by W. L. Thomas. Chicago: University of Chicago Press, 1956.

Daumas, Max. 'L'équipement hydroélectrique des Pyrénées espagnoles.' *RGPSO* XXXIII (1962), 73–106.

Daveau, Suzanne. *Les Régions frontalières de la montagne jurassienne; étude de géographie humaine*. 'Mémoires et Documents', no. 14. Lyon: Institut des études rhodaniennes de l'Université de Lyon, 1959.

Deffontaines, Pierre. 'Parallèle entre les économies de l'Ampourdán et du Roussillon: le rôle d'une frontière.' *RGPSO* XXXVIII (1967), 243–58.

'Participation des Pyrénées au peuplement des pays de la Plata.' *Actas*, I CIEP, V. 269–77.

Defourneaux, Marcelin. *Pablo de Olavide ou l'Afrancesado (1725–1803)*. Paris: Presses Universitaires de France, 1959.

Dejean, P. 'Un centre de vie montagnarde dans la Vallée d'Aspe: Le plateau de Lhers.' *RGPSO* III (1932), 466–88.

Dendaletche, Claude. 'Le peuplement végétal des montagnes entre les pics d'Anie et d'Orhy (Pyrénées occidentales): notes écologiques, floristiques et phytocénotiques.' *Pirineos*, CV (1972), 11–26.

Descheemaeker, Jacques. 'La Bidassoa et l'Île de la Conférence.' *Eusko-Jakintza*, II (1948), 649–80.

'Le droit public actuel des faceries pyrénéennes.' *Actes du soixante-dix-septième-congrès des Sociétés savantes* (Grenoble, 1952), 591–9.

'Les faceries pyrénéennes et du Pays Basque.' *Eusko-Jakintza*, I (1947), 355–93.

'La frontière dans les Pyrénées basques (organisation, antiquité, fédéralisme).' *Eusko-Jakintza* IV (1950), 127–78.

'La frontière du Labourd et les enclaves du Baztan.' *Eusko-Jakintza*, II (1948), 265–83.

'Une frontière féodale au XXe siècle.' *Pyrénées*, no. 12 (1952), pp. 289–97.

'Une frontière inconnue: Les Pyrénées de l'océan à l'Aragon.' *Revue générale de droit international public*, 3e série, vol. XVI (XLIX, vol. II) (1941–5), 239–77.

'La Frontière pyrénéenne de l'Océan à l'Aragon.' 2 vols. (Unpublished) Thèse (droit). Université de Paris, 1945.

'La frontière pyrénéenne entre le Bidasoa et Itxassou.' *Actes du soixante-dix-septième congrès des Sociétés savantes* (Grenoble, 1952). *Bulletin de la Section de Géographie*, LXV (1952), 43–50.

'La question d'Ondarrolle.' *Eusko-Jakintza*, III (1949), 237–61.

'Le statut du Pays-Quint.' *Eusko-Jakintza*, I (1947), 213–29.

'Une survivance de la juridiction du diocèse de Bayonne sur le nord de l'Espagne.' *Eusko-Jakintza*, III (1949), 262–6.

'Le tribut de la vallée de Barétous.' *Eusko-Jakintza*, III (1949), 399–428.

Detton, Hervé. *L'Administration régionale et locale de la France*. Paris: Presses Universitaires de France, 1964.

Dion, Roger. *Les frontières de la France*. Paris: Hachette, 1947.

Douence, A. 'L'élevage ovin dans les Basses-Pyrénées.' *L'Union ovine*, X (1938), 124–27.

Douglass, William A. *Death in Murélaga: funerary ritual in a Spanish Basque village*. American Ethnological Society, Monograph 49. Seattle: University of Washington Press, 1969.

'Opportunity, choice-making, and rural depopulation in two Spanish Basque villages.' Ph.D. dissertation. University of Chicago, 1967.

Dralet, M. *Déscription des Pyrénées, considérées spécialement sous les rapports de la géologie, de l'économie politique, rurale et forestière, de l'industrie et du commerce . . .* 2 vols. Paris: Arthus Bertrand, 1813.

Dravasa, E. *Les privilèges des Basques du Labourd sous l'Ancien Régime.* Unpublished Thèse de Droit; Université de Bordeaux, 1950.

Druène, Bernard. 'Les lies et passeries, spécialement pendant la Guerre de Succession d'Espagne.' *Actes,* II CIEP, VII. 5—37.

Dubosq, F.; P. Chimits; H. Gout. 'Une zone témoin en vallée de montagne pyrénéenne: La zone-témoin de la vallée de Baïgorry (Basses-Pyrénées).' *Bulletin de la Fédération française d'économie montagnarde,* Nouvelle série, No. 11, 1960—1, pp. 567—76.

Duby, Georges. *L'économie rurale et la vie des campagnes dans l'Occident médiéval.* 2 vols. Paris: Aubier, Ed. Montaigne, 1962.

Duhourcau, Bernard. 'Sur les chemins de Saint-Jacques de St. Palais à Roncevaux.' *Sanctuaires et Pèlerinages,* X (1964), offprint.

Duloum, Joseph. *Les Anglais dans les Pyrénées et les débuts du tourisme pyrénéen (1739—1896).* Lourdes: Les amis du Musée pyrénéen, 1970.

Dumège, Alexandre. *Statistique générale des départements pyrénéens . . .* 2 vols. Paris: Treuttel et Wurtz, 1828—9.

Dumont, Arsène. 'Natalité des Basques de Baïgorry.' *21e session de l'Association française pour l'avancement des sciences* (Pau, 1892), II. 597—612.

Dumont, Jean, Baron de Carels Croon. *Corps universel diplomatique du droit des gens ou recueil des traitez d'alliance, de paix, de trêve . . . qui ont été faits en Europe depuis le règne de l'Empereur Charlemagne jusqu'à présent.* 8 vols. Amsterdam: P. Brunel, R. et G. Wetstein, etc., etc., 1726—31.

Dupont, P. 'Herborisation aux confins basco-béarnais.' *Actes,* II CIEP, III. 23—43.

Enjalabert, Henri. 'Le commerce de Bordeaux et la vie économique dans le bas Aquitain au XVII siècle.' *Annales du Midi,* LXII (1950), 21—35.

Espesset, M. 'L'exploitation des forêts des Basses-Pyrénées.' *Annales de la Fédération pyrénéenne d'économie montagnarde,* XI (1944—5), 158—71.

Espinasse, Gisèle. 'Le rayonnement d'une industrie agricole locale: le Roquefort.' *RGPSO* II (1931), 377—430.

Estornes Lasa, Mariano. *Oro del Ezka,* San Sebastian: Auñamendi, 1958.

Etcheverry, Louis. 'L'émigration des Basques en Amérique.' *La Réforme sociale,* 2ème série, I (1886), 491—515.

Etcheverry, Louis. 'L'émigration des Basses-Pyrénées pendant 60 ans.' *Mémoire, 21ème session de l'Association française pour l'avancement des sciences* (Pau, 1892), pt. I, pp. 363—4; and pt. II, pp. 1092—1104.

Etcheverry, Michel. 'Une page d'histoire frontalière.' *Eusko-Jakintza,* II (1948), 633—47.

Etcheverry-Aïnchart, Jean. 'Les Aldudes autrefois', in *Traditions des Aldudes.* Bayonne: Gure Herria, n.d. but *c.* 1964.

   'Une vallée de Navarre au XVIIIe siècle, Baïgorry; II—Les gens.' *Eusko-Jakintza,* II (1948), 65—95.

   'Une vallée de Navarre au XVIIIe siècle, Baïgorry; III—Les institutions.' *Eusko-Jakintza,* II (1948), 209—28.

Eyre, S. R. *Vegetation and soils; a world picture.* Chicago: Aldine, 1963.

Fairén Guillén, Victor. 'Contribución al estudio de la facería internacional de los valles de Roncal y Barétous.' *Principe de Viana,* VII (1946), 4—28.

   Facerías internacionales pirenaicas. Madrid: Instituto de Estudios Políticos, 1956.

   'Notas sobre la actualidad de las facerías internacionales pirenaicas.' *Actes,* II CIEP, VI. 215—45.

   'Las facerías quinquenales internacionales del Valle de Baztán.' *Pirineos,* XII (1956), 113—58.

   'Notas para el estudio de las facerías internacionales pirenaicas.' *Pirineos,* XVII—XVIII (1961—2), 145—64.

'Sobre las facerías internacionales de Navarra.' *Principe de Viana*, XVI (1955), 507—24.

Faucher, Daniel. 'Le bocage pyrénéen.' *RGPSO* II (1931), 362—5.

'L'agriculture des Pyrénées françaises. Caractères généraux.' *RGPSO* XI (1940), 39—54.

'Les Pyrénées: aperçu géographique.' *RGPSO* XIV (1943), 204—36.

and Cavaillès, Henri. 'Lefebvre, Th., "Les modes de vie dans les Pyrénées atlantiques orientales".' *RGPSO* V (1934), 337—48.

Ferrer, Manuel. 'La industria navarra.' *Actas*, V CIEP, III. 121—36.

Fleury, Michel, and Valmary, Pierre. 'Les progrès de l'instruction élémentaire de Louis XIV à Napoléon III, d'après l'enquête de Louis Maggiolo (1877—1879).' *Population*, XII (1957), 71—92.

Floristán Samanes, Alfredo. 'Los communes en Navarra.' *Actes*, IV CIEP, IV. 74—86.

'La desamortización de bienes pertenecientes a corporaciones civiles y al estado en Navarra', in *Homenaje al Excmo. Señor Don Amando Melon y Ruiz de Gordejuela*. Saragossa: Instituto de Estudios Pirenaicos, 1966.

'Juntas y mestas ganaderas en las Bardenas de Navarra.' *Actas*, I CIEP, V. 111—30.

'Las transformaciones modernas de la agricultura navarra', in *Aportación española al XXI Congreso geográfico internacional*. Madrid: Consejo superior de investigaciones científicas, 1969, pp. 89—110.

and Torres Luna, María Pilar de. 'Distribución geográfica de las facerías navarras.' *Miscelanea ofrecida al Ilmo. Sr. D. José María Lacarra y de Miguel*. Saragossa: Universidad de Zaragoza, 1968.

and Torres Luna, María Pilar de. 'Influencias pastoriles en el paisaje rural del valle de Baztán.' *Pirineos*, vol. XXVI, no. 95 (1970), pp. 5—46.

Ford, Richard. *A Handbook for Travellers in Spain*. 2nd ed. London: John Murray, 1847.

Fornier, Emile. 'Le déneigement des cols pyrénéens.' *RGPSO* XXXVIII (1967), 309—24.

'Les passages frontaliers en Cerdagne et Haute-Ariège.' *RGPSO* XL (1969), 225—42.

Fourcassié, Jean. 'Comment on voyageait aux Pyrénées à l'époque romantique.' Pau: 1936 (extrait du *Bulletin pyrénéen*, 1936).

'Luxe et misère aux Pyrénées, il y a cent ans.' *Annales de la Fédération pyrénéenne d'économie montagnarde*, XI (1944—1945), 42—5.

Foursans-Bourdette, Marie-Pierrette. *Économie et finances en Béarn au XVIIIᵉ siècle*. Collection de l'Institut d'economie régionale du Sud-Ouest, VII: 'Études d'économie basco-béarnaise', t. V. Bordeaux: Ed. Bière, 1963.

France. Institut national de la statistique et des études économiques. *Résultats statistiques du recensement général de la population effectué le 10 mars 1946; population légale.—état civil et activité professionnelle de la population présente—familles—immeubles—ménages et logements: Département des Basses-Pyrénées*. Paris: Imprimerie nationale, 1951.

Recensement général de la population de mai 1954; résultats statistiques: population-ménages—logements maisons: Département des Basses-Pyrénées. Paris: Imprimerie nationale, 1959.

Recensement de 1962. Population légale et statistiques communales complémentaires: Basses-Pyrénées. Paris: Direction des Journaux Officiels, 1963.

Recensement général de la population de 1962; Résultats du dépouillement exhaustif; population—ménages—logements—immeubles. Basses-Pyrénées. Paris: Imprimerie nationale, 1966.

Recensement général de la population de 1962: Basses-Pyrénées; resultats du dépouillement exhaustif: population par région agricole.

Recensement de 1968. Population du département des Basses-Pyrénées; arrondissements, cantons, et communes. Paris: Direction des Journaux officiels, 1968.

France. Institut national de la statistique et des études économiques. Direction régionale de Bordeaux. *Population par commune de 1876 à 1954. Département des Basses-Pyrénées.* (Mimeographed) Bordeaux: I.N.S.E.E., n.d.

    Nomenclature des écarts et lieux-dits des Basses-Pyrénées, 2 vols: I. Liste alphabétique départementale avec indication de la commune. II. Listes des écarts dans chaque commune et renseignements statistiques. (Mimeographed) Bordeaux: I.N.S.E.E., 1958.

France. Ministère de l'Agriculture. *Statistique agricole de la France, annexe à l'enquête de 1929; Monographie agricole du département des Basses-Pyrénées.* Pau: Imp. 'L'Indépendant', 1937.

    Monographies agricoles départementales—64—Les Basses-Pyrénées. Paris: La Documentation française, 1961.

France. Ministère des Postes et Télécommunications. *Annuaire officiel des abonnés au téléphone: Basses-Pyrénées, 7 mars 1968.*

France. Ministère des travaux publics, de l'agriculture et du commerce. Direction générale des ponts et chaussées et des mines. *Recueil de documents statistiques.* Paris: Imprimerie Royale, 1837.

Frazer, Sir James George. *The new golden bough.* Abridged edn. by Theodore H. Gaster. Garden City, New York: Doubleday, 1961.

Gachitéguy, Adrien. *Les Basques dans l'ouest américain.* Bordeaux: Éditions Ezkila, 1955.

Gaussen, Henri. 'Les châtaigniers japonais au Pays basque et dans le Sud-Ouest pyrénéen.' *Travaux du Laboratoire forestier de Toulouse,* t. I, vol. IV, art. XIII (1946).

    'Les châtaigniers japonais au Sud-Ouest pyrénéen.' *Travaux du Laboratoire forestier de Toulouse,* t. I, art. XVI (1932).

    'Les forêts de la vallée d'Aspe.' *RGPSO* III (1932), 5—17.

    'Les forêts du Pays basque.' *Travaux du Laboratoire forestier de Toulouse,* t. III, vol. I, art. XVI (1941).

Guadinos, L. 'L'industrie familiale du lin et du chanvre.' *Annales de la Fédération pyrénéenne d'économie montagnarde,* IX (1940—1), 100—16.

George, Pierre. 'Structure agraire et problèmes démographiques dans la vallée d'Aspe (Basses-Pyrénées).' France. Institut National d'Études Démographiques. *Travaux et documents.* Cahier no. 8: 'Dépeuplement rural et peuplement rationnel'. Paris: 1949, pp. 91—100.

Germán, P. 'El camino de peregrinación jacobea Bayona—Urdax—Velate—Pamplona.' *Principe de Viana,* XXV (1964), 213—33.

Giesey, Ralph E. *'If not, not'; the oath of the Aragonese and the legendary laws of Sobrarbe.* Princeton: Princeton University Press, 1968.

Gilfillan, S. O. 'European Political Boundaries.' *Political Science Quarterly,* XXXIX (1924), 458—84.

Girard, Albert. 'L'émigration espagnole.' *Annales de Géographie,* XXI (1912), 418—25.

Gómez-Chaparro, Rafael. *La Desamortización civil en Navarra.* 'Collección historica de la Universidad de Navarra, XIX.' Pamplona: Ediciones Universidad de Navarra, 1967.

Gómez-Ibáñez, Daniel. 'The rise and decline of transhumance in the United States.' M.A. thesis, University of Wisconsin, 1967.

Gómez de Llarena, Joaquín. 'La magnesita sedimentaria de los Pirineos Navarros.' *Actas,* I CIEP, II, 381—95.

Goron, Lucien. 'Les migrations saisonnières dans les départements pyrénéens au début du XIXe siècle.' *RGPSO* IV (1933), 230—72.

Great Britain, Air Ministry, Meteorological Office. *Tables of temperature, relative, humidity and precipitation for the world, Part III, Europe and the Atlantic Ocean North of 35°N.* M.O. 617c. London: Her Majesty's Stationery Office, 1958.

Guilera, Josep Maria. *Unitat històrica del Pirineu.* Barcelona: Aedos, 1964.

Guitard, Monique. 'Les forêts d'Aspe et d'Ossau.' Diplôme d'études supérieurs de géographie. Université de Bordeaux, Faculté des Lettres, 1954.

Hartshorne, Richard. 'Geographic and political boundaries in upper Silesia.' *Annals of the Association of American Geographers*, XXIII (1933), 195–228.

Herrmann, Albert. 'Das Land der Basken. Eine historisch-geographische Studie.' *Zeitschrift der Gesellschaft für Erdkunde zu Berlin*, 1944, pp. 20–35.

Higounet, Charles. 'L'habitat rural dans les Basses-Pyrénées.' *Bulletin Pyrénéen*, no. 215 (1935), pp. 17–21.

'Un mapa de las relaciones monasticas transpirenaicas en la Edad Media.' *Pirineos*, VII (1951), 543–53.

'Esquisse d'une géographie des châteaux des Pyrénées françaises au Moyen âge.' *Actas*, I CIEP, VI, 9–20.

Hourcade, Bernard. 'La transhumance hivernale du bétail du Haut-Ossau.' *RGPSO* XL (1969), 253–65.

La vie rurale en Haut-Ossau (Pyrénées Atlantiques). Pau: Société des Sciences Lettres & Arts de Pau, 1970.

House, J. W. 'The Franco–Italian boundary in the Alpes Maritimes.' *Transactions and papers of the Institute of British Geographers*, XXVI (1959), 107–31.

Idoate, Florencio. 'La comunidad del valle de Roncal.' *Actas*, V CIEP, III. 141–6.

'Notas para el estudio de la economia Navarra y su contribución a la Real Hacienda (1500–1650).' *Principe de Viana*, nos. 78–81 (1960), pp. 77–129, 275–318.

'Poblados y despoblados o desolados en Navarra (en 1534 y 1800).' *Principe de Viana*, nos. 108–9 (1967), pp. 309–38.

Isaac, Erich. 'On the domestication of cattle.' *Science*, CXXXVII (1962), 195–204.

Jaulerry, Gérard. *L'Électrification de la region pyrénéenne*. Paris: Girard, 1933.

Jimenez-Castillo, Margarita. *La población de Navarra; estudio geográfico*. Saragossa: Consejo superior de investigaciones científicas, 1958.

Joanne, Adolphe Laurent. *Itinéraire descriptif et historique des Pyrénées de l'Océan à la Méditerranée*. 1st ed. Paris: Hachette, 1858.

Jonasson, Olof. 'The agricultural regions of Europe.' *Economic Geography*, I (1925), 277–314.

Jones, Stephen B. 'Boundary concepts in the setting of place and time'. *Annals of the Association of American Geographers*, XLIX (1959), 241–55.

Jorré, Georges. 'L'aménagement hydroélectrique des lacs pyrénéens français.' *RGPSO* V (1934), 5–28.

Jovet, P. 'Influence de l'écobuage sur la flore des pâturages basques.' *Annales de la Fédération pyrénéenne d'économie montagnarde*, XVIII (1952), 23–94.

Juste, C., and Dutil, P. Les sols d'altitude du Pays Basque. *Bulletin de la Fédération française d'économie montagnarde*, nouvelle série, no. 17 (1966–7), 355–64.

Kristof, Ladis K. D. 'The nature of frontiers and boundaries.' *Annals of the Association of American Geographers*, XLIX (1959), 269–82.

Krüger, Fritz. *Die Hochpyrenäen. A. Landschaften, Haus und Hof; Band I*. Hansische Universität Hamburg: Abhandlungen aus dem Gebiet der Auslandskunde, Band 44 (1936) and Band 47 (1939). (Reihe B. Völkerkunde, Kulturgeschichte und Sprachen; Band 23 and Band 26.) Hamburg: Friederichsen, de Gruyter, and Co. m.b.H., 1936 and 1939.

'Die Hochpyrenäen. B. Hirtenkultur.' *Volkstum und Kultur der Romanen; Sprache, Dichtung, Sitte* [Hamburg], VIII (1935), 1–103.

'Die Hochpyrenäen. C. Ländliche Arbeit, Band I: Transport und Transportgeräte.' *Butlletí de dialectologia catalana* [Barcelona], XXIII (1935), 39–240.

Die Hochpyrenäen. C. Ländliche Arbeit, Band II: Getreide, Heuernte, Bienenwohnung, Wein- und Ölbereitung. (Hamburger Studien zu Volkstum und Kultur der Romanen;

Herausgegeben vom Seminar für romanische Sprachen und Kultur. No. 32.) Hamburg: Hansischer Gildenverlag, 1939.

'Die Hochpyrenäen. D. Hausindustrie, Tracht und Gewerbe.' *Volkstum und Kultur der Romanen; Sprache, Dichtung, Sitte* [Hamburg], VIII (1935), 210–328; IX (1936), 1–106.

'Sach- und Wortkundliches vom Wasser in den Pyrenäen.' *Volkstum und Kultur der Romanen; Sprache, Dichtung, Sitte* [Hamburg], II (1929–30), 139–243.

Laborde, Pierre. 'Les travailleurs frontaliers sur la Côte basque française.' *RGPSO* XL (1969), 243–52.

Structure agraire et économie rurale du bassin de St. Jean Pied-de-Port. Unpublished Mémoire, Diplôme d'études supérieures de géographie; Université de Bordeaux, 1960.

Lacarra, José María. 'À propos de la colonisation 'franca' en Navarre et Aragon.' *Annales du Midi*, LVX (1953), 331–42.

'Notas para la formación de las familias de fueros de Navarra.' *Anuario de historia del derecho español*, X (1933), 203–72.

'Rutas de peregrinación: Los pasos del Pirineo y el camino de Santa Cristina a Puente la Reina.' *Pirineos*, I (1945), 5–27.

Lacasa Lacasa, Juan. 'Electricidad pirenaica.' *Actes*, IV CIEP, IV, 156–68.

Lamare, Pierre,. 'Introduction et aperçus: Pays basque français et espagnol', in *Pays basque français et espagnol*, 'Les Guides Bleus illustrés.' Paris: Hachette, 1963, 47–112.

'Milieu physique et condition humaine en Pays basque.' *Munibe*, VI (1954), 70–81.

'La structure physique du Pays basque (quatrième article).' *Eusko-Jakintza*, V (1951), 165–75.

'Sur la toponymie dans les cartes géographiques.' *Eusko-Jakintza*, III (1949), 450-5.

Lambert, Elié. 'Le livre de Saint Jacques et les routes du pélerinage de Compostelle.' *RGPSO* XIV (1943), 5–34.

'Le pélerinage de Compostelle et le pays basque français.' *Pirineos*, XI (1955), 135–47.

'Les relations entre la France et l'Espagne par les routes des Pyrénées occidentales au Moyen âge.' In: *France méridionale et pays ibériques: Mélanges géographiques offertes en hommage à M. Daniel Faucher* (Toulouse: Ed. toulousaines de l'Ingénieur, 1948), vol. I, pp. 319–28.

'Les routes des Pyrénées atlantiques et leur emploi au cours des âges.' *Actas*, I CIEP, VI. 121–64.

Larramendi, M. *Corografía o descripción general de la muy noble y muy leal provincia de Guipúzcoa.* Barcelona: 1882.

Lassalle, Robert. 'Les maïs hybrides dans les Basses Pyrénées.' *RGPSO*, XXV (1954), 78–80.

Lautensach, Hermann. *Geografía de España y Portugal.* Barcelona: Vicens-Vives, 1967.

Laxalt, Robert. *Sweet promised land.* New York: Harper, 1957.

Lefebvre, Théodore. *Les Modes de vie dans les Pyrénées atlantiques orientales.* Paris: A. Colin, 1933.

'La transhumance dans les Basses-Pyrénées.' *Annales de Géographie*, XXXVII (1928), 35–60.

Le Gall, André. 'Les types de temps du Sud-Ouest de la France.' *Annales de Géographie*, XLII (1933), 19–43.

Léon, Antoine. *Histoire de l'enseignement en France.* Paris: Presses Universitaires de France, 1967.

Lerat, Serge. 'L'économie des Pyrénées basques et béarnaises.' *RGPSO* XXXIX (1968), 435–57.

'L'introduction du maïs hybride dans les pays de l'Adour.' *RGPSO* XXXII (1961), 97–117.

Leremboure, Michel. 'La chasse à la palombe au Pays basque.' *Eusko-Jakintza*, IV (1950), 215–18.

Le Roy Ladurie, Emmanuel. *Times of feast, times of famine; a history of climate since the year 1000*. Garden City, New York: Doubleday, 1971.

Loubergé, Jean. 'L'industrie du marbre dans les Pyrénées occidentales.' *RGPSO* XXXIX (1968), 411—28.

Lowenthal, David, and Comitas, Lambros. 'Emigration and depopulation: some neglected aspects of population geography.' *Geographical Review*, LII (1962), 195—210.

Loze, Axel. *Déforestation et reboisement dans la région pyrénéenne*. Paris: Lib. Recueil Sirey, 1910.

Lucas Alvarez, Manuel, and Miralbés, María Rosario. 'Una carta de paz entre los valles de Tena y Ossau (1646).' *Pirineos*, VIII (1952), 253—95.

Madariaga, Salvador de. *Spain*. New York: Scribner's, 1930.

Madoz, Pascual. *Diccionario geográfico—estadístico—histórico de España y sus posesiones de ultramar*. 16 vols. Madrid: Imprenta del Diccionario . . . de Madoz, 1848—50.

Martín Duque, Angel J. *La comunidad del valle de Salazar; origenes y evolución histórica*. Pamplona: Junta general del Valle de Salazar, 1963.

Martín Galindo, José Luis. 'El caserío vasco como tipo de explotación agraria.' *Estudios geográficos*, XXIX (1968), 205—44.

Menendez Pidal, Gonzalo. *Los caminos en la historia de España*. Madrid: Ediciones Cultura Hispánica, 1951.

Mensua Fernández, Salvador, and Soláns Castro, Manuela. 'El mapa de utilización del suelo de Navarra.' *Geographica*, XII (Enero—Diciembre, 1965), 9—15.

Michelin et Cie. *Carte Michelin de la France*. 1:200,000, no. 85: St. Sébastien—Tarbes, edition of *c*. 1925.

Carte au 200,000ème. no. 85: Biarritz—Luchon, edition of 1970.

Minghi, Julian V. 'Boundary Studies in Political Geography; review article'. *Annals of the Association of American Geographers*, LIII (1963), 407—28.

Moodie, Arthur E. *The Italo—Yugoslav Boundary; a study in political geography*. London: G. Philip, 1945.

Moreau, Maurice. 'Les forêts béarnaises au XVIIIe siècle.' *Pyrénées*, no. 7 (juillet-sept., 1951), pp. 9—13.

'L'habitat rural dans la vallée d'Ossau.' *Bulletin Pyrénéen*, no. 241 (1946—7), 30—42.

Morineau, Michel. 'Y a-t-il eu une révolution agricole en France au XVIIIe siècle? ' *Revue historique*, CCXXXIX (1968), 299—326.

Muthuon, J. M. 'Rapport sur les forges du pays conquis en Espagne, dans les Pyrénées occidentales.' *Journal des Mines*, no. XI (Thermidor, an. III [1795]), 1—18.

Nadal, Jorge. *La población española (siglos XVI a XX)*. Barcelona: Ariel, 1966.

Nagore, Daniel. 'Geografía botánica de Navarra.' *Estudios geográficos*, VI (1945), 241—59.

Navarre. Diputación foral. *Las cañadas en Navarra*. Pamplona: Diputación foral de Navarra, 1936.

Provincia de Navarra [map]. 1:200,000 (año 1962).

Navarre. Diputación foral. Dirección de industria. *Catálogo de la industria de Navarra*. Pamplona: Diputación foral, 1968.

Programa de promoción industrial de Navarra (texto refundido) año 1966. Pamplona: Diputación foral, 1966.

Navarre. Diputación foral. Servicio de caminos. *Mapa de Navarra*. 1:200,000. Formado por el Teniente Coronel del Cuerpo de Estado Mayor D. Frederico Montaner Canét (año 1926).

Navarro Gonzalez, Victoriano. 'El turismo, nuevo aspecto de la economia pirenaica.' *Actes*, IV CIEP, IV, 169—78.

Olphe-Gaillard, G. 'Le paysan basque du Labourd à travers les âges.' *La Science sociale*, 20ᵉ année; 2ᵉ période, fascicule 17 (sept., 1905), 433–532.

Orwin, C. S., and Orwin, C. S. *The open fields*. 2nd ed. Oxford: Clarendon Press, 1954.

Ospital, A., and Eppherre, G. 'Les Aldudes, un fleuron du Pays basque', in *Traditions des Aldudes*. Bayonne: Gure Herria, n.d. but *c.* 1964.

Palassou, Pierre Bernard. *Mémoires pour servir à l'histoire naturelle des Pyrénées, et des pays adjacentes*. Pau: Imp. de Vignancour, 1815.

Paquereau, Marie-Madeleine. 'Étude palynologique de la tourbière d'Ogeu (Basses-Pyrénées).' *Actes*, IV CIEP, I. 99–103.

    and Barrère, Pierre. 'Palynologie et morphologie quaternaires dans les environs d'Arudy.' *Actes* IV CIEP, IV. 18–25.

Parrot, Aimé G. 'L'incinération des landes au Pays basque français.' *Bulletin de la Société des sciences, lettres, et arts de Bayonne*, no. 66 (jan., 1954), pp. 1–11.

    'Le paysage forestier au Pays basque français.' *Eusko-Jakintza*, VI (1952), 85–100.

Payne, Stanley. *Franco's Spain*. New York: Crowell, 1967.

Perpillou, Aimé Vincent. 'L'évolution de l'utilisation du sol par l'agriculture dans huit départements du Midi de la France.' (France. Centre National de la Recherche Scientifique, Centre de documentation cartographique et géographique) *Mémoires et Documents*, VII (1960), 119–34.

Pinède, Christiane. 'L'émigration dans le Sud-Ouest vers le milieu du XIXᵉ siècle.' *Annales du Midi*, LXIX (1957), 237–51.

    'Une tentative d'émigration pyrénéenne organisée en République Argentine.' *RGPSO* XXVIII (1957), 245–74.

Pitrau, Jean. 'Le paysan montagnard; sa vie et son destin.' *L'information agricole* (Edition du Loir-et-Cher) No. 354; 2ᵉ No. d'avril, 1966, pp. 5–8.

Plandé, R. 'La formation politique de la frontière des Pyrénées.' *RGPSO* IX (1938), 221–42.

    'L'utilisation industrielle de la vallée d'Aspe (Pyrénées occidentales).' *Revue de géographie alpine*, XVII (1929), 41–54.

    'La vallée d'Aspe.' *Revue de géographie commerciale*, XLVIII (1923), 73–118.

Planté, Adrien. 'De l'émigration des Pays basques.' *21ᵉ Session de l'Association française pour l'avancement des sciences* (Pau, 1892), pt. I, pp. 359–60.

Platt, Robert S. *A geographical study of the Dutch–German border*. 'Landeskundliche Karten und Hefte der G.K.W.; Reihe, Siedlung und Landschaft in Westfalen', no. 3. Münster: Geographischen Kommission für Westfalen, 1958.

    'The Saarland, an international borderland. Social geography from field study of nine border villages.' *Erdkunde*, XV (1961), 54–68.

Pounds, Norman J. G. 'France and "les limites naturelles" from the seventeenth to the twentieth centuries.' *Annals of the Association of American Geographers*, XLIV (1954), 51–62.

    'The origins of the idea of natural frontiers in France.' *Annals of the Association of American Geographers*, XLI–XLII (1951–2), 146–57.

Prescott, J. R. V. *The geography of frontiers and boundaries*. Chicago: Aldine, 1965.

    The geography of state policies. Chicago: Aldine, 1969.

Puigdefábregas, J., and Balcells R., E. 'Relaciones entre la organización social y la explotación del territorio en el Valle de Roncal (Navarra oriental).' *Pirineos*, vol. XXVI, no. 98 (1970), pp. 53–89.

Raymond, Paul. *Dictionnaire topographique du département des Basses-Pyrénées, comprenant les noms de lieu anciens et modernes*. 'Dictionnaire topographique de la France.' Paris: Comité des travaux historiques et scientifiques, 1863.

Real Academia de la Historia. *Diccionario geográfico-histórico de España ... comprehende el Reyno de Navarra. Señorío de Vizcaya, y Provincias de Alava y Guipúzcoa*. 2 vols. Madrid: en la Imprenta de la viuda de D. Joaquin Ibarra, 1802.

Reclus, Elisée. 'Les Basques: un peuple qui s'en va.' *Revue des Deux-Mondes* 15 mars 1867.

Remy. *La Ligne de démarcation; histoires du Pays basque, de Béarn et de Bigorre.* Paris: Librarie Académique Perrin, 1973.

Ritter, Raymond. 'Documents pour servir à l'histoire militaire de la frontière des Pyrénées (1692–1707).' *Actes*, II CIEP, VI, 183–97.

Rodriguez Garraza, Rodrigo. *Navarra de reino a provincia (1828–1841).* Pamplona: Universidad de Navarra, 1968.

Ros Jimeno, José. 'El decrecimiento de la natalidad y sus causas.' *Revista Internacional de Sociología*, VI (1944), 79–123.

Roussel & La Blottière. *Carte générale des Monts Pyrénées et partie des Royaumes de France et d'Espagne.* [Map, engraved on 8 sheets; 1:330,000 scale.] Paris: 1720.

Sanjuán Cañete, A. *La frontera de los Pirineos occidentales.* Toledo: Imprenta Sucesor de Rodríguez, 1936.

Sanson, J. *Recueil de données statistiques relatives à la climatologie de la France.* 'Mémorial de la Météorologie Nationale, No. 30'. Paris: Office National Météorologique, 1945.

Sansous, Gisèle. *La transhumance dans les vallées aspoise et ossaloise.* Unpublished Mémoire, Diplôme d'études supérieures de géographie; Université de Bordeaux, 1965.

Sanzchasco, B. *Yanci: estudio de un municipio navarro.* Unpublished Memoria, Licencia de estudios geográficos; Universidad de Zaragoza, 1961.

Sarrailh, Jean. *L'Espagne éclairée de la seconde moitié du XVIIIᵉ siècle.* Paris: Imprimerie nationale, 1954.

Sermet, Jean. 'Le Centenaire des traités des limites et la commission internationale des Pyrénées.' *Revue de Comminges*, LXXXIII (1970), 234–55.

'Communications pyrénéennes et transpyrénéennes.' *Actes*, II CIEP, VII. 59–193.

'L'extraction des bois pour la mâture dans les Pyrénées françaises et espagnoles.' *RGPSO* XXV (1954), 84–91.

'Île des Faisans, Île de la Conférence.' *Annales du Midi*, LXXIII (1961), 325–45.

'Nouveaux dolmens des Pyrénées basques.' *RGPSO* XXV (1954), 84.

'Le problème de la limite géographique occidentale des Pyrénées.' *Mémoires de l'Académie des Sciences, Inscriptions, et Belles-Lettres de Toulouse*, 3ᵉ série, IX (1958), 99–144.

'Problèmes pastoraux frontaliers du Pays Quint.' *Actas*, III CIEP, Resumen de las comunicaciones presentadas con anterioridad al congreso, pp. 64–5.

Les Routes transpyrénéennes. Toulouse: Société d'histoire des communications dans le Midi de la France, 1965.

Le Tricentenaire de la paix des Pyrénées, 1659–1959. Saragossa: Instituto de Estudios Pirenaicos, 1960.

Shepherd, William R. *Historical Atlas.* 7th ed. New York: Henry Holt, 1929.

Silen, Sol. *La historia de los vascongados en el oeste de los Estados Unidos.* New York: Las Novedades, 1917.

Slicher van Bath, Bernard H. *The agrarian history of Western Europe, 500–1850.* London: Arnold, 1963.

Solé Sabarís, Luis. *Los Pirineos; el medio y el hombre.* Barcelona: Alberto Martín, 1951.

Sorre, Maximilien. *Les Pyrénées.* Paris: A. Colin, 1922.

Les Pyrénées méditerranéennes; étude de géographie biologique. Paris: A. Colin, 1913.

Souttou, Pierre. *Le Barétous: étude des structures agraires et de l'économie rurale dans le canton d'Aramits.* Unpublished Mémoire, Diplôme d'études supérieures de géographie; Université de Bordeaux, 1968.

Spain. Comision de Estadística general del Reino. *Censo de la población de España según el recuento verificado en 21 de Mayo de 1857.* Madrid: Imprenta Nacional, 1858.

Junta general de estadística. *Censo de la población de España según el recuento verificado en 25 de diciembre de 1860*. 2 vols. Madrid: Imprenta Nacional, 1863.

Dirección general del Instituto geográfico y estadístico. *Censo de la población de España según el empadronamiento hecho en 31 de diciembre de 1877*. 2 vols. Madrid: Instituto geográfico y estadístico, 1883, 1884.

Dirección general del Instituto geográfico y estadístico. *Censo de la población de España según el empadronamiento hecho en 31 de diciembre de 1887*. 2 vols. Madrid: Instituto geográfico y estadístico, 1891, 1892.

Dirección general del Instituto geográfico y estadístico. *Resultados provisionales del censo de la población de España según el empadronamiento hecho en la península é islas adyacentes el 31 de diciembre de 1897*. Madrid: Instituto geográfico y estadístico, 1899.

Dirección general del Instituto geográfico y estadístico. *Censo de la población de España, según el empadronamiento hecho en la penínsulaé islas adyacentes en 31 de diciembre de 1900*. Tomo 3. Madrid: Instituto geográfico y estadístico, 1903.

Dirección general de estadística. *Censo de la población de España según la inscripción de 31 de diciembre de 1940. Clasificaciones por sexo, edad, estado civil, instrucción elemental, fecundidad y profesión de la población presente (hecho)*. Madrid: Dirección general de estadística, n.d.

Instituto nacional de estadística. *Censo de la población de España y territorios de su soberanía y protectorado según el empadronamiento realizado el 31 de diciembre de 1950. Tomo II: Clasificaciones de la población de hecho de la peninsula é islas adyacentes, obtenidas mediante una muestra del 10 por 100*. Madrid: Instituto nacional de estadística, 1954.

Instituto nacional de estadística. *Censo de la población y de las viviendas de España según la inscripción realizada el 31 de diciembre de 1960. Tomo I: Cifras generales de habitantes*. Madrid: Instituto nacional de estadística, 1962.

Instituto nacional de estadística. *Censo de la población y de las viviendas de España de 1960. Nomenclator de las ciudades, villas, lugares, aldeas y demas entidades de población. Provincia de Navarra*. Madrid: Instituto nacional de estadística, 1963.

Instituto nacional de estadística. *Reseña estadística de la Provincia de Navarra*. Madrid: Instituto nacional de estadística, 1950.

Instituto nacional de estadística. *Estadística de propietarios de fincas rusticas de España. Cuaderno 2: Provincias vascongadas y Navarra*. Madrid: Instituto nacional de estadística, 1951.

Instituto nacional de estadística y Ministerio de agricultura. *Primer censo agrario de España, año 1962*. Serie B. vol. 31: 'Navarra'. Madrid: Instituto nacional de estadística, 1964.

Ministerio de Hacienda. *Acuerdos fronterizos con Francia y Portugal*. Madrid: Ministerio de Hacienda, 1969.

Sulzlée, C. 'Le problème du reboisement au Pays basque.' *Annales de la Fédération pyrénéenne d'économie montagnarde*, XI (1944–5), 172–6.

Theret, M. *Le Béarn: agriculture et élevage*. Paris: Vigot, 1960.

Torres Luna, María Pilar de. *La Navarra húmeda del noroeste; estudio geográfico de la ganadería*. Madrid: Consejo superior de investigaciones científicas; Instituto de geografía aplicada del patronato 'Alonso de Herrera', 1971.

Toutain, J.-C. 'La population de la France de 1700 à 1959.' Supplément no. 133 aux *Cahiers de l'Institut de science économique appliquée*. 1963.

Trutat, Eugène. *Les Pyrénées; les montagnes, les glaciers, les eaux minérales, les phenomènes de l'atmosphère, la flore, la faune et l'homme*. Paris: J.-B. Baillère, 1894.

Tucoo-Chala, Pierre. 'Forêts et landes en Béarn au XIVe siècle.' *Actes*, II CIEP VI. 161–73.

Histoire du Béarn. Paris: Presses Universitaires de France, 1962.
'Notes sur la peste noire de 1348 en Béarn.' *Revue régionaliste des Pyrénées*, XXXIV (1951).

Ubieto Arteta, Antonio. 'Las fronteras de Navarra.' *Principe de Viana*, XIV (1953), 61—96.
Urabayen, Leoncio. *La casa navarra.* Madrid: Espasa Calpe, 1929.
Una geografía de Navarra: investigación sobre las residencias humanas de Navarra. Pamplona: Libe, 1959.
Uranga, José Javier. 'Fuegos de la Merindad de las Montañas en 1350.' *Principe de Viana*, XV (1954), 251—94.
Urrutibéhéty, Claude. *Voies d'accès en Navarre et carrefour des chemins de Saint Jacques.* Bayonne: Imprimerie S. Sordes, n.d.

Van Valkenburg, Samuel, and Huntingdon, Ellsworth. *Europe.* New York: Wiley, 1935.
Veyrin, Philippe. *Les Basques.* 2nd ed. Paris: Arthaud, 1955.
Les Basques du Labourd, de Soule et de Basse Navarre; Leur histoire et leur traditions. Bayonne: Musée Basque, 1945.
Vicens Vives, Jaime. *An economic history of Spain.* Princeton, New Jersey: Princeton University Press, 1969.
Viers, Georges. 'Le climat et les types de temps dans la vallée de Baïgorry.' Unpublished typescript. Université de Bordeaux. Faculté des Lettres. Mémoire secondaire pour le diplôme d'études supérieurs de géographie. Bordeaux: 1950.
'Les études toponymiques dans les Pyrénées occidentales.' *RGPSO* XXVI (1955), 151—4.
'La forêt d'Irati.' *RGPSO* XXVI (1955), 5—27.
Mauléon-Licharre: la population et l'industrie; étude de géographie sociale urbaine. 'Collection de l'Institut d'économie régionale du Sud-Ouest, VII; Études d'économie basco-béarnaises, II.' Bordeaux: Bière, 1961.
'Le Pays des Aldudes.' *RGPSO* XXII (1951), 260—83.
Les Pyrénées. 3rd ed. Paris: Presses Universitaires de France, 1973.
'Le Relief de la Haute Soule et du Haut Barétous et les influences glaciaires.' *RGPSO* XXIV (1953), 73—95.
Le Relief des Pyrénées occidentales et de leur piémont; Pays basque et Barétous. Toulouse: Edouard Privat, 1960.
'La vallée de Baïgorry; les paysages, la vie rurale.' Unpublished typescript. Université de Bordeaux. Faculté des Lettres. Mémoire pour le diplôme d'études supérieurs de géographie. Bordeaux: 1950.
Viers, Georges, *et al.* 'La XLIe excursion géographique interuniversitaire (8—13 mai 1959).' *Annales de Géographie*, LXVIII (1959), 486—524.
Vignau, R. 'Aspect historique et juridique du Pays Quint', in *Traditions des Aldudes.* Bayonne: Gure Herria, n.d. but *c.* 1964.
Violant y Simorra, Ramón. 'Notas de etnografía pastoríl pirenaica—la trashumancia.' *Pirineos*, IV (1948), 271—89.
El Pirineo español; vida, usos, costumbres, creencias y tradiciones de una cultura milenaria que desaparece. Madrid: Plus-Ultra, 1949.
Yanguas y Miranda, José. *Diccionario de antigüedades del Reino de Navarra.* [reprinted] Pamplona: Institución Príncipe de Viana, 1964.
Diccionario de los fueros del Reino de Navarra, y de las leyes vigentes promulgadas hasta las Cortes de los años 1817 y 18 inclusivo. [reprinted] Pamplona: Institución Príncipe de Viana, 1964.

Young, Arthur. *Travels during the years 1787, 1788, and 1789, undertaken more particularly with a view of ascertaining the cultivation, wealth, resources and national*

prosperity of the Kingdom of France; to which is added, the register of a tour into Spain.
2 vols. Dublin: printed for Messrs. R. Cross, P. Wogan, L. White, P. Byrne, A. Grueber,
J. Moore, J. Jones, W. McKenzie, and J. Rice, 1793.

    Travels during the years 1787, 1788, and 1789; undertaken more particularly with a
view of ascertaining the cultivation, wealth, resources, and national prosperity of the
Kingdom of France. 2nd ed. 2 vols. Bury St. Edmonds: printed by J. Rackham for
W. Richardson, Royal Exchange, London, 1794.

Yrizar, J. de. *Las casas vascas.* San Sebastian: Librería Internacional, 1929.

Zudaire, E. 'Facerías de la cuenca Baztán—Bidasoa.' *Principe de Viana*, nos. 106, 107
(reprint dated 1967), pp. 61—96. 161—241.

ARCHIVAL MATERIALS

Bayonne. Chambres de commerce et de l'industrie. Lists of industrial establishments.

France. Administration des contributions directes. Cadastre. 'Matrice des propriétés
foncières de la commune de . . .' The 'Napoleonic' cadaster. MS. ledgers and maps kept in
the archives of the Service du cadastre at Bayonne and Pau.

    Direction départementale de l'agriculture des Basses-Pyrénées (Pau). Typescript lists of
'bons de carburants', used to determine the number of tractors in the study area.

    Direction générale des contributions directes et du cadastre. 'Cadastre . . . Matrice des
propriétés non-bâties.' The 1914 revision of the cadaster. MS. ledgers kept in the
archives of the Service du cadastre at Bayonne and Pau.

    Institut national de la statistique et des études économiques. 'Enquête agricole de
printemps 1946 (Basses-Pyrénées).' Computer print-out kept at Bordeaux office of
I.N.S.E.E.

    Institut national de la statistique et des études économiques. 'Enquête agricole—année
1951: Basses-Pyrénées.' MS. kept at Bordeaux office of I.N.S.E.E.

    Institut nationale de la statistique et des études économiques. 'Recensement agricole,
1956, Inventaire communal (Basses-Pyrénées).' Computer print-out kept at Bordeaux
office of I.N.S.E.E.

    Ministère de l'agriculture. Direction générale des eaux et forêts. Inspection de Bayonne.
'Rapport de M. Georges Duplan, Ingenieur des travaux des Eaux et Forêts à Bayonne,
sur la Forêt Syndicale de la Vallée de Baïgorry, dite d'Hayra—Rapport de son histoire
et du projet d'aménagement (1961—1975).' Typescript kept in Centre de Gestion,
Office national des forêts, Bayonne. n.d. but *c.* 1966.

    Ministère de l'agriculture. Direction générale des eaux et forêts. Inspection d'Oloron.
'Notice descriptive des services, 1948.' Typewritten report kept in Centre de gestion,
Office national des forêts, Bayonne.

    Ministère de l'agriculture. Service central des enquêtes et des études statistiques.
'Basses-Pyrénées: enquête communautaire sur la structure des exploitations agricoles
(sept. 1967—jan. 1968).' Data kept at Direction départementale de l'agriculture, Pau.

    Ministère des travaux publiques, des transports, et du tourisme. 'Recensement de la
circulation sur les routes nationales en 1965.' MS. map in Bayonne office of Ponts et
chaussées.

    Ministère des finances. Administration des contributions directes et du cadastre.
'Matrice cadastrale des propriétés bâties et des propriétés non bâties. Commune de . . .'
The cadastral revisions of 1932—69. MS. ledgers kept in the Service du cadastre at
Bayonne and Pau.

Navarre. Archivo general de Navarra. Sección catastro (Planos). Cadastral surveys for each
municipio, dating from the 1890s.

    Diputación foral. Dirección de industria. Typescript 1966 census of industry, and MS.
municipal questionnaires (30 November 1967) relating to employment in industry,
both kept in the files of the Dirección de industria, Pamplona.

Diputación foral. Servicio catastral. 'Estadística de riqueza pecuaria; años 1946—1968.' MS. ledger kept in the office of the Servicio catastral, Pamplona.

Diputación foral. Servicio catastral. 'Estadísticas de resumen de extensiones superficiales de las riquezas agricola, pastos, forestal e improductivos.' MS. ledgers kept in the office of the Servicio catastral, Pamplona.

Diputación foral. Servicio catastral. 'Estadística de las extensiones superficiales de las riquezas agricola y de pastos.' MS. ledger kept at office of Servicio catastral, Pamplona.

Diputación foral. Servicio catastral. 'Estadística de las extensiones superficiales de riqueza forestal.' MS. ledger kept in the office of Servicio catastral, Pamplona.

Pau. Chambre de commerce et de l'industrie. Lists of industrial establishments.

Spain. Instituto nacional de estadística and Ministerio de agricultura. Primer censo agrario de España, 1962. Typescript and MS. tables of results (by municipios) for unpublished data, kept in the Ministerio de agricultura, Madrid.

Ministerio de agricultura. Annual (May and Sept.) municipal questionnaires on agricultural production and acreages. The individual 'hojas declaratorias' and the ledgers aggregating them according to categories of crops are kept in the Pamplona office of the Jefatura Provincial de Agricultura.

Ministerio de obras públicas. Dirección general de carreteras y caminos vecinales. Mapa de tráfico: Navarra, 1967. 1:400,000 MS. map of traffic density in 1967 and 1961 kept in the Pamplona office of the D.G.C.C.V.

Patrimonio forestal del estado. 'Informe de Don Lucas de Olazábal, Ingeniero de Montes; 26 de enero 1860; Pamplona.' MS. of 8 folios kept in the archives of Patrimonio forestal del estado, Pamplona.

Patrimonio forestal del estado. 'Proyecto de ordenación de los montes "Aezcoa" y "La Cuestion". (Madrid: P.F.E., 1904) Typescript kept at Pamplona office of Patrimonio forestal del estado.

Patrimonio forestal del estado. 'Proyecto de ordenación de los montes "Erreguerena", "Vertiente meridional de Quinto Real", y "Legua Acotada".' (Madrid: P.F.E., 1903) Typescript kept at Pamplona office of Patrimonio forestal del estado.

INDEX

Abaurrea Alta, landforms, 11
Administration (*see* Government, Minor civil divisions)
Aézcoa (forest), 65, 67, 112—3
Aézcoa, road, 72
Aézcoa/Cize *facería*, 52
Agriculture, 36—9, 116—124
  and climate, 14—16
  and landforms, 10, 25—7
  and population, 38—9
  seasonal activities, 26—7
  statistics, 139—141
  subsistence, 96, 116—17
Agricultural education, 89
Agricultural revolution, and common lands, 57—67 (*see also* Maize)
Aïnhoa, road, 69
Aldudes, landforms, 8, 10
  settlement, 35
Alfalfa, 119
Altitude (*see* Elevation above sea level)
Ampurdán, 2, 5
Andorra, boundaries, 54 n. 20
Anie, Pic d', 8, 53
Animal husbandry (*see* Livestock, Cattle, Sheep)
Anué, 64, 66
Arable, 96, 109, 119
Arán, Vall d', 2—3
Arce, population decline, 97
Architecture, traditional, 11, 33, 136
Arette, climate, 15
  tourism, 125
Arga (river), 11—12
Arlas, Pic d', 8
Armouries, 110—11
Arnéguy, 50—2
  road, 78
Aspe (valley), 113
  architecture, 11
  forests, 112
  roads, 77
  vacation homes in, 125
Aspect (micro-climate), 16, 22 n. 22
Assarts, 30, 34—5, 65, 96 (*see also* Common)
Athas (Lees-Athas), 112
Autonomy of valleys, 24, 30—2, 45, 47—8
Aydius, population decline, 97

Baïgorry (valley), 35, 50—2
  forges, 111
  hotels, 125
  railway, 79

Banca, climate, 15
  forge, 111
Bardenas Reales, 27, 117
Barétous, architecture, 11
Barétous/Roncal *facería*, 47, 52—3
Bastides (new villages, 1282—1358), 29
Basques, culture, 126—7
  farm, 33
  house names, 35, 40 n. 20
  language, 2
  language and literacy, 84—8
  migration, 107—8
  nobility, 32
  place names, 21 n. 2
Bayonne, climate, 14
  roads from, 70—1, 77—8
Bayonne, Treaty of, 48—9
Baztán (valley), 35, 49—52
  assarting in, 65
  electric power, 82
  roads, 69—72, 79
Beech, 17, 19
Behobia, road, 69
Beorzubuztán (mountain), 50
Berra (river), 49
Biarritz, climate, 12—14
Bidasoa (river), 8, 11, 43, 49
  (valley), forests, 116
  forges, 111—12
Bidasoa, Montes de, 65, 137
Bilbao, 6
Birch, 17
Biriatou, 49
Birot, Pierre, 5
Black Death (1348), 34
Bojeral, 20
Borda (shepherd's summer cabin), 26, 65
  transformed into farms, 33, 35, 51
Boundary, 1, 3, 8, 43—53, 126
Bozate (Arizcun), 41 n. 29
Bracken, 18, 26—7, 45
Burghardt, Andrew, 4
Burguete, landforms, 11
  road, 69

Cadaster, 139—40
  and land tenure, 41 n. 32
  in Pays Quint, 52
Cagots, 41 n. 29
Cantabrian Mountains, 5
Car ownership, 124
Caro and d'Ornano Treaty, 51—2
Catalan language area, 2